RUSSIA SPEAKS

RUSSIA
SPEAKS

An Oral History
from the Revolution
to the Present

RICHARD LOURIE

 Edward Burlingame Books
An Imprint of HarperCollins*Publishers*

FIRST EDITION

Designed by Cassandra J. Pappas

Library of Congress Cataloging-in-Publication Data
Lourie, Richard, 1940–
 Russia speaks: an oral history from the Revolution to the present / Richard Lourie.—1st ed.
  p. cm.
 "An Edward Burlingame book."
 Includes index.
 ISBN 0-06-016449-2
 1. Soviet Union—History—1917– 2. Oral history. 3. Soviet Union—History—1917– —Biography. 4. Oral biography.
I. Title.
DK266.L67 1991
947.084—dc20 —dc20   89-46544

91 92 93 94 95 CC/HC 10 9 8 7 6 5 4 3 2 1

*To all the Russians who gave me tea on cold nights
and told me the story of their life
with the same courage
they had lived it*

Contents

Introduction

This book of stories came about because of stories never told me. When I was a boy I used to ask my father to tell me about Russia, where he was born. "What was it like there?" He'd look back through the decades to his childhood, shake his head, and say: "Terrible."

Satisfied that he'd found the one word that said it best, he'd move on to subjects dearer to his heart—business, the Red Sox, the fights. But I wasn't satisfied in the least! Why hadn't he told me anything? Was I still too young? Was he irritated to be reminded that he hadn't always been an American? After what seemed the proper interval, I'd put the question to him again: "Come on, tell me, really, what was it like in Russia?" After a long and thoughtful pause, he'd shake his head and say: "Awful."

Then my father would look up to see if I had finally understood and must have always been disappointed to see that I hadn't. But how could I? I had not been born in Russia; if I had, one word would have been plenty.

Apart from a few ear-blistering curses my grandfather taught me, I knew no Russian as a child. English was the only language spoken at home (Hebrew just a holy boredom that ruined afternoons). Good English was as important as good teeth or good posture. And the Boston public schools of the forties taught it unimaginably well.

By the time I was seventeen I was devouring Russian novels in translation and convinced I was a writer. My father was against it. To him it was no accident that poetry and poverty were spelled almost the same.

Two years later, Robert Lowell awarded me the Sneath Poetry Prize for 1960 by slipping a crumpled envelope containing a check from his inside jacket pocket and handing it to me as we were descending a concrete stairwell at Boston University. So stunned to have won, I failed to appreciate the fantastic casualness of it all. Later, in his office, Robert Lowell told my future, his rich voice a sing-song of ordinary prophecy. "You'll get a B.A. in English, specializing in Dryden or Herbert then go on for an M.A. in Creative Writing. You'll start publishing in the little magazines . . ."

Oh no I won't, I vowed to myself, anything but Dryden and little magazines! I'll study Russian, I'll read Dostoyevsky in the original!

I kept the vow. Along the way I translated some thirty books from Russian and Polish and wrote five of my own, three of them novels, the land of my father's birth coloring them all.

In 1988 Arthur Samuelson, then an editor at what was then Harper & Row, called me up and said: "Look, you're a novelist, a translator, a Soviet specialist, why not go to Russia with a tape recorder and do a sort of oral history novel. You're smart, you're a writer, I trust you to figure it all out."

And so, out of a silence, a prophecy, and a suggestion this book was born.

It was not an easy birth. My first impulse was to attempt to be representative in a balanced, sociological sort of way, but Russia is too vast and complex, volume upon volume would be the result. Besides, some people would not speak to me. Others lied. And what of the millions who had perished in the camps and whose silence outlines every voice in that nation where all the living are survivors?

Some levels of society—like the wealthy peasants known as kulaks or the businessmen called NEPmen who flourished in the late twenties—had been rendered extinct by edict and bullet. After strenuous effort, I finally located not a NEPman but a NEP-man's wife, close enough. An elderly woman, she kept postponing our meeting because of ill health. Finally, she had a turn for the better and an appointment was made for a Thursday afternoon. On the preceding Wednesday I received a call informing me that she had passed away that morning. Death was this book's first editor.

It soon became clear that the truth about Russia in this century might be told but never the whole truth. And that meant that the techniques of art—the flash of lightning that illuminates the landscape as Pasternak called it—would have to be brought into play. Form is that lightning. And selection is what triggers it. Though I strove to be faithful to the hardness of facts and the severity of real time, I knew that in the end all the visions I had collected would have to be aligned into a design for which I bore the responsibility.

Still, key segments of that design would inevitably be missing and I would have to join the extant fragments with narrative just as the skeletons of prehistoric behemoths are connected with plaster where bones are missing. But nothing was made up and only the most minuscule of liberties were taken, like referring to the secret police as the KGB whereas in fact its initials had changed often, its nature never.

A new set of working principles emerged. The art was to be all in orchestration and all in service of a new way of telling history. The narrative would focus on a core of about a half dozen people whose lives had been formed and deformed by Russia's century of faith and violence. These would not be famous people though some had risen to prominence. The only exception to that rule was Andrei Sakharov who enters the story by entering the life of one of the main characters and who, by walking away from his privileged position, by "going to the people" as the Russians used to say, belongs in this history of Russia, not as it was made, but as it was lived.

Cassis, France
October 1990

No. 6 Sretensky Boulevard (1988)

"I WILL NEVER FORGIVE THE COMMUNISTS FOR IN-VENTING COMMUNAL APARTMENTS!" says Lusya with a fury that surprises even her. A fury that must be subdued, but not quite yet. It is still too painful to remember the fact that ten years of waiting have not been able to change: that she, her husband, and their three children have two rooms in a five-room apartment where they share all common space—the kitchen, the bathroom, the hallway—with eight other people. And their two rooms aren't even adjacent, which means that if she wants to check on the children, she must go out into the hall where she may encounter any one of those eight neighbors, their relatives, or their guests.

"Of all the horrible perversions invented by the Soviet system, the communal apartment is the most horrible perversion of them all. It destroys the boundary between the outer world and the inner, the public and the private. You open the door of your room and you're in Red Square."

Red Square itself is close enough so that Lusya's children

have a very good view of the fireworks over the Kremlin on Revolution Day. But Dzerzhinsky Square is even closer. There, all the buildings, old and high-rise new, belong to the KGB with the one exception of the largest Child's World store in the city. At one end of the square is the infamous Lubyanka Prison, and in the center of the square is the monument to Felix Dzerzhinsky, the founder of the secret police, wrapped in heroic solitude.

D zerzhinsky Square being so close has always made our building a favorite for people working in the KGB, *says Lusya.* There's even a rumor that under Stalin a tunnel was built from this building to KGB headquarters so that people could get to work quickly and comfortably. We have one of those families in our apartment. I'm not sure if he's KGB, or just has ongoing relations with them.

I have absolutely nothing in common with him. I wouldn't have wanted to spend a day on a train with a person like that, let alone live under the same roof with him for two years. But somehow you manage, I haven't gone mad yet.

He's so haughty and smug. He acts like we're some inferior race and he's the white man. He's even capable of spilling some water and saying to me, "Wipe that up, will you, Lusya."

His wife Vera's more likable. She's about the same age as him, forty-six, forty-seven. There's no meanness in her and sometimes she can be very kind. Still, the other day she was watching television in the kitchen and when Sakharov started speaking she said, "Sakharov, that old devil's senile already, what good is he, all he does is babble."

I was boiling inside but I didn't say anything. You're forced to live with total strangers.

Lusya is in her early thirties, her hair, eyes, and eyebrows all the same dark, woodland brown, a raccoonish darkness even gathering under her deep-set eyes. She wears no makeup, her long hair her only luxury, the snarls brushed out with a will. Her fury is that of patience finally enraged. But she does not dwell on grievance, always preferring serenity or the laughter that evens the balance. "And to think the famous French architect Le Corbusier once called this the most beautiful building in Moscow!"

Number 6 Sretensky Boulevard reaches for a city block, its might offset by a facade of light brown brick iced with columns, a turreted and gabled castle transported stone by stone from the architect's mind.

"The building was built around the turn of the century as apartments for the very well-to-do," continues Lusya. "After the revolution they became communal apartments. Red Army artillery headquarters were located in this building, and so was the first Ministry of Education, where Lenin's wife worked. Lenin used to visit this building quite often and that's why there's a plaque to him on the front of the building."

The plaque is an old-fashioned futurist rhomboid, all in white, with Lenin in profile, goateed, alert as a hawk. It is near the building's front door and is slightly above eye level. The front door itself is high, heavy, thick with coats of paint, a maroon turgid with lead. The front hall is vast and dim. Its walls are tattooed with rock 'n' roll graffiti in misspelled English, but the writing by the elevator buttons is in grammatically correct Russian: DEATH TO KIKES AND TARTARS.

The elevator always begins its risky ascent with a thud and a lurch, one corner of the cabin dependably damp with urine. The doors to Lusya's fifth-floor communal apartment are nine feet tall, their scale all that remains of the old luxury. There are thirteen overcoats hung in the hall, thirteen pairs of boots. A brown-gold light obscures the corners of the rooms.

I n a communal apartment, everyone is a potential enemy, *says Lusya, calmer now.* I wouldn't want to live with my closest friends in a communal apartment. But one of my neighbors is wonderful, Praskovya. She's a simple country woman, in her eighties now, and just waiting to die. She came to the city to find work fifty-five years ago and she worked as a maid in this apartment, she's been here all those fifty-five years. She's a woman of great patience, and what you could call Christian humility.

She's illiterate, and still a virgin too. One time she told me a story about her attack of appendicitis. She called an ambulance. They came and one of them said, "Maybe you're pregnant." "How could I be pregnant?" says Praskovya. "I've never been with a man."

An old maid, illiterate, very kind and good-humored. I'm awfully fond of her.

Death is her dream now. Praskovya wants so very much to die. She says she's tired of living. Her life's nothing but boredom. She doesn't see well enough to leave the apartment anymore. And she can't read. She just sits in her room and stares into space.

Still, Praskovya likes living in a communal apartment. She says even if they offered her an apartment of her own, she wouldn't take it. She likes having neighbors around. She says, "I'm bored and sad and lonely, but in the evening when I hear doors closing and people talking and the phone ringing and the kids shouting, then I don't feel so all alone."

Of all our neighbors in the apartment, Vera and Dima are the closest to us in the way they look at the world. They're not pro-Soviet, not communists. They're both physicists in their mid-twenties. Dima's from Moscow. He's very phlegmatic and never notices what's happening around him in the apartment. But Vera notices. She's from Siberia, a redhead, and very temperamental.

Most of the fights start over the children. I have three, Vera has two, and the KGB man's wife has one. Most of the fights are between the women. They start in the kitchen, which we all share—four refrigerators, three tables, two stoves, and laundry always dripping from the ceiling.

Hearing women's voices rising, edging toward rage, Lusya runs down the hallway toward the kitchen, worried that one of her children might be involved. What she sees makes her gasp.

Vera, the redheaded Siberian, is just about to hurl a pot of boiling water into the KGB man's wife's face. Suddenly, Praskovya, the half-blind old country woman, rises from her table and stands between them, large and imperturbable in her housedress. Doubly furious now, Vera slams the pot back on the fire, splattering water hissing into the gas flame. The KGB man passes Lusya at the doorway as if she were not even there, reaches into the kitchen to replace his yogurt in the refrigerator, then is gone in a single movement.

That March evening in 1988 Lusya and Alyosha have a guest, Mark, a man in his early thirties with close-cropped hair and the tensed stillness of a bird about to depart a footing in which it has just lost confidence. A glass-fronted bookcase divides their room into two: the front half is the kitchen they would be sitting in if they had a place of their own, the other half of the room contains their bed, the youngest child's crib, a mighty, wooden wardrobe, and several icons, all very small, miniature flashes of gold and gold brown.

Tall, bearded, snaggle-toothed, with eyes that are a sleepy grey or suddenly sky blue, Alyosha is glad not to talk. He talked all day, working as a guide for Soviet tourists visiting the Kremlin, and now if he wants to get any writing of his own done he will have to work late at night in the kitchen, the best possible solitude the apartment can offer him; and even then someone could stray in, woken by a bad dream, wanting a glass of water.

It is after midnight and Moscow is monumentally still. These are the blessed hours between the long day and sleep, a time for drinking tea and for telling stories of life, which, in Russia, by some power always turn into fables of fate.

Lusya serves tea and pastries she has baked that day, which have the raisin-sugar sweetness of the south.

Y ou know our neighbor Vera, the redhead from Siberia, *says Lusya to Mark, who nods his head quickly several times while munching on a pastry.* One time when we were still open with each other she said to me, "You know I can really be mean."

And she can be. She likes to hurt children's feelings.

A few weeks ago Vera started yelling at me because my daughter Masha had started crying and woken up her daughter Masha. But my daughter was crying because she had slammed her foot in the door. It'd hurt her a lot.

Vera started screaming that I had stupid, retarded children.

I said, "My daughter's crying because she hurt herself."

"I don't care," says Vera. "Make her stop."

"I don't have a magic wand," I said. "If your Masha was hurt she'd cry too."

"My Masha is smarter than all your three children put together."

Vera knows I practice Russian Orthodoxy. She's always testing me, as if to say, Your humility's not real. It's only outward. But what Vera doesn't understand is that not even the saints could always maintain their outward humility. Even outward humility is a difficult task.

And since then Vera and I haven't spoken. I always thought it would be very hard not to be on speaking terms with any of my neighbors in the apartment, but in fact it turns out to be much easier that way.

Lusya pauses to fill tea cups and to check how quickly her pastries are going.

"It looks like I'll be getting the new apartment I told you about," says Mark, his dark eyes suddenly widening, "but one thing makes me very nervous. I've heard that there's up to a ten-year wait to get a telephone there. And having three little children and no telephone makes me very nervous."

"Horrible," says Lusya with angry compassion. "Let me tell you what happened here today. Alyosha, you don't know about this either. I heard some noise in the kitchen and I ran to the door. There was Vera just about to throw a pot of boiling water in the face of the KGB man's wife when Praskovya gets in between them, and makes them stop, can you imagine that, Praskovya."

Mark seems more startled by the image of violence than

taken by Praskovya's kitchen heroism, but Alyosha smiles as he imagines that tableau of Innocence Taming Those of Wicked Temper.

"But," continues Lusya, "all those fights only happen because this is a completely unnatural way for people to live. It isn't natural to live with total strangers under the same roof. Collective farms and communal apartments don't work for the same reason—they're not natural.

"God, all I want out of life is a place of our own so the children's childhood memories won't be of this nightmarish communal apartment! I'll never forgive the communists for inventing them!"

"Speaking of communists," says Mark, very alert, his tea cup jiggling against the saucer, "my uncle Ilya, the old Stalinist, is coming in from Minsk tomorrow. You should hear his stories."

Revolution

T hree times I saw Tsar Nicholas in the flesh! Three! *says Mark's uncle Ilya Jaffee, holding up three fingers for emphasis.*

In 1915 Russia was at war with Germany and Tsar Nicholas had appointed himself commander in chief of the army. His headquarters were in Mogilev, and the Petersburg–Mogilev line ran right through Vitebsk, where I lived.

The Hebrew school I went to was located on the second floor of a building that overlooked the tracks. A couple of times I noticed a special train going by, its cars were light blue and very beautiful. One day I saw the imperial crown on the side of one car and I thought to myself, That might even be the Tsar!

I shouted to the teacher that I had a stomachache. As soon as he dismissed me, I ran out and hopped the fence.

And it was then I saw the Tsar. He turned out to be a

small man, with a reddish beard and traces of smallpox on his face. He was standing by the window, smoking.

I ran home and immediately shared my great happiness with my older brother, Misha, who informed me I was an idiot. "What are you so happy about, Nicholas is against the Jews. That's why you can't go to high school." My father just thought I was making the whole thing up.

Ilya Jaffee, the old Stalinist, in his early eighties now, is so vital he can barely sit still on the couch as he tells his stories to a dozen people—nephews, nieces, their children, their friends—who have formed a natural amphitheater around him. He is tall and powerfully built, a man incapable of dawdling. His grey hair looks brushed back by wind resistance and he wears oversize, wraparound glasses. He is restive on the couch because he is resisting what has become second nature to him—standing and addressing groups.

Mark is among those listening, both drawn by and recoiling from his uncle's energy, for Ilya is an old man in nothing except his fussiness about dates, which is more than historical scrupulousness—it is the will imposed on time.

Ilya Jaffee checks his audience. Yes, he has their undivided attention. Who could help but admire the sheer nerve of that schoolboy, jumping to his feet and lying to his teacher's face. Who could resist a story about seeing the Tsar not once, not twice, but three times.

Ilya had been afforded that vision of God's regent in Russia grabbing a nervous smoke because Tsar Nicholas II had made the fatal mistake of appointing himself commander in chief of Russia's armies. He was Tsar by birth and psychology but not by instinct. That psychology prompted him to believe that his presence at the head of Holy Russia's army meant more than the fact that a quarter of his soldiers were being sent into battle unarmed, told to take weapons from the dead.

The Nicholas whom Ilya saw was lurching into the last of his disasters in a reign that had been marked with disaster from the start. His coronation in 1894 had somehow turned into a stampede, and the populace that had come for cold beer and celebration was treated instead to panic and carnage.

The Russia that Nicholas had inherited as his patrimony had changed greatly at the end of the nineteenth century. The Industrial Age came to vast, sleepy Russia dreaming the dream of the ages. A country of lords and peasants suddenly had industries and a working class, new professionals and businessmen making a middle class. It was a time of open borders in Europe, and revolutionary ideas traveled easily. It was a time when many people, one individual at a time, crossed some ultimate boundary in themselves, the boundary between belief and disbelief, the boundary between obedience and rebellion.

Although there were revolutionaries in Russia printing leaflets and assassinating officials, the country was not ripe for revolution; a few more lurches into disaster were required for that. The next one came in 1904, when Russia's relentless eastward expansion brought it into conflict and war with Japan. Within fifty years Japan had gone from a nation of archers to a military power whose navy's state-of-the-art dreadnoughts sank the Russian fleet in the Tsushima Strait, between Korea and Japan.

But Nicholas lost something even more important than the war, which ended in 1905. In that year the contract between him and his people was fractured. On Bloody Sunday, January 22, 1905, a peaceful demonstration of common people carrying icons went to the Winter Palace to petition their Tsar. They were cut down by mounted police, over a hundred dying and countless others stumbling through the snow with saber slashes.

Nicholas's authority had been fatally breached. The sailors on the battleship *Potemkin* in the Black Sea mutinied and trained their guns on the Russian Empire. And in October 1905 all of Russia went on a ten-day strike that has been called the greatest and most effective in all history. The strike was particularly well organized in the capital city of St. Petersburg, where the workers had spontaneously formed executive councils, which they called soviets, a word with a future.

The Tsar was forced to surrender a portion of his power to a legislature. The liberals were satisfied, the radicals were not, and they continued to assassinate at least a thousand officials a year. The radicals lived in a world of secrecy and conspiracy, in fear of betrayal. For many of them youth was prison and exile.

Though Nicholas had assented to the creation of a legislature without believing it necessary and then attempted to thwart it, liberty was gaining ground in Russia. High-minded zealots spread the gospel of progress, evolution. Tsardom was old-fashioned, corrupt, inept, but Russia could be regenerated from within if only it were allowed time and peace. It was allowed neither.

In 1914 the world lurched into war, in much the same fashion as Nicholas had lurched from one disaster to the next. It was not a war that began with a planned invasion but with a series of slipshod increments. A slide, not a drive.

It was the first war in which great numbers of men were simply mashed by machines and projectiles, a terrible war that Russia was soon losing badly. And, as in the war with Japan, something else was being lost in addition to territory and lives: loyalty was withering. And, as the *Potemkin* had demonstrated in 1905, Russia's guns could point in any direction.

Believing himself the only person able to rouse the troops, Nicholas appointed himself commander in chief in 1915 and began traveling from St. Petersburg to staff headquarters, a route that took him through Ilya's hometown of Vitebsk.

T he second time I saw Tsar Nicholas was on my way home from Hebrew school. His train had stopped further up, not far from my house. But the fence was too high to hop. So, I climbed a little set of stairs that went out over the tracks. I saw the Tsar in a lit window, he was standing at the window and smoking.

I ran home and got my brother. "Come on, run, the Tsar's here." But while we were running back, the train started pulling away. Still, we did catch a glimpse of the light blue cars with the imperial crown.

Disappearing into a distance formed of tracks and sky, the train was also disappearing into history. Each time Nicholas returned to the front, he left his capital, and his country, in the hands of his wife, the Empress Alexandra. Her only son, the future Tsar, was a hemophiliac, and his bleeding could only be stopped by Rasputin, a mystical holy man who had walked from Siberia to Jerusalem in his youth. The Empress was entirely in Rasputin's spell until he was assassinated in December 1916; poison, knives, bullets, and drowning were required to kill that man of insane vitality.

In early 1917 Tsar Nicholas yet again rode the light blue train from the capital to the front, with a pause in Vitebsk.

The third time I saw Nicholas was right before the revolution. He looked bad, huge circles under his eyes.

Then some soldiers started shoving me aside. A couple of generals were coming. "Out of the way!"

And that was the last time Nicholas and I got to see each other, *says Ilya Jaffee with a roguish smile. But then he becomes serious when adding,* Still, those were rare visions.

With his own eyes Ilya had seen what for many others would be a purely intellectual conclusion—that the Tsar was not a divinity but a man like any other; one bullet could kill him. One at a time thousands of Russians were shifting allegiance toward rebellion.

One of those who did not so much cross the line but found it moving beneath his feet was Ivan Vrachov. His parents were peasants who became workers and needed no pamphlets to know that poverty was bitter. From them he must have inherited his peasant stubbornness that kept his loyalty to Lenin from ever wavering. Ivan was unyielding. All his rural simplicity and jam-like Russian sweetness disappear when he speaks of the hardships that made him a revolutionary.

There were hundreds just like me. My father was a stoker, my mother a cook and a washerwoman. I had three years of the local parochial school. There were hundreds like me from the working class who took an active hand in the revolution. And some of us even ended up in the highest echelons of the party. The revolution flung open doors for people with energy and questioning minds, minds that were of course taken by the revolution's ideas.

I was born in 1897 in the south, in the Kuban Cossack region, but I'm not of Cossack descent. The Cossacks always saw us as outsiders. My father was a former peasant from the province of Voronezh and my mother was a peasant from the province of Tula. There were many children in the family and so of course she had to go looking for work: sometimes she cooked, sometimes she did laundry.

All the education I ever got was those three years at the parish parochial school. My parents tried to enroll me in the city elementary school, which had first through eighth, but I wasn't accepted. I wasn't accepted because I was from a poor family. And when one of my teachers tried to get me assigned to the high school—I was a good student—there turned out to be an insurmountable obstacle. The Tsar's minister of education had decreed, it was right there in black and white, that the children of cooks were not to be admitted to high schools.

There were many mouths to feed in the family and, at the age of eleven and a half, I had to go to work. I worked in a brewery, then in a noodle factory. I improved my situation by learning to cut hair. Finally, I ended up doing hair and makeup in a theater. I worked in the theater and in film, right at its inception, when film was still silent.

Among the Russian intelligentsia there were a great many teachers who were utterly devoted to serving the people. And I had the good fortune to have a teacher like that. She instilled the love of reading in me. *He smiles, remembering her with fond gratitude, then switches to speak of himself in the third person as if that passion for reading had already made him a part of history:*

And suddenly that little boy began reading the best works of Russian literature, the classics, Gogol, Turgenev, until he got to Gorky, his contemporary. That boy was very taken with Gorky and when the war started in 1914, he was a regular subscriber to Gorky's very progressive magazine, *Chronicle*.

It all helped me rid myself of the chauvinism that had

infected me when the war began. Gradually I grew hostile to the war, then hated it and was antiwar.

By then I was earning fairly good money in the theater. I would scour all the bookstores, buying up all the literature by the People's Will terrorist organization. I was preparing myself to play a role in the revolution. And by the time the Tsar was deposed in February 1917, I was 100 percent prepared.

*

Not only was Russia losing the war, but the cities were starving and cold. There were demonstrations for bread and coal in St. Petersburg that turned into mob riot. But when the troops of the garrison were called out, they refused to fire and fraternized with the rebels. The lines that had been crossed within people were now being crossed out in the streets. Nicholas had lost what he never really had—authority. He assented to abdication as he had assented to everything, without really consenting.

After the February Revolution, Russia was no longer ruled by tsars. Until a government could be formed through representative election, the legislature appointed a Provisional Government. Ultimately to be led by the socialist Alexander Kerensky, the new government was very liberal and immediately introduced equal rights for all before the law and all freedoms of expression. There was rejoicing in the land that reached deep into the countryside and even affected children, like a nine-year-old tomboy of gentle birth named Margarita Ivanovna Zarudny, known as Mulya.

All I knew was a platform covered with red cloth was built in the village square. People went to the platform and spoke, congratulating everyone on their new freedoms. The Tsar had abdicated. He had not been killed and was in no danger. There was going to be a democratic government. Everybody was very happy. One of the speakers that day was my mother.

My mother had gone to the university and was very much the young revolutionary. She became a member of an organization called Committee on National Education and she set up various schools for adults. My father was the son of a

Russian senator and had attended the Naval Academy. But the Navy wasn't for him. He became an engineer and worked on the first streetcars in St. Petersburg, which were built by Westinghouse. He didn't like routine work and so he quit and found himself a job in the Urals. There he was involved in trying to protect some Jewish families from a pogrom. He was beaten up by the mob *and* arrested by the police. Both! He spent three months in solitary confinement until finally his connections in the capital helped him get out.

That's mostly why my mother married him, out of admiration for the stance he had taken and for what he went through. The story goes that after they got married they went to some coffeehouse and played chess, and my mother beat him sixteen times in a row.

By the time of the February Revolution, Mulya's father had taken another position. Now he was running a steel mill in the small town of Vyksa, a backwater of old Russia. They were of the sort of gentry that led a cozy but spartan life. The world was the family and the servants and a few other children—the occasional visitor staying, as was the custom, for weeks—the holidays, summers glorious but brief, and long winters of magical icicles and sleigh rides.

I t was the old Russian life, even though there was a war on with the Germans, *says Mulya.* Life was very measured and serene.

My mother never set foot in the kitchen. She didn't even know how to cook. We had a cook, a Latvian woman named Suzanna. And we had Manya, a peasant girl in her early twenties whose village used to belong to my grandfather. So, we had a maid, a governess, Manya, Suzanna, women who came to do the heavy washing, and a coachman. It was twenty miles to the nearest railroad station, a team and a coachman were an absolute must.

When I turned six my father decided that it was imperative that I study a foreign language. Both my parents were a bit on the revolutionary side, my mother more than my father. They considered French the language of "society" and settled on my learning German, more the language of science.

Mother didn't want to send us to school and decided that she would teach us at home herself. There was a classroom on the second floor and we had to be there at a certain time after breakfast. Mother would teach us reading, arithmetic, geography. Father usually came back from the mill at one o'clock and he'd play loud marches on the piano, which meant classes were over.

Then after lunch Mulya could run out and play with the boys, climb trees, build tree houses. And they had to watch out for her. Small and quick, soft of manner, she competed in earnest and was never happier than when besting her brother. Good at math and building blocks, Mulya didn't care much for religion, especially the monastery she visited the week before Easter, the holiest time for the Russian Orthodox, who give the greatest glory to the Resurrection, not the Birth. The services were interminable, Mulya would be dizzy with hunger. And the little orphan girls who lived there looked like they had never learned to play.

"Everything was black and white. All the priests dressed in black robes and the nuns wore black and the buildings had white cupolas and golden crosses and white walls and black pine trees all around. And the food was awful."

*

Life was rich and stately for Mulya in the eternal backwoods of Russia, but for another little girl, Ruth Bonner, born in Siberia the same year as the twentieth century, life always tasted of exile. Her ancestors had been forcibly sent to Siberia in the eighteenth century by Catherine the Great. Not as convicts, but as forced labor, to populate the land and work it.

" 'On foot to Siberia under the lash,' that was the expression used back then," says Ruth Bonner with a bitter appreciation of the phrase's concision. She laughs at herself when remembering her youth and the youth of the century, both so full of spirit and so innocent, not that hers was in the least pampered. Some brutal truths became familiar early.

M y father's clan was very different from my mother's. Nearly everyone on my father's side of the family was fired up about revolution. They were all against the Tsar and for the poor. The children were split up into Socialist Revolutionaries, Bolsheviks, Mensheviks, anarchists, whatever you like, anything but monarchists. After the revolution of 1905 some of them even ended up in prison, or doing hard labor, or in exile.

No sooner was my childhood over than I began making the acquaintance of those . . . institutions. I visited relatives in prisons and labor colonies. I had aunts in them all.

One of my aunts was even sentenced to capital punishment. During the 1905 revolution, it was either in Tomsk or in Kiev, she had organized soldiers to mutiny, nothing more, nothing less. And she was tried as a traitor and sentenced to death. But then the defense proved that she was still a minor. At that time, a person was a minor until twenty-one. Her death sentence was reduced to life at hard labor. And she was in prison from 1905 until 1917. Twelve years.

Once a year my grandfather's clan got together to sit down at the table for dinner and long discussions. About the revolution, persecution, prison, exile, whatever. The older children had theoretical arguments. The Socialist Revolutionaries argued with the Bolsheviks, and the Mensheviks argued with the Socialist Revolutionaries and the anarchists. There were as many party positions at the table as there were children, each one trying to win the day. They discussed land reform, the working class, the situation of the working class, the need to increase the number of workers, the influx of workers from the country to the city. They all argued ferociously and sometimes fist fights broke out. Then my grandfather would step in.

When I was fourteen we started a little magazine at school. The others were a little older than I was, fifteen, sixteen. But they took me on because I could draw well. This was during the First World War. In one issue we ran an article about rich people making money in the black market trade in opium. The hashish and opium came from abroad, from Manchuria and China. And from Mongolia. We said that one of those black marketeers had just built a house near our town and if you dug up around it, you'd find nothing but opium. And we wrote about the war too, about the generals. We said that our governor general Kiyashka spent more time on beauties than on business.

And we did satire, fairly childish stuff. Once we wanted to depict German war atrocities. There was an exercise bar out in the yard. Two posts, a crossbar, with rings hanging down. The children pretended to be hanging me. They put a rope around my neck and made it look like it was tied to the crossbar. But it was really slack. I was up on a little bench. They knocked the bench out from under me, and at the same instant they took a picture. And there I was—a German war atrocity!

By the time I was sixteen I was an out-and-out Socialist Revolutionary. A real terrorist. I had a fairly elementary program—kill the bad people and let the good ones live. Kill all the bad people, or throw them in jail, and let the good ones enjoy life. Though I couldn't have defined what "good" meant.

My mother corresponded with her brother, who was a professor at Moscow University. Mother's family was completely different than father's, who hadn't had much education. They were clearly wealthier because the children had studied abroad. To study abroad meant you had money. And they were all gifted musicians. For a long time my grandfather's brother was second violin at the Bolshoi. Mama's brother had graduated from a university in Germany and was well known as a psychologist. Now he was a professor at Moscow University.

Those relatives were more conservative, more educated, more interested in art, literature, poetry, and science. And they were somewhat removed from social problems and politics. Liberal democrats. By that time I couldn't have been much farther left.

So, my mother wrote to her brother and said, "I'm sending my little terrorist to you."

That was at the beginning of 1917. Just in time for the February Revolution.

The rejoicing that the revolution induced did not, however, last long. Recognized by the United States and other Western democracies, the Provisional Government was soon in trouble. It not only continued the war but continued to lose it. Nor could it halt the slide toward economic ruin. Provisionary in nature, it did not feel empowered to give land to the peasants, who only wanted peace and land. Kerensky, the head of the government, became derisively known as "persuader in chief," for he lacked soldiers and police to enforce his will. In fact, in his capital (which, for patriotic reasons during the war, had been renamed Petrograd, Russian for Petersburg) he had a very real rival for power—the organization of workers known as the Petrograd Soviet. If push came to shove, the troops stationed in the capital would obey the Petrograd Soviet and not Kerensky.

Germany, wishing Russia out of the war, allowed the dangerous radical Vladimir Lenin to return to Russia in a sealed train, hoping he would foment revolution. Lenin, the leader of the Bolshevik faction of the communists, had been caught off guard by the February Revolution, having despaired of seeing the overthrow of tsardom in his lifetime. With his keen sense of power, Lenin recognized that now there were only two forces, the government and the soviets, which existed in every city and army regiment. And he made his position clear when he launched the slogan: ALL POWER TO THE SOVIETS!

As early as 1902 Lenin had formulated his dream and ambition: "Give us an organization of revolutionaries and we shall overturn the whole of Russia!" He had that organization, and Russia had been half-overturned already. And among his followers there were none who would prove more unswerving in his devotion than Ivan Vrachov.

Ivan had been drawn to Marxism, the philosophy that did not explain the world but sought to change it, and to Lenin's party, the Bolsheviks, as those smart and tough enough to do just that. He was still cutting hair in the theater. Now it was time to declare himself.

I had a friend, a printer by trade. We were on such close terms that he didn't hide the fact that he was a member of the Bolshevik wing of the Social Democratic Workers' Party.

And so I said to him, "Help me join the party."

But he said, "To become a revolutionary you need to steep yourself in the working class. You move in cultured circles, you deal with theater people. That's not where you belong! You have to go over to the working class!"

"Alright," I said, "I'll quit the theater!"

My friend the printer promised to get me a job in a factory, but soon afterwards he was sent out of Moscow and the job didn't come through. Then I was called up by the army. The February Revolution found me in a military hospital suffering from pleurisy. And it was there in the hospital that I began using all the arguments I had to win the wounded soldiers over to the cause of the revolution. That's how it all started. And from then on, it was all just like a fairy tale.

When I had recovered, I was transferred to the garrison in the Russian town of Voronezh on the Don River. Before I left I went to see the wife of my friend the printer. She knew many revolutionary songs and could sing them. I asked her to teach me them. I went there every day and learned the basic songs. And on the train to Voronezh I taught all the young soldiers those songs. We sang the "Marseillaise," "Bravely, comrades, keep step," "Let us renounce the old world," and other revolutionary songs.

And when we arrived in Voronezh, we marched through the main streets of town, singing those revolutionary songs so beautifully that people stopped and applauded. That was my entrance into Voronezh. A fairy tale.

I only did two days of boot camp. I was immediately elected a member of the company revolutionary committee, and soon I was chosen to serve as a deputy of the Voronezh Soviet

of soldiers and workers. Now I joined the Bolsheviks. And
from then on I was acting on instructions from the Voronezh
party committee.

In June 1917 a province conference of Bolsheviks was
held in Moscow and the Voronezh party organization sent me
there as a delegate, me, a twenty-year-old! That conference was
an education in itself. One of the main points on the agenda
was the issue of the party's new platform. In April Lenin had
called for the party to be transformed into a revolutionary
organization. We discussed the issue and what we decided was:
We want to turn this bourgeois democratic revolution into a
proletarian revolution. Then we'll be able to carry out Lenin's
slogan—ALL POWER TO THE SOVIETS!

At that time in Voronezh I could walk freely about the
city with my armband that read: Member, Executive Committee
of the Voronezh Soviet. I wasn't afraid of anything. And
nothing happened to me or to any of my colleagues. At that
time there were really two governments in Voronezh and other
large cities. In practice, the governor of Voronezh Province
could not undertake anything of importance without the
consent of the Voronezh Soviet. The commander of the
garrison could not issue any significant orders without the
consent of the Voronezh Soviet. Not to mention the mayor.

Fearing the increasing power of the soviets, the commander in
chief of the Russian army, General Kornilov, marched grandly into
Moscow in August 1917 to stage a coup against the Provisional
Government of Alexander Kerensky and to restore order by crushing the rebellious soviets. But this gambit depended on the arrival
of Cossack troops from the south, and one of the men blocking that
move was Ivan Vrachov.

A very serious task had been thrust on us, the Bolsheviks of
Voronezh. Kaledin, the leader of the Cossacks of the Don
army, was rushing to Kornilov's aid. Voronezh lay on his path,
he couldn't reach Moscow without passing through Voronezh.

The Voronezh Soviet formed a military committee.

Lookouts were posted at all the important stations on the southeastern rail line, working closely with the main railroad trade unions. We took control of all the more important stations. And no matter how hard Kaledin tried to send troops to aid Kornilov, he failed, we blocked the tracks. Us Bolsheviks would go up to those trains full of Cossacks and argue with them until they saw the light—"Brothers, Cossacks! What are you doing!? Do you have any idea of what you're being sent to do!?"

None of this had changed Mulya's life a bit. News was always late in coming to that little backwoods town, and by the time the news did arrive it had lost most of its freshness and urgency. The rhythms of the old life were strong—tea, lessons, snowmen, chats with the servants, the occasional holy wanderer begging a meal. But Ruth Bonner's life had changed drastically, or so at least it appeared. Exiled by her mother to Moscow—to culture, education, good behavior—the "little terrorist" proved only half-corrected.

W hen I arrived in Moscow my uncle immediately placed me in a good high school. And he helped me prepare for my degree exams, which I passed. It was a very rare thing for a woman to get a high school degree in that day and age.

I lived in two different worlds. In my uncle's world everyone had season tickets for the theater, and especially for symphony. They were all very musical in that family, but an elephant must have stepped on *my* ear. They took me to see *Peer Gynt,* which was considered a very daring and progressive work, I had to fight to keep my eyes open.

And they also had concerts at home, well-known people came, people sang or recited poetry. Alexander Kuprin, a famous writer, even attended one New Year's there and I took it upon myself to tell him that his novel *The Pit* was immoral. He held himself by the stomach and laughed and laughed. "Where did you dig up this treasure?" he said. "In Mother Siberia," I said, "as far east as it gets."

But I lived in two worlds because that aunt of mine

who'd been sentenced to death was now living in Moscow. She had been received with honor in Moscow for having suffered twelve years of hard labor for the cause of revolution. She and a few others like her were given a whole house on Lyalin Lane. They were very much in vogue. They were given food and a stipend, and lived quite nicely there on Lyalin Lane.

I'd run over there whenever I had a moment free from being tutored by my uncle, from my exams, my Latin, Greek, and all the rest of my classical education. I always felt more at home with those people who'd been exiled and had done hard labor. And they always greeted me with love and hugs.

In that house every word printed in the papers and press was discussed, every aspect, every pro and con.

In October, when the revolution erupted and the fighting started, none of us children were allowed to set foot outside the house. My uncle had four children, the oldest was the same age as I, seventeen, and the rest were younger.

From the window I could see Karetno-Sadovaya Street. There was no fighting there but the sounds of fighting carried from Gorky Street. Big crowds would go by, shouting, sometimes fights would break out. Sentries from one side or another would go past, you couldn't tell who was who.

It was turmoil. But after a few days some order was established. Armed house committees were formed because break-ins were occurring. There was petty crime right from the start.

The hunger was boundless. There I was living in a well-to-do professor's home and for the whole mob of children, there were five of us, my aunt would cut up tiny pieces of bread and say, "Bite off a little and chew it slowly and wash it down with water so you feel like you ate something. That's all you're getting."

They were also swapping belongings for food. Not at the market, with private persons. Moscow immediately became a closed city. Nobody came in, nobody went out. But still, what they used to call "bag men" would bring in some food from the country. One time my aunt and uncle brought home a little round sack of sunflower seeds. They'd swapped a dress for them. And so every day I'd spend a couple of hours husking sunflowers and eating seeds until I felt full. It was better than studying Greek.

Another time they swapped a clock for a bag of oats, the kind horses are fed. You had to steam the oats for a long time until the skin broke and then you'd suck out the little seed inside. We had butter, egg whites. Mushrooms and berries too, but at fabulous prices and only bought direct.

They wouldn't let us out of the house for a minute, and so the "little terrorist" had to watch the October Revolution from the window of a professor's house.

The fighting that Ruth glimpsed in Moscow was fiercer than that in Petrograd, where Bolshevik-led troops suffered only six casualties in taking the Winter Palace, seizing power from the Provisional Government, which by then was protected by troops consisting largely of women and youths. Kerensky had already fled and there was really no one in charge. Lenin had his fulcrum to move Russia, but the revolution would have to be repeated in city after city before it would really be won.

Ivan Vrachov, who always speaks for the record, to correct the endlessly distorted record that perverts both the revolution's glory and its truth, says:

S ome people still believe that the party's Central Committee sent a directive to prepare for the October uprising. And they think that then the provincial committees met, discussed the issue, passed a resolution, worked out a plan—who to mobilize, where to send them—and that's how the revolution was made. Utter nonsense!

There was no directive from the party's Central Committee, nor could there have been. The party was torn by dissension. On October 16 when the Central Committee held an illegal meeting and Lenin proposed that it prepare for an armed uprising, some of the old Bolsheviks didn't support him. And so there was no directive.

People had to figure things out for themselves. All by themselves. We were aware that an uprising was in preparation but when, or how it would take place, that we didn't know. And when the October Revolution took place in Petrograd we had no way of knowing about it because the relations between the various factions had taken a turn for the worse. The Socialist Revolutionaries, the SRs, had control of the telegraph and concealed the information from us.

Still, rumors did reach us that something important was in the works. We started preparing. We formed a temporary revolutionary committee in one of the larger army units. We held a meeting. Since we had no information to go on, we adopted the proposal made by the old Bolshevik Kartashev to prepare for action but to abstain from taking any for the time being. Kartashev the old Bolshevik said, "We can spoil things badly by acting prematurely."

All the same, we formed an action squad, just in case—if something happened, it would be able to make important decisions in the name of our party. The squad was composed of five people—three Bolsheviks and two left SRs. And one of those Bolsheviks was me.

I decided to spend the night of October 30 in the office of the soviet. I had no place of my own and I sometimes spent the night in the soviet. Then all of a sudden a special messenger arrives from the army camp in Voronezh and informs me that counterrevolutionary officers had started disarming part of the garrison. The regiments had been given an ultimatum—turn in your machine guns and ammunition. They'd gotten the jump on us!

I dashed outside like a madman and caught up with Moiseev, the head of the action squad. His response: "Let's get over there!"

We hired a horse-drawn cab and set off for the garrison.

The counterrevolution was on the move and it had to be resisted, it had to be stopped.

Relying on the revolutionary committee of the 5th Machine Gun Regiment, nearly all of whom supported the Bolsheviks, we began preparing an armed action with the goal of capturing and disarming the officers.

And it was the garrison commander's own fault that he was killed. He resisted, he opened fire first, he gave the order to open fire and he fired himself. He was killed along with a few other officers.

And that's how the October Revolution was launched in Voronezh, all because two members of the action squad went ahead and took the initiative.

The next morning we called on the workers to revolt and they responded by seizing the telegraph office, the train station, and the other important facilities like the telephone exchange. And when that was done they declared, ALL POWER TO THE SOVIETS!

Civil War

Part One

They were quick on their feet in that family. No sooner had Ilya Jaffee spotted the Tsar's train than he had tricked his teacher and was out the door; no sooner had Lenin and Dzerzhinsky formed the Cheka, the secret police, than Ilya's uncle joined it.

The Cheka itself had been founded quickly. Born on December 7, 1917, six weeks after the revolution, minutes in terms of historical gestation, the Cheka was the revolution's twin, fraternal if not identical. As an acronym, Cheka stands for Extraordinary Committee to Combat Counterrevolution and Sabotage; as a word it means "linchpin." The creation of the Cheka was the Bolshevik's declaration of civil war, although the actual military engagements between the Whites and the Reds would not come until the next year, 1918.

As a Marxist, Lenin was convinced that history was a force that, like physics or chemistry, could be understood. Unlike these sciences, however, it could not be exploited, only directed and hastened, toward its inevitable end, communism. His dedication to his vision was itself a form of ruthlessness, but, like most Bolsheviks, he could be human in his off-hours.

Having seized power, he formed a government that included Leon Trotsky, orator, author, and soon to be creator of the Red Army, and Joseph Stalin, a moustached Georgian with the right background and organizational skills to head up the department of ethnic affairs. The Russia that Lenin now ruled was composed of many nations, nearly all of which were seeking to break free, but Lenin had not the slightest intention of surrendering even one milligram of the power he now had.

After the revolution, the long-promised election had come, and people from all over Russia freely elected a representative body that was known as the Constituent Assembly. Three-quarters of the country voted far left, Lenin's Bolsheviks coming in third. The Assembly met for the first time on January 5, 1918, and for the last time on January 6, when Lenin sent armed sailors to close that bourgeois charade down. This was not a popularity contest, this was the serious business of history, where your enemy is best killed.

At the end of January, the Bolsheviks changed from the old Russian calendar to that of the West, leaping thirteen days forward in time, causing the anniversary of the October Revolution to fall in November. They at once began nationalizing industry and seizing grain from the peasants to feed the workers of the cities and the soldiers of the armies. Not that the Bolsheviks had any interest in continuing the war. In March they signed the disastrous Brest-Litovsk peace treaty with the Germans that cost them the Ukraine, Poland, Finland, Lithuania, Latvia, and Estonia—sixty million people.

As it had under Tsar Nicholas and under Kerensky, Russia now needed time and peace, and, as under Nicholas and Kerensky, Russia was again given neither. By the early spring, the counterrevolutionary Whites, composed of several, largely uncoordinated armies, were attacking Soviet Russia from its southern and eastern peripheries. The Whites were tsarist officers, nobility, conservative Cossacks, peasants, the middle class, intellectuals, even some leftists who were more anti-Bolshevik than anything else. The Whites had passion but no vision of the future. The Reds had both.

The Reds also had control of the Russian heartland, including the big cities and their industry. But they were besieged from every side because now the Allies, still fighting Germany, invaded Russia as part of their persecution of the war. Some, like the sixty thousand Japanese who entered from the Far East, had territorial aims in mind. The forty thousand British and ten thousand Americans were there mostly for strategic reasons, though the British did lend matériel and consulting officers to the Whites.

There were several theaters of war, never a united front. And within those theaters the lines were very fluid, a city never knowing under whose power it would wake in the morning. The fighting had all the passionate heat and cruelty of fratricide. White atrocities were excesses of sentiment, while the Reds had a more deliberate weapon, the Cheka.

The Cheka's job was spot welding with terror. Enemies of the revolution were to be eliminated. A member of the Cheka, a Chekist, was a man of action, his mind unclouded by doubt or scruple, able to pass a death sentence in less time than it took to load a rifle, aim, and fire. Ilya's uncle had some of that quickness and iron, qualities which Ilya had never once glimpsed in his three visions of the Tsar.

When the Civil War broke out, my uncle the Chekist was on his way back from Petrograd to the Ukraine. He stopped by to see us. On that very day my youngest sister died of starvation. My uncle, a man of tremendous energy, said, "You're all going to die like flies here!"

And the Whites were coming. My uncle sent our whole family away from Belorussia, to Zaporozhye in the Ukraine. We traveled in a heated cattle car. When the train stopped at a station called Sinelnikov, my parents went out to buy food. My mother came back with a jug of milk and my father was carrying a big loaf of white bread that must have weighed ten pounds. They handed up the bread to my brother Misha and me. And while they were climbing back up into the cattle car, my brother and I started tearing the bread to pieces. By the time my mother was back in the car with the milk, the bread was all gone.

We stayed with my uncle's family in Zaporozhye. Since he was in the Cheka, he lived well and there was plenty to go around. Then Denikin's White Army took the city and my uncle fled. The Whites came to his apartment but he wasn't there. That infuriated them and they beat my father so savagely he was crippled for life.

My father couldn't work anymore. As the brightest of the five children, I had been singled out to study to become a rabbi. But now at age thirteen I went to work. Through the synagogue they found me a job in a bakery. The bread I brought home kept my family from dying of hunger.

Ilya's uncle the Chekist had saved the Jaffee family from hunger and from the Whites in the north only to deliver them to hunger and crippling White cruelty in the south. There would be no more schooling for Ilya, but the lessons kept coming and he was still a fast learner.

Ilya would have made a good rabbi because faith for him was not an idea but oxygen for the very fire of his metabolism. And he would not have been shy about standing before his congregation and projecting his voice and instructions into every heart. Still, he would have also had an aptitude for the Talmudic, a finesse for hairsplitting.

But it wasn't hairs that were being split in the Russia of 1918. When Ilya went to work in the bakery, he was thirteen, the age at which, in Jewish tradition, a boy becomes a man. And Ilya had become a man, the man of the house, supporting his family on bread, the last staple before starvation. In his case, the transition was not marked with the ancient readings but with the modern ceremony of political violence, which had more power over the mind of a child than any holy book. Ilya himself had no politics yet, but he did have a political enemy—the Whites, the tsarist officers, the aristocrats, the Cossacks, the anti-Semites, all the sons of bitches that had ruled Russia for a thousand years.

I worked nights in the bakery and I started reading to keep from falling asleep, *says Ilya.* I read Sherlock Holmes, that sort of thing. Still, it made me a better reader.

I started wondering what the scientists had to say. I'd come across the name of Darwin in some book and so I decided to start with Darwin. I went to the library and asked for Darwin. They told me, You won't understand a word of it. But I took the books out anyway.

I read Darwin all through the night, night after night. I had taken out two of his books—*The Origin of Species* and *The Descent of Man.*

I immediately got the feeling that Darwin's against God. He doesn't tell you not to believe in God, but he proves that man was not created on the seventh day but was the gradual product of evolution.

One of the books had color illustrations. Pictures of hands—a monkey's, a primate's, prehistoric man's, modern man's. They had clearly evolved over the generations. This proved that God did not create man. I ceased believing in God.

*

Nikita was lucky, his faith never wavered. Perhaps that was because he was a Cossack to the marrow, bred for the only two occupations worthy of a man—farming and fighting. His loyalties were clear, a ladder that led from the chief of the Cossacks, the ataman, to the tsar of Russia, to heaven and the God of the Russian Orthodox. Originally, the Cossacks were Russians too proud and brave to live in servitude. They fled to the south, where Turkish-speaking tribes still marauded. The name Cossack—*Kazak,* free warrior—was given them by one of those tribes, or taken by the Cossacks the way they took territory.

They settled in the rich lands of the south and prospered as farmers. The Cossacks were a people apart, a people that on very short notice could become an army of cavalry whose specialty was the charge and saber slash, cutting an enemy diagonally in two, from the base of the neck to the waist at the opposite side.

In time the Russian Empire had extended its authority to

the Cossacks' lands. In return for military service the Cossacks were allowed to maintain their independent lives. In the Civil War most of them fought with the Whites. For the Cossacks the restoration of the old ways was vision of future enough.

A wistful anguish overcomes Nikita when he remembers the days of his Cossack youth, the fields golden as icons in his memory, the sky sweet blue and arched.

Nikita seems to have been born at attention. His posture accentuates his cheekbones, not massive, two sharp facets under the skin. He has the warrior's nonchalance, and at times his light blue eyes sparkle with Cossack mischief. But when he speaks of his life he at once becomes Lieutenant Nikita Ivanovich Yovich of the Kuban Cossack Army, reporting:

I was the sixteenth child. Ten died early, leaving seven of us—two sisters, five brothers.

I was born in 1900, in the land of the Kuban Cossacks. Our settlement was called Voznesensk. It stretched for seven miles along the Shamlyk River, which feeds into the Laba, a tributary of the Kuban River that empties into the Black Sea. Cossacks never lived in the city unless they were serving and had been posted there.

According to the census of 1913, Voznesensk had a population of some twenty-two thousand. A little less than half the population were Cossacks. The rest were what we called outsiders.

My father was an ordinary Cossack, a noncommissioned officer. Every Cossack had to serve four years active duty in the army and you were in the reserves until you were thirty-three. A Cossack was responsible for his own horse and equipment, everything except for weapons. Once a year there'd be a general meeting and a Cossack would have to show what shape his equipment was in.

Every Cossack worked the land. There were no factories where we lived. Just grain mills, sugar plants, creameries. Cossacks were farmers. The Cossacks were different from the rest of Russia and all the rest of the world—Cossacks didn't own their land. The land belonged to the Cossack community and when a male Cossack reached seventeen, he was apportioned his share. Women were not given land.

It was all up to you. If you worked hard and were serious about it, you'd make money, get wealthy. You'd have horses and good cows and machines to plow the land. The lazier you were, the harder you had it. But no one went begging in Voznesensk.

Maybe it was because the climate was good or because Cossacks were hardworking people, but life was good in Voznesensk. Drunkenness and brawls were very rare, and a murder would have been unthinkable. Still, some of the Cossacks did love to play cards. If a man was playing cards too much his wife would go to the ataman, the Cossack leader. The Cossacks elected their own ataman and could boot him out too.

The woman would go to the ataman, fall to her knees and burst into tears: "My husband's been beating me, the children are going hungry and all he does is play cards." An hour later the husband would be brought before the ataman: "If you play cards again, I'm sending you to Siberia."

That's how it was—if a Cossack neglected his family, if he drank and brawled and his children went around dirty, the assembly, the elders, would petition the emperor to strip the man of his rank of Cossack, and then he'd be automatically sent to Siberia.

Cossacks were churchgoing. In our settlement of twenty-five thousand there were three Russian Orthodox churches, two Old Believers, and two United Faith churches for Old Believers who wanted to rejoin the Orthodox. I went to church too. It was all very strict.

There were no illiterate people in Voznesensk. We had a boys' high school and a girls', a technical institute, and an agricultural institute. There was even an elementary school for girls, a rare thing.

I graduated from high school. I had eight years of German, seven of French, and six of Latin. In early 1918 I entered the Polytechnical Institute in the city of Ekaterinodar.

I was called up in March 1918. And by April I was an officer in the White Army.

I received three wounds and two promotions.

At first the war went well for the Whites. In the summer of 1918, the Whites were close to the Siberian city of Ekaterinburg, where Tsar Nicholas and the royal family were being held prisoner by the Reds. The cause of restoration could have been strengthened if the Tsar were to stand at the head of the White Army. As was often to be the case, a political equation equaled execution. On the night of July 16, 1918, the entire royal family and a few loyal servants were put to death. The question of succession was also thereby settled, two birds with one stone.

*

Nikita the Cossack was entering battle against men full of furious determination and keen hatred, like Starinov, who was not only born on the wrong side of the tracks, but spent most of his youth walking between the rails with his father, a track inspector at Zavidovo-Redkino on the Moscow–Petrograd line. They looked for cracked rails, broken ties, loose rivets, any flaw in the miles and miles of steel that knitted Russia together. The young Starinov saw more track than trees. But what he loved to see most of all was a hurtling locomotive brought to a hissing stop by his father, standing right by the tracks holding in one uplifted arm a red lantern or flag.

"Oh, I was for the Reds right from the very start," says Starinov. "I was in the city of Tver when the February Revolution broke out and I marched in the demonstrations. And after the October Revolution when those, what do you call them—bourgeois—and the aristocrats started sabotaging, I was immediately given a very important post: I was put in charge of supplying boots to the army throughout the province of Tver. And I was only eighteen years old."

The immense updraft of the revolution lifted Starinov to a position of prominence. And the opportunities he was given were themselves proof that the revolution was made by people like him and for people like him. People who were willing to fight for what they had now tasted.

Wto hen the Civil War started I could have been exempted because I was doing an important job—supplying the army with boots. But I refused the exemption and went to fight with the Red Army, *says Starinov.*

We were in the southern town of Korochi, and on the defensive, being attacked by White cavalry. Then they sounded retreat.

I hid in a root cellar. The White cavalry went by and I was stranded behind enemy lines. I spent five days behind enemy lines with enemy troops everywhere you looked.

Fortunately, I had read a good deal of literature about partisan warfare before I joined the army, articles telling how Russian soldiers had escaped from the Germans.

I traveled at night and slept by day. The first day I settled down to sleep in some nettle bushes. The Whites were letting the horses graze near there. One horse walked right over to where I was. I gave it a poke on the nose and it went away. Otherwise, it would have been all over.

Then night came and I set off. There were White guards out walking around, singing songs. A good thing it was a dark night. I gave them the slip.

The next day I found an empty barn on the outskirts of the town and went in. There was straw in the barn and I slept the day there. When I got up that evening I found that the door had been locked. I went out through the roof, it was thatched with straw and no problem to get through.

A while after I climbed down from the roof, I ran into a peasant. I told him I was a White and on my way to such and such a place. He said, "You're no White, you're a Red."

He gave me some food and told me, "The Reds retreated about twelve miles, they're on the other side of the river. That's where to go."

I walked for three days until I got there. Then I buried

my Red Army uniform, two grenades, and my rifle in a hemp field. I swapped my greatcoat to a peasant for some peasant clothes. I thought I'd be able to cross the lines if I was dressed like a peasant, carrying hay rakes. What a fool!

The Reds and Whites let peasants cross through the lines. On the way, I met a peasant woman who said to me, "Where do you think you're going? The Whites already hung two Reds over there, you want to be the third?"

I spent the rest of the day lying in some tall tomato plants. That night I got up and went to where I'd buried my rifle and took the two grenades and my ammunition. But I couldn't get my greatcoat back. The peasant had already dyed it to make it look like a civilian coat.

I swam across the river with my rifle and grenades. It wasn't a big river and I knew how to swim. Then I was grabbed by our own soldiers. Red Army uniform, rifle, civilian coat, no documents—a spy!

But I was lucky, my own regiment was nearby, they sent me over there, and the whole thing was squared away. And it wasn't long before I was back in battle again. And it was in that battle that I got my first wound.

It was a hot, summer day and our rifle division was taking a licking from the Whites. But we stayed on the attack even though the machine guns never stopped cutting us down, until all of a sudden it was the officers and gentlemen who found themselves in a tight spot.

We were seasoned by then and full of hatred.

A piece of shrapnel came out of nowhere, went through my puttees and into my right shin. My puttees were red with blood and my leg was on fire. I pulled out the shrapnel and bandaged up the leg. I didn't lose consciousness. I kept going. Everything was fine and dandy.

Nikita the Cossack was lucky with his first wound too; unfortunately, it wasn't in battle with the real enemy, the Reds, but with the underworld element who found the revolution a holiday for crime.

A gang had taken over a brewery near Voznesensk and they were running wild in there. Fifteen of us were issued rifles and sent to arrest them.

They had a guard posted at the gate but he ran away at the sight of us.

My friend and I were dispatched to the office. He went in first, I was right behind him. The man inside the office opened fire. I had my rifle in my right hand and threw up my left hand. Either it jolted him or he just missed, but the bullet whistled past my eye and grazed my temple. This was the first time anyone had shot point-blank at me.

Nikita rubs the tips of his fingers along the left side of his head, then looks at them as if expecting to see blood. It was not the sort of incident a young Cossack would dream of as his initiation, but what mattered most was that he had stared into the zero of a muzzle and been blooded as a brave.

*

Everything was not so fine and dandy the day after Starinov was wounded by shrapnel, which could have just as easily nicked open an aorta as pierced his shin.

W hen I woke up the next morning, my leg was swollen and inflamed. I tried to get up. Forget it! My head was swimming and I was seeing spots in front of my eyes.

They took me to the field hospital, one car of a military hospital train that smelled of iodoform, festering wounds, and dried blood. People were groaning and raving.

It took the train a day to get to the hospital in Tula.

The doctors said, "We'll have to amputate, young man. Above the knee. Do you consent?"

I didn't want to be a cripple at nineteen. "No, I won't let you do it."

"Gangrene will set in and you'll die."

"Let it, I don't care."

I lay there in the ward and I couldn't believe it—shrapnel, a scratch, and all of a sudden it's costing me a leg.

There was an old military medic there, a man named
Ivan Sergeevich. He lifted up my blanket and looked at my
swollen leg. After a minute he said, "That a boy, you did the
right thing not letting them amputate! We'll get you fixed up.
I'm going to wrap your leg with a compress made of plantain
to bring down the swelling and the fever. The medical men say
it's just an old wives' tale, but it works."

It was a miracle—my temperature started to fall and the
burning in my leg gradually went away.

Not only was his leg saved, but while convalescing Starinov also
found what would be his life's work. In the arguments among the
soldiers as to which branch of service was the best, he liked the
bravado of the military engineers who built bridges and blew
bridges up, laid track and derailed trains. As soon as he was on
his feet again, Starinov requested and was granted a transfer to the
27th Engineering Company of the Red Army.

*

Ivan Vrachov, as part of the Bolshevik action squad, had made the
revolution in Voronezh by acting on his own initiative, no problem
since his impulses were in harmony with Lenin's. Vrachov kept
rising higher in the party ranks, his life now entirely taken up with
party congresses, plenums, presidiums, delegations, issues, positions. At the age of twenty he was elected to the party's Central
Executive Committee and in Petrograd he caught the eye of the top
Bolshevik leaders.

During a session of the 10th Party Congress, there was an
announcement: "Comrade Vrachov, to the rostrum, see
Comrade Gorbunov."

I walked over and Gorbunov said, "Lenin wants to see
you."

"When?" I said.

"Right now."

"What are you talking about? We're still in session."

"Go see Lenin."

I went.

I introduced myself in a hushed voice. Someone brought
me a chair.

Lenin said to me, "At the party conference in Grozny,
did you come out in favor of leasing our oil refineries to
foreigners?"

"I did," I said.

On his desk in front of him Lenin had a reprint of the
minutes of the party meeting in Grozny. That I had spoken in
favor of concessions was underlined in red pencil.

"And what decision did the conference reach on your
report?"

"They were positive toward it. The ideas in my report
were the basis of the resolution issued by the conference."

Then Lenin leaned closer and put special emphasis on
what he was saying. "The country's going through a severe fuel
crisis. We can't get through this crisis without help from
abroad. And this is why we in the Central Committee intend to
lease out concessions to the oil industry in Grozny and Baku. I
want you to do something. Call a meeting of the Baku and
Grozny delegations and discuss the issue with them. Then
report to me. I'll give you a pass."

And he wrote: Let Comrade Vrachov in to see me.

But the capitalists were hostile to our country. The
capitalist corporations didn't want to come to our aid. Armand
Hammer was an exception. He set up a pencil factory in
Moscow. But that wasn't what Lenin wanted. And, in the end,
we succeeded in getting the oil industry back on its feet all by
ourselves.

A short while after being singled out by Lenin, Vrachov was approached by one of the key Bolshevik leaders, the brilliant orga-
nizer Yakov Sverdlov, who proposed that Vrachov remain in Petrograd.

" 'But what about Voronezh?' I said.

" 'They'll find someone to replace you in Voronezh. We
need people here too.' "

Bolsheviks knew how to make quick decisions, and how

to obey them without question. Ivan Vrachov remained in Petrograd.

I n March Sverdlov summoned me, *continues Vrachov,* and said that the Central Committee was sending him and another one of Lenin's closest associates, Grigory Zinoviev, to Moscow in order to, as he put it, make "good Christians out of the Moscow Bolsheviks." They were categorically against making peace with the Germans, and had said that if a peace were concluded they'd even break it.

"But what do you need me for?" I asked Sverdlov.

"We'll find something for you. Get ready. Quick as you can!"

We traveled in a single dining car attached to a locomotive. There was Sverdlov, Zinoviev, a Latvian communist, myself, and a group of sailors from Sverdlov's personal guard.

On the way Sverdlov told me that he had another task. Lenin and the Central Committee had decided to shift the capital, from Petrograd, which was in danger from the German army, to Moscow. It was Sverdlov's task to effect the transfer. A commission would be formed to do the groundwork for transferring the government. And I was to be on that commission.

How could the Bolsheviks have anything but faith in themselves if even a twenty-one-year-old, the son of a stoker and a woman who hired herself out to cook and do laundry, could have a hand in moving the capital of all Russia from the imperial city founded by Peter the Great two hundred years before.

*

The historical axis of Russia was shifting and the shock waves even reached the Ural Mountains, the traditional divide between Europe and Asia, where Mulya's restless father had taken a job running one of three steel mills in the city of Magnitogorsk. But even though the whole family, servants, silver, portraits, and all had moved with him, it was now 1918 and the "old Russian life" was over.

By then Mulya, the gentry tomboy, already knew a good deal about her father's profession. She was curious, observant, inquisitive. Like him, she had a better handle on the technical problems of the mill than on the political mood of the workers.

There were strikes at the blast furnaces, *says Mulya.* Blast furnaces can't stand strikes because they have to be emptied before you stop feeding them. Otherwise, a crust forms on top of the molten iron, creating a vacuum underneath. But my father and the others couldn't convince the workers of this. Blast furnaces exploded and a lot of workers were killed.

There was a tremendous rumble of displeasure from the workers after the first explosion. The second time a blast furnace exploded many people were badly burned and the workers beat up the foreman of that particular mill. When the third explosion happened we were sure that father would be the first one to be attacked. But, fortunately, no workers were killed.

Finally, these disturbances among the workers reached a climax and some people came one night and arrested both my father and my mother. All of the influential people of the town were arrested. Mother because she was known for her educational work, and father because he was the head of the mill and perhaps because of his gentry origin.

The people who came had guns and were very rude. They just took my parents away. There were no charges against them, the only charge against my father was that he was the head of the mill. They put mother and father on a train and sent them to prison in the town of Ufa.

The power to arrest people was given to the head of the communist party in the town. Later he stopped sending people to Ufa and just shot them in his own cellar. My parents had been lucky to be arrested and sent off to Ufa. After about three months in prison they were released, but they couldn't come back. So they asked Manya the maid to bring the children to Ufa.

Manya packed everything she could. But the paintings were left behind, the furniture, everything. We fled to Ufa. Five of us children, Manya, and the old nurse.

We traveled in a freight car that had just been emptied of coal. The side walls were covered with coal dust—the ceiling, the floor, everything. So, Manya put all of our things in the middle of the floor and told us to sit there on our trunks and not to touch the walls. Still, we were pretty black by the time we arrived.

Father was without a job. And the interesting thing is that in Ufa my parents happened to meet the Jewish family my father helped to escape the pogrom before he was married. That family had an apartment in Ufa and invited us to share it with them. And we moved in with them.

Bravery and generosity were rewarded as in a fairy tale and Mulya was free to go back to her childhood again, leading the children in games for the whole summer, until suddenly the Reds deserted the city and a new army marched in with a military band. Ufa was now under White control.

F ather was offered the job of heading a series of steel mills around Ufa. There were three members of the board, appointed by whatever White government it was. Father was one of the three.

And so we went to Asha Balashovsk, where there was a small steel mill. There was a river there that was dammed and both sides of the river were covered with the slag from the blast furnaces. Slag from a blast furnace is a beautiful thing, all shades of blue, aqua.

My brother and I used to go out and collect pieces of slag, crystal, river stones. One day mother asked us to go find her a smooth river stone that she could use for a darning egg. We made a competition out of it, but it wasn't really fair because I had already spotted the perfect stone and ran right out and got it. But my brother had to really go out and look until he found one. Mother was very nice about taking both of the stones.

The whole situation was rather uncertain there. One of the three members of father's board had been killed while sitting at his desk reading the Bible. Shot through the window. Probably by one of the communists who were trying to disrupt the mills, which were now under White control.

Then the Red Army approached and we had to leave. Father ordered one of the freight cars fixed up inside. The carpenters really fixed it up very nicely, making living quarters with folding beds. By then it was wintertime, approaching Christmas. We were fairly warm in the freight car, which had a wood-burning stove. I was very disturbed that we did not have a Christmas tree. I kept saying, "Can't we stop somewhere and cut one of those trees?"

But they couldn't stop in that Siberian landscape of snow and immense evergreens until they finally reached safety in Chelyabinsk, a few hundred miles due east of Ufa.

Chelyabinsk in winter, and it was impossible for us to find any living quarters. Ten or fifteen miles from Chelyabinsk was a little village, all of those villages were Cossack villages in Siberia. Father found a family that was willing to rent us two rooms. Afterwards, my father remained in Chelyabinsk. Eight of us—the old nurse, Manya, my mother, and the five of us children—all lived in two rooms. The family of the Cossacks all moved to the kitchen, where they had sleeping shelves around the big Russian stove.

An engineer and his family also lived in that hut. One of the girls was blind and became my very good friend. She had a lot of imagination. I could tell her stories and she believed everything. We'd walk along the frozen lakes pretending we were in the jungle being chased by tigers and lions.

Mulya's family had achieved another makeshift safety. But Russia was a chaos of armies; towns would be taken and retaken by Reds and Whites a dozen times, each victor inflicting reprisals. In the south, anarchist bands, marauders with wild politics, appeared in the interstices, only to slaughter and vanish. Allied with the Whites, an entire Czech army of forty thousand former POWs was fighting its way eastward out of Russia.

But the multiplicity of their enemies only strengthened the Reds' unity. The Red Army forged by Leon Trotsky was winning victories now, recovering territory. They had industry, which plays a huge role in modern war, and they had faith, which plays a huge role in any war.

Ilya Jaffee had lost his faith in God while reading Darwin. War had shown him that, underneath it all, life was violent struggle. The Whites had become his enemy when they beat his father so savagely that he would be too crippled even to support his family. But hatred of the enemy was not enough for Ilya Jaffee. He needed a picture of the world that was true to life's atrocious grandeur. His innate need for faith was as maddeningly organic as the hunger that had caused Ilya to devour the bread on the train, leaving nothing for his parents.

"Wrangel's White Army was nearby. A Red propaganda train had stopped in our city. The man in charge of the train was named Potemkin and he later became minister of education. Posters went up announcing a series of lectures. I started attending them. Potemkin was a wonderful speaker, he made everything so clear. And in fact he was the one who got me thinking about the problems of society."

Propaganda trains were painted with oversize slogans and bright pictures to catch the eye of the many illiterates. Some of the country's best artists had greeted the revolution as an elemental force that would transform Russia and had sacrificed their art in service to the revolution.

Comrade Potemkin, Ilya's first guru of communism, may have been related to the Potemkin who was the lover of Catherine the Great, the eighteenth-century empress, and who was rewarded for his services with the governorship of a vast province in the south. Potemkin remained a popular Rabelaisian figure. A battleship was named after him, the very one on which the sailors mutinied in 1905, turning their huge guns on the Black Sea port city of Odessa. In Russia the past is always present and never more so than in names and words.

One day, *says Ilya,* there was supposed to be an open-air lecture under a tent by the river. I get there, and there's a big audience, mostly Red Army men, but no speaker. We wait and we wait, and then someone comes out and says, "Instead of a lecture, there's going to be a court of revolutionary justice presided over by Comrade Potemkin."

In the first case, four people were tried—a father, his two sons, and some relative. They had murdered the chairman of the Poor Peasants' Committee. He'd been collecting taxes, which they stole after murdering him. The sentence—Firing squad, no right of appeal!

The next case was of two people accused of forging documents in order to receive three freight cars of food products, which they had dumped on the private market. And the food belonged to the army. One of the defendants, Engelhart, lived right near us. He was a little old man, a seventy-year-old notary. The other defendant was a big guy. Engelhart could have told the big guy what blank documents to steal.

But there's another act in this play. All of a sudden the big guy claims he fought in the revolution of 1905 and even was on the battleship *Potemkin.* A real hero! They start asking around the audience, "Anyone here from the battleship *Potemkin?*" Three men get up. One sailor says, "I don't remember him." They start asking him questions—how they sighted the battleship's guns, what parts of Odessa they had fired at. And of course he didn't know. He was just a crook who had done time for theft under the Tsar. Those two got the same sentence—Firing squad, no right of appeal!

Then Potemkin asked if there was anyone who wished to take part in executing the sentence of the proletarian court.

A forest of hands! Those were Red Army men. Forty were selected, and they took the prisoners over to the side of the road and executed them right there on the spot. I had a strong sense of moral satisfaction at seeing proletarian justice meted out. But still I slept badly that night.

Nikita the Kuban Cossack was in Wrangel's army, attacking the area where Ilya Jaffee had just witnessed the living theater of revolutionary justice. But Nikita could never get close enough to the Reds to fight the way a Cossack was supposed to. There was no valor at such distances and no glory in random wounds.

The second time I was wounded, *says Nikita,* we were in an open car. It was incredibly icy, a field of ice. We couldn't see the enemy. But he was firing cannon at us from the distance.

I was in the passenger seat. I don't know just what happened. A shell burst right near the car. Maybe the driver pulled too hard on the wheel, I don't know, anyway, the car flipped over. And went onto my arm. I was holding onto the side when it turned over.

They took me to a doctor. At first they wanted to cut off the arm but then they started irrigating the wound and didn't have to amputate.

Another time, in the Crimea, we were attacking in file. The enemy was firing on us from a distance. It looked like they were preparing to withdraw. They were firing artillery to explode high, high up. In order to hit more of us.

Artillery can function in two basic ways. A shell can explode on impact, or it can explode up in the air. They clearly wanted to fire over a greater area and the shells were bursting high, high up. The shrapnel from an exploding shell came by and caught me. I fell, they grabbed me and picked me up. I looked down and saw the blood flowing again. All so stupid.

Nikita was disappointed that the enemy was always so far away, always under cover of artillery; and Starinov was disappointed, to say the least, at being captured before he could even begin practicing his newfound art of demolition.

I t was outside the city of Korochi. We didn't sleep that night, we had bonfires all night.

We thought the enemy was retreating, but somehow the enemy broke through our lines that night and by morning they had us surrounded. One of our own officers had betrayed us, he was with the Whites. Our whole company was taken prisoner, me included.

There I was, a prisoner, and me without a cross. If you weren't wearing a cross, the Whites'd consider you a communist. They kept us in a school under guard.

Then a priest comes to the school and says, "Who are you fighting against!? The Whites are trying to set people free. And you people are out there fighting for the Kikes!"

Our commanding officer was a communist but no one betrayed him. That night he led an escape. We disarmed the guard when he dozed off and the other guard'd gone to answer the call of nature. Then we went into the barracks where the rest of them were sleeping. We seized their rifles and escaped with all their weapons. I was a prisoner of war for less than twenty-four hours, the only time I was ever captured.

Starinov had already shown an affinity for finding himself in the most dangerous place of all—behind enemy lines. If they hadn't escaped, they might well have all been shot. Cross or no cross, the Whites and Reds could smell each other, and a brawling railroad man's son like Starinov would have smelled wrong to the former tsarist officers and Jew-hating priests. But, like one of the delayed-action mines that would later become Starinov's specialty, this incident's danger did not end with capture and escape.

*

Nikita the Cossack had received his three wounds and two promotions and was now Lieutenant Yovich. Yet, it wasn't rank he thirsted for but close engagement.

T hings weren't going too well in the Crimea, and our commanding officer General Wrangel thought it might be worthwhile to give the Bolsheviks a little surprise from behind their lines.

Landing operations were done in the Crimea. This time we went out on the Sea of Azov and made a landing near Novorossiisk. We left as soon as it was dark, and by dawn we were approaching the Kuban shore.

We went from the ships to flat-bottomed boats, then jumped into the water, holding our rifles and ammunition up out of the water.

We began the landing under machine gun fire. There were two machine guns on shore. The military vessel accompanying us fired once, then again, and both machine guns went flying. So, they weren't firing any more by the time we came out on shore. And we took about five prisoners.

In the next two days we covered about twenty-five miles, fighting as we went. We marched in chain formation, about fifteen or twenty feet apart, rifles over our shoulders. As a rifle division we were right in the center. On August 5 we entered a large Cossack settlement and held a parade. But then on August 9 a lot of Bolsheviks appeared, more and more all the time. They forced us out of the center of the settlement.

We were a platoon of about thirty men cut off from our left flank. We retreated at a fast pace, then stopped by the road, the one we'd come on from the sea. We could hear people shouting Hurray! I said, "That's our men counterattacking."

We ran from the roadside into some tall weeds, quite tall. From there we could see the Reds starting to move out. A whole mass of them, 200–250 men, a grey mass beginning to withdraw.

And we came up behind them, firing from the hip.

For once, it was up close, and with the Reds on the run to boot.

*

When Mulya wasn't out on frozen Siberian lakes with her friend the little blind girl, pretending to be chased by lions and tigers, she took pleasure in observing the Siberian Cossacks' way of life. "They'd bake enough bread for a week and store it in an unheated pantry, where it would immediately freeze solid. Whenever they needed a loaf they'd take one out and let it thaw. And just before Shrovetide, the Cossack boys would show off their skill in horseback riding—some of them would ride standing up on the horse's back, others would snatch small objects from the ground while galloping at breakneck speed. But I didn't play with the Cossack children, I played with the engineer's daughter."

Mulya's father was an engineer too, one of those aristocrats whom education and commitment had transformed into progressive professionals. He was in a terrible position. Sympathetic to the revolution, he had been identified by the Bolsheviks as a member of the ruling, managerial class and had already been arrested once. Now he had to keep moving to remain under the protection of the White Army, which came with its own costs, as the family learned on the day the Whites arrived in that Siberian Cossack village.

T he Whites had to house their people, their officers, *recalls Mulya.* They came and announced to us that we had to get out. There was no place to go, absolutely none, and mother was almost ready to give birth to another child. The White officer shouted and screamed that we had to get out or they'd throw us out.

Outside the village there was a small, winterized summer place, a dacha, that had been abandoned. We moved in there. That night mother was taken to the dining room and gave birth to her sixth child on the dining room table.

It was beautiful there. We went tobogganing, we built castles of snow, houses of snow that had rooms inside and a roof over them, and we played inside.

Then the Red Army moved in again and we moved out again. To Omsk. Omsk was built around a huge prison for political prisoners and other kinds, but the city had a big opera house, and several schools, one very nice private school.

We lived on a little side street which was particularly well known because there was a huge puddle there all summer long, it was almost like a lake. Our house was made of logs but it was wallpapered inside. In the winter the wallpaper would flutter in the air when the wind blew through the logs.

We did not have a toilet or a bathroom in the house. Water had to be gotten from the well or from the river. There was an outhouse, a wooden plank with holes. In the winter all the excrement had to be chopped out and taken away. We did that ourselves. We chopped out the excrement, lay it on a sled, and took it down to the river.

Omsk was the capital of Admiral Kolchak's White Army. Kolchak happened to have been my father's classmate in the Naval Academy. Father met Kolchak there in Omsk. But it was obvious that Kolchak was going to lose. People started escaping further east. East and east and east.

Father had to leave, he would certainly be arrested as soon as the Reds entered the city. Mother and the children, some of whom were sick, couldn't travel in a freight train. Father spent two days at the station before he could squeeze into one of the boxcars. It would be two years before we heard from him.

We were left with mother, six children, Manya the maid, and the Latvian cook. The money father left us ran out almost immediately. It was money issued by Kerensky's Provisional Government and just about worthless. And during the first Christmas we spent in Omsk, we cut up all that money and made Christmas decorations out of it. At least it was colorful.

Mother got a job teaching history at the private school. It was a very good school and she sent us there. In order to make money she taught morning sessions, afternoon sessions, and evening sessions.

One evening people were saying, "The Bolsheviks are coming, the Bolsheviks." Manya the maid went out and saw soldiers lined up on the other side of the river. There was some shooting going on. We went to bed and in the morning we woke up wondering what government we were under—was

it White or Red? So, we had to go out and see what kind of
uniform they were wearing. It was the Bolsheviks—they were
wearing pointed caps with a big, red star.

At first they left us pretty much alone. Then all the
complications started, worse than ever. Mother was a socialist
and belonged to the Socialist Revolutionary party. There was
supposed to be some kind of anti-Bolshevik uprising in Omsk
and she was involved. She had also hid some people in our
house who were being pursued by the communists, the
Bolsheviks.

One night there was a search. People came in the
middle of the night with guns, searched through everything,
and arrested mother.

We still hadn't had any word from father and didn't
know whether or not he was alive. After mother was arrested,
it was Manya who took care of us. Manya was only twenty-five
years old. She came from a village that at one time belonged to
my grandfather. Manya had gone to the school that mother had
founded there.

We had two cows that father had bought just before he
left. Manya milked the cows. I learned how to milk a cow too.
The cows were very important, they meant we children had
milk. Mother kept sending notes from prison, asking "Did the
cow have a calf?" But the prison people thought it was some
kind of a code and they wouldn't let us send an answer to her.

Manya would line all six of us children by height in
front of the windows of the prison, hoping that mother would
see that all of the six children were together and well. The
guard in the big tower right next to the prison usually tried to
prevent prisoners from looking out the window. First, he would
use a mirror and cause a reflection to flash on the window. And
if that didn't work, he would shoot at the windows. Not exactly
at the windows but at the wall around the windows. The white
walls of the prison were riddled with holes, *says Mulya, her
eyelids wincing in remembrance of that mirror flashing the purest
cruelty.*

*

Free after his brief stint as a prisoner of war, Starinov was now able to see the craft of military engineer at work in the field.

The Whites had tanks. That's right, English tanks. And they were attacking us in those English tanks. We had to do something about it.

There was a river not far from the city of Orel. I had just joined the sappers. There were some pretty smart guys in that company. What should we do? Blow up the bridge? But the tanks would just pull up, stop, and fire on us. And then they'd rebuild the bridge. Or find a way to outflank us. That wouldn't hold them up for very long.

It was a wooden bridge. With wooden supports.

So, we saw partway through the supports. The Whites come. They see the bridge is in one piece. The tank goes racing out onto the bridge. The supports give, the bridge collapses, and the tank goes tumbling down—baboom!

That held them up for quite a while. And the main thing was that the tank fell into our hands. The tank crew escaped, they didn't suffer. The river wasn't deep and the tank men were able to get away. The tank was empty but it was ours.

And oh did the whole thing do our hearts good!

Mulya was in anguish, never knowing if her mother had spotted them lined up in front of the prison before the light reflected from the guard's mirror blinded her eyes or before his bullets sent her scurrying.

After she had been in prison three months we were told that mother had been shot. She was executed along with two hundred others. Some people saw two women in a crowd that was being marched through the street. They usually dug a big ditch, put these people on the side of the ditch and shot them so they fell into the ditch. Of course we always hoped that maybe someone had survived. We were never given the body.

By then we received a postcard from father. It was signed—Your Cousin, Sontseva. But it was father's handwriting and we knew it was from him. He was in Harbin, in Manchuria. He didn't know mother was dead.

Manya managed to support us. Whoever the government was, they wanted to put us children in orphanages. And Manya said, "Give me some more children, I already have the beginnings of an orphanage myself." And they did.

Manya was a person with a very strong sense of what's right and what's wrong. And a very strong feeling for children. She felt they were the most important thing in life. She had gotten hold of some land outside the city where she could have a vegetable garden. She grew enough cabbages to make sauerkraut, she salted cucumbers, and kept potatoes and carrots in the sand in the cellar. She milked the cow.

And the children kept getting sick. Everybody had measles. Everybody had German measles, and the youngest girl had mumps. Manya managed to treat them by reading old books with old remedies.

Their mother dead, their father in Manchuria, the children were cared for by a peasant woman whose sole loyalty was to them. Only once did she leave them in anyone else's care, and that was when Manya traveled from Siberia back to Tula in Central Russia to see her parents. Using forged documents that said she was a military nurse, she ended up treating the wounded more than once. On the way back to Siberia, Manya contracted malaria and ran a fever of 105°. The train was so cold inside that Manya's hair froze to the window and it took boiling water to get her free.

Even though she was still only twelve herself, Mulya now felt second in command: "When mother left, the last thing she told me was, 'Now, remember, you're the oldest.' I decided to follow her example and give my younger sisters lessons. I locked one of my sisters in a closet because she wouldn't do what I told her.

"Of course I had nightmares that I was sitting in prison and thinking I was going to be executed. I'd look at the clock and watch the hour approach."

The hour of defeat for the Whites was approaching. Mulya's father's instincts had been right. Everyone was fleeing, east, east, east.

∗

Starinov was still learning the lessons of war and finding he liked learning nothing better, especially when he discovered that sly cunning, with which he was himself imbued, could be a combat weapon.

We captured two English officers who were with the Whites. Those officers were tall and arrogant and looked at us with contempt. But nobody laid a hand on them. They were given plenty to eat and drink, which surprised them. Then after a while something amazing happened—it was decided to send those two officers back across the front line to the enemy. They couldn't believe it themselves. But they were sent back.

We couldn't see the point of it. Those officers were so repulsive you were just itching to hang them. But then the commissar explained it all to us. "Well," he says, "if we executed them, there'd be two officers less. But what good would that do us? But this way we're sending them back to the Whites, the counterrevolutionaries who say that Bolsheviks are animals, the worst animals in the world. And then those two are sent back and everybody sees there's not a scratch on them and that they've been well fed. But then everyone'll think they must have been won over by the Bolsheviks. They'll come under suspicion, and so will everyone they're connected with. But at the same time it will be great propaganda that the Bolsheviks aren't animals."

Starinov liked the logic. It was like sawing partway through the bridge supports. In fact, the whole White cause was collapsing now, the Reds had them with their backs to the Black Sea. The final battle took place in the Crimea. And Starinov was there.

"The Whites were in a panic. We were shelling them but we couldn't have killed many of them because they were firing at us too, and you couldn't get very close. They fled under artillery cover from naval vessels. They boarded ships, any ship they could find."

One of the retreating Whites was Nikita the Cossack from the Kuban region. As always, his report is concise:

The remnants of the White Army were evacuated through Novorossiisk and the Strait of Kerch. We continued to offer the Red Army resistance. On October 29, 1920, we were ordered to go down to the shore and begin boarding the steamers. We waited a few days until the shelling stopped, and on November 1 and 2 the ships departed at various times from Kerch, Theodosia, and Sevastopol, all heading for Constantinople.

I was leaving Russia forever, and only twenty at the time.

Part Two

But wars, especially civil wars, never end with the cease-fire. Nikita the Cossack had begun a retreat that would last seventy years. And it was precisely that—a retreat, not flight, not surrender in absentia.

T he White Army was divided up as follows: what was called the real White Army was sent to the peninsula of Gallipoli, and the Kuban corps of which I was part was sent to the island of Lemnos in the Aegean Sea. The Don Cossacks, and there were more of them than Kuban, were first stationed south of Constantinople, then they all were concentrated on Lemnos with the Kuban. There were fifty thousand Cossacks on the island. What were they going to do with all these people?

One fine day they announce that a boat'd be coming to take people to Baku. A Soviet government representative had come inviting people to sign up for six-months' work in the oil fields of Baku.

After the Reds beat us, some of the Cossacks didn't care

anymore—what mattered to them was their homes and their children. Their real interest was their farms. Most everybody was just tired of the whole thing. About three thousand Cossacks signed up to go to Baku, including three of my friends from high school. I requested to be assigned to that group too. But then my commanding officer said, "If Yovich can leave then I can leave too." That did it. I requested to be reassigned back out of the Baku group. The boat left, the men did indeed work in the oil fields for six months, and then they were all executed.

Many of the Cossacks were far from having any ideology. The more educated ones had some ideas, some convictions, and the majority of them were against the Bolsheviks of course. Though there were also those who believed you could somehow come to terms with the Reds.

By the way, anti-Semitism was unknown among the Cossacks. The Cossacks never saw any Jews. Jews weren't allowed to live in Cossack regions. And then later in life when they met up with Jews they'd see they were people like anyone else. In the Crimea I ran into a lieutenant I knew and asked him, "What are you doing here?" And he says, "I'm staying with some Jewish friends." And I said, "But you're an officer in the White Army!" It turned out he was a Jew himself, he'd fought with the Volunteer Army, and had been promoted to officer for merit in combat.

Still, there are some things I just can't fathom. Why, as soon as the revolution broke out, did Jews, Jews, Jews, start rushing to Lenin from everywhere, from Austria, from America, from France. . . . Why did all those Jews come to Russia? Lenin must have promised them something. But the fact of the matter is that Trotsky and Bukharin, and endless other Jews, made up the ruling elite in the Soviet Union. Why didn't they go to develop Israel, why did they go to Petersburg and Moscow? If they had been religious Jews, they would have gone to help build a Jewish state. But these Jews were internationalists, and that means they're as much a Jew as I am. They didn't give a damn for anything. They were people without religion, without a God. A fact is a fact—the overwhelming majority of them were against religion and that's what connected them to Lenin. And then later on they ended up running important parts of industry and government. And naturally that causes people to be against the Jews. And so, for what's called anti-Semitism, the Jews have only themselves to blame.

*

Mulya was still trapped in Omsk. "There was no wood to heat the house. We wore mittens and coats all day long. And then all of a sudden life turned into a fairy tale."

Mulya's father arranged for his family to be sent to Harbin in Manchuria. Once again they traveled in a heated freight car, for three weeks across Siberia. They were met in Harbin by a boy who was around the same age as Mulya, now fourteen.

The boy said my father was crazy, absolutely crazy. I thought that father might have lost his mind out of grief for my mother. I was terrified, taking my five brothers and sisters to be with a crazy father! We hadn't seen him for two years. But then we found out that father had rented a room and screened off one half of it and filled it with birds. And that was why the boy thought he was crazy.

We hadn't had a bath for three weeks. We looked terrible, very bedraggled. Father had us all washed and cleaned, then dressed us all in Japanese kimonos, lined us up by height, and took our picture.

Once again life reverted to home, school, and play. The present had not caught up with Harbin.

Harbin was an enclave of old Russia, a completely Russian city, *says Mulya*. It was originally built as a continuation of the Trans-Siberian Railway, to make a straight connection to Vladivostok. In the center of Manchuria, Harbin was built as a Russian city, a planned city, with a Russian Orthodox church constructed entirely without nails. The tsarist government rented a strip of land for ninety-nine years from China, a strip of land on which they could build a railway, one that widened around the stations and around Harbin.

The Chinese did not recognize the Soviet government. After the revolution the city began to be filled with refugees. There were many commercial people who established banks, shops, and so on, but a lot of intellectuals also came. The city had a rich cultural life, a permanent opera, a permanent symphony.

It was still an old-fashioned Russian city, the schools were run like prerevolutionary Russian schools. We had to curtsy to the director of the school, and the boys were supposed to click their heels.

Father decided to settle in Harbin because he felt it was possible for his children to get a Russian education there. He believed that it was a temporary situation and that one day we'd be able to go back home to Russia.

But Soviet Russia came to them instead. The Chinese and Soviet governments concluded an agreement to share the facilities in Harbin. The school where Mulya was studying science with a will and learning to operate a lathe in her spare time was now under Soviet control.

First the church was removed from our school when the school became Soviet. There was no more curtsying.

And the whole language was different, cruder, swear words, a deliberate flaunting of lower-class speech. The whole atmosphere changed. Wall newspapers appeared. Sometimes they printed accusations of people not being quite loyal to Soviet Russia.

Very active Young Communist League and Pioneer people appeared. "The International" was played on special occasions and the people in Pioneer uniform saluted while it was played. I always felt out of it. You wanted to belong, to do what the others did.

We lived in a house given us by the railway. Father

worked for the railway. We made a tennis court ourselves. We didn't have enough money for a net so we learned how to weave a fisherman's net. We had to save up for the string. We really had no money at all.

But we had a flower bed, it was made in the shape of Africa, and the flowers were planted accordingly—blue flowers for the Nile, yellow flowers for the Sahara Desert.

In winter we flooded the tennis court to skate on. The temperature could go down to 40° below but there was very little snow. The wind would bring some very fine reddish dust, which was said to be from the Gobi Desert. By the time the dust reached Harbin it was so extremely fine that it could penetrate sealed windows. Even the snow had a little reddish tinge to it.

Mulya's father was playing loud marches on the piano again. When Mulya wasn't studying science in high school, she was applying science to the family fun, devising a means to flood the tennis court all at once so the ice would freeze evenly.

But then there was also the exceedingly delicate matter of citizenship. The Soviets and the Chinese had normalized relations, and that meant Harbin's bubble of Old Russia was about to burst. Everyone had to choose citizenship now—either Soviet or Chinese. Somehow unable to envision themselves as Chinese citizens, Mulya's family applied for Soviet citizenship. The children were granted theirs right away, but Mulya's father's case was still pending. And then, before anyone knew it, the Soviets and the Chinese were at war.

The Chinese Eastern Railway for which my father worked was now being used to transport Chinese troops to the front against Russia. That was an impossible situation for the Soviet employees on the railway—transporting enemy troops. So the Soviet citizens and those who had applied for citizenship were all told they had to go on strike. So did schools, teachers, everyone.

Father continued working on the railway.

We were supposed to come to the first lecture of the school year and then demonstratively leave the lecture. I didn't go to that class, and the second day I went back to school. So I definitely broke all my Soviet ties. I had to stand by my father.

And it was just when Mulya's father had lost his railroad job and the housing that went with it that Mulya was offered a dazzling and painfully impossible chance. Mr. Craine, a wealthy American acquaintance, the former ambassador to China, whom her father had met in Peking and who had helped get the family to Harbin, now offered to pay for Mulya and her brother to study in an American university. But the offer had to be regretfully rejected—Mulya could not leave her family now that her father had no income, no housing, nothing but a lump sum retirement payment.

Twenty years old now, her tutoring providing the family's only income, Mulya understood that the most important thing was for the family to have a home of their own. And she insisted that the lump sum be used for that purpose.

When the house was built and her father began making some money by doing translations, Mulya was able to accept Mr. Craine's kind invitation to visit Peking, where he renewed his offer to send Mulya and her brother to America to study. Now that the family was provided for, she had to face the choice for what it really meant:

The idea of being a foreigner, a person forever without a country, just seemed very terrible to me. The choice was either to become a countryless person or go back to Russia. I was afraid to go back to Russia and I knew that Harbin had no future. This was obvious to everyone by then. No future whatever.

There were two alternatives that both sounded very sad—being a foreigner in one place and a foreigner in your own country.

And finally I dreamed a very strange dream. I thought I was in a big square, somewhere in America, something like Times Square, which I had heard about, or seen pictures of.

There was a very large crowd there. And suddenly in the crowd I saw my mother's face. Maybe she had escaped, I had never seen her dead. I ran, trying to get her. She disappeared. I was very disappointed. I started out of the square and went into a narrow street surrounded by tall buildings on both sides. Suddenly I saw my mother coming toward me. She took me by the shoulder and turned me around and she said, "Don't go back to Russia, you won't be accepted there."

And that was the turning point. I decided to accept Mr. Craine's invitation.

A train trip across Korea, a visit to the temples of Kyoto, two weeks at sea, and Mulya was standing surrounded by California redwoods. In time the rest of the family, except for her father, who died in Harbin, would follow—even Manya came, ever loyal. Mulya attended MIT, married an American, and had children who grew up American. A widow now, she lives in Belmont, Massachusetts, a mildly patrician suburb of Boston where she would be in no way distinguishable from the other genteel, older women of the town, except for a slight tendency to make mistakes when using the definite and indefinite articles, which Russians can never quite master.

Her home, though light, airy, even Californian, still retains something of gentry Russia in its preference for the darker tones of brown, the serious tomes in the bookcases, the presence of fateful memorabilia—a pencil drawing of Mulya as a girl in Omsk, the photograph of all six of the children scrubbed clean, wrapped in Japanese kimonos and lined up by height.

"And I still have the smooth stone I got for my mother," says Mulya with astonishment and tender horror. But then she quickly adds, with gingerish humor, "And I still use it for darning."

On the other side of Boston, where the red brick is sullen, and black children are brought in from the inner city in large, yellow buses, there is a small Russian church with pale green cupolas, golden crosses, and a panoply of bells. Beside the church there is a dilapidated house, barely visible from the street because of the tall evergreens in front. It is church property and given over to the use of elderly Russians, one of whom is the Kuban Cossack Nikita Ivanovich Yovich.

The retreat from the island of Lemnos has led to Roslindale, Massachusetts, to a room both spartan and littered—temporary quarters, a billeting. The only decorations on the wall are portraits of Tsar Nicholas and Tsarina Alexandra hung reverentially above eye level.

As old as the twentieth century, eighty-nine in 1989, Nikita is still as straight as a bayonet and still handsome, his silver hair brushed straight back, his silver moustache still twirled with Cossack dash. His movements are quick and smooth, except when they snag on one of his old scars. And when Nikita glances at the too-white scar-tissue twisted at his elbow, he even gasps slightly, the wounds of defeat always fresh.

Nikita and the Cossacks on the island of Lemnos were caught in a slow-motion explosion that would suddenly speed up and send them flying like human shrapnel in all directions. To France and Australia, to Yugoslavia, Argentina. Nikita had sailed back into the Black Sea from which he had just retreated, to Bulgaria, the first of many lands and languages.

After Bulgaria, there was Czechoslovakia, Austria, France. In 1942, when the Nazis demanded a contingent of workers, Nikita was among the foreigners sent to Germany by the French government. He had to survive and had no regrets about working in Albert Speer's transportation ministry, but he would not fight alongside the other Whites who joined the Nazis against the Soviets. After the war he worked for twelve years as an auto mechanic in a Renault plant in Casablanca. He moved to Boston in 1960 and is still a Cossack at his post, his voice still crisp:

The last commander of the White Army in the south was General Wrangel. In 1924 he merged all the groups that still maintained a military spirit and created the R.A.S.U., the

Russian Armed Services Union. Grand Duke Nikolai Nikolaevich, the late Tsar's uncle, was still alive, and was invited to be honorary president.

General Wrangel lived in Belgium. But the Bolsheviks got to him, killed him with poison. Wrangel had a deputy, Kutepov, but he was abducted by the Bolsheviks in 1933. And his deputy, Muller, was also abducted.

Years passed, gradually people began dying off. In 1986, the most senior man still alive turned out to be Captain Ivanov who lived in Detroit. Captain Ivanov received a communication from Paris saying that as the most senior man he was now obliged to assume the presidency of the R.A.S.U. He was ninety-one. He needed a deputy and I was recommended to him.

I received a letter from this Captain Ivanov whom I had never met, an official letter—Dear Nikita Ivanovich: As of such and such a date, I have become the president of the Russian Armed Services Union. I am alone and am requesting your help.

And so I answered the letter—Dear Captain Ivanov: I was brought up to be a soldier—that means, never volunteer for duty, but never shirk it.

A week later I received orders from him, stating that as of such and such a date, Lieutenant Nikita Ivanovich Yovich would be serving as his deputy. He gave me various orders, xeroxing lists and so forth, which I carried out. After a few years I began having problems with my health and I wrote to Captain Ivanov requesting to be relieved of my duties. I received no reply. I wrote again. All of a sudden I receive a letter saying that Captain Ivanov has had a stroke and is paralyzed. I phoned him but there was no answer. And then I received orders from him, which he had somehow been able to sign—I had been appointed president of the Russian Armed Services Union.

As if concluding a report to his commanding officer, Nikita raises his eyes to the portrait of Tsar Nicholas, as young, red-bearded, and serene as when Ilya Jaffee had hopped the fence and beheld him for the first of three times. Three!

The Twenties

Part One

"I was trouble from the start," says Natalya Viktorovna, scraping cracker crumbs from the table with the edge of her hand. Her knuckles are large with arthritis. The black stone in her ring is an elongated oval, like her odd eyes, whose pupils seem stood on end.

The guns of August 1914 issued their salvos as she was born to a father who would die in the first days of the war. Natalya Viktorovna was left with her mother, a former aristocrat who had no other wish in the world but to transform herself into a "fiery communist" and always kept almost succeeding.

Natalya's mother threw herself into party work, leaving her six-year-old daughter alone day and night even though she was suffering from tuberculosis and her legs were in casts that prevented all movement.

I adored my mother so much that I wouldn't eat if she wasn't there. And she wouldn't come home until late at night and we'd have those twenty minutes together. Later on that adoration changed into opposition, confrontation, and I caused her a lot of grief in this life.

I was alone all the time. She'd feed me and make my breakfast for the next day when she came home at night. Once she placed me in a sanatorium but I went on a hunger strike. I refused any and all food and after three days they told her to take me home or I would die.

Finally, my mother pleaded with the party to assign her to a children's tuberculosis asylum, and she was reassigned. The asylum was a series of barracks in a dense pine forest. Every night I'd look out the window and see wolves walking right up to the house. In keeping with the old Russian tradition, the bathroom was not in the house. The children used chamber pots but the adults had to go out to the courtyard, with rifles in hand to use against the wolves. Starving people were always passing by there on their way to the city and if one of them froze to death the wolves would devour his body.

The Reds had won the Civil War but the fighting had ruined the country. Fields were burned, bridges blown, factories bombed, and there was starvation in the land. Using the slogan ALL POWER TO THE SOVIETS, Lenin had seized power for his party, the Bolsheviks, who had become so unpopular that they changed their name to the communists. The peasants hated the communists because they requisitioned food at gunpoint for the industrial workers of the cities. The workers hated them because the food they were fed barely kept them alive. And there were grumblings from the army and navy. Most of the soldiers and sailors were peasants simply because Russia was then still 80 percent peasant, and they didn't like what they saw when they went on leave to their native villages. The communists had no mandate, but they had the guns and the will to use them. They needed all that will when the sailors on Kronstadt Island, which guarded Petrograd, rose up in a fury against the betrayal of their dream. It was a painful moment for Lenin and his party because the sailors of Kronstadt were famed as the most heroic of the fighting Reds.

All the same, the party faithful went out to slay the revolution's finest sons.

And it was the sailors' own spontaneity that led to their undoing. Their indignation reached a fever pitch in early March 1920; they could not even wait the few weeks until the ice had melted and would no longer be able to support their adversary's trucks, howitzers, troops. Trotsky led the Red Army over the ice to Kronstadt.

Still, the sailors had made their point. The ruling communists were going to have to sue for peace with the Russian people. But it was reality that was dictating the terms, even though those terms still had to pass through the Kremlin before becoming official. Food would no longer be requisitioned. There would be a tax, in money or in kind. Anything remaining beyond that could be sold by the peasant at market. Small private enterprise was allowed.

The New Economic Policy (NEP) was a sobering humiliation for the Bolsheviks, but they prided themselves on their ability to swallow any pill, no matter how bitter. NEP was formally worked out at the 10th Party Congress. And, needless to say, Ivan Vrachov was there, stubborn and clear-minded except for the moments when he remembered how high the revolution had lifted him, a poor boy with only three years of parish parochial school education who had helped transfer the capital of Russia on orders from Lenin himself. At these memories he would suffer vertigoes of gratitude and reverence.

T he 10th Party Congress took place in March 1921, *recalls Vrachov.* It was a situation of extreme crisis, a revolt had flared up on Kronstadt. That was a very disturbing event. The sailors of the Baltic Fleet had always been in the vanguard of the revolution, and then all of a sudden there's a counterrevolutionary uprising there? And there were peasant uprisings too, acquiring significant dimensions in Tambov and Saratov provinces, and in the Ukraine as well.

The 10th Congress passed a bill of extreme importance—the repeal of food requisitioning. And what did

that mean—food requisitioning? It meant sending detachments
of armed workers out to the countryside. There was even a
special Food Army formed. They went through the countryside
under the pretext of taking the surplus while emptying the
barns clean. The country was going hungry. There was hunger
in all the cities, and that included Moscow and Petrograd.
People's lives had to be saved.

And so, the Congress passed a resolution to repeal food
requisitioning and replace it with a food tax. This, along with
small-scale private enterprise, formed the basis of what later
became known as the New Economic Policy.

But as devoted to the revolution and passionate about politics as
he was, Ivan Vrachov still found the time to relax. Since Vrachov
was unmarried and had no family in Moscow, he went visiting
frequently and was always particularly happy in one house, that of
his friend Mikhail Boguslavsky.

Ivan Vrachov had a lot in common with Mikhail Boguslavsky, who had also risen from working-class poverty to high
political office, chairman of the Red Union of Printers, a place on
the Moscow Soviet. And there was no shortage of subjects for
political men to discuss in the Moscow of 1921. Mikhail's home
was also a pleasure for Ivan to visit because Boguslavsky had a
wonderful little dark-eyed seven-year-old daughter, Revekka, who
always went running into Ivan's arms and loved him madly, almost
as much as she adored her father.

I loved my father so much it didn't matter who I was with, if
my father came home and said, Come to the Kremlin with
me, Revekka my darling, I'd abandon anyone, just to spend
those few minutes with him. He was a very witty man, he
never came into the house without making a joke. His charm
was that he was so wonderfully human. He did have one
defect—he was short, even small, with a slightly hunched back.
But his eyes were always sparkling with wit and intelligence
and they were such charming eyes. He was full of fun, very
gentle, and loved people.

If there is anything good in me, anything positive, I consider that my father's legacy. He instilled me with internationalism, the belief that all peoples are of equal value.

And he never punished me. There was one time . . . Papa said to me, "I'll be coming back at four o'clock, please be home then." I was an eight-year-old girl out playing with the girls and didn't have my wristwatch on. I was fifteen minutes late. I rang the bell and Papa opened the door, took me by the shoulders and said, "Vladimir Ilich Lenin is a little bit busier than you but he's never late."

Papa always told me to try to make intelligence prevail over feeling, otherwise you'll be a slave to your feelings. He'd say, "Put a piece of chocolate that you really like in front of you and tell yourself not to eat it before evening. Walk by it but don't touch it."

Or—you have to speak out but you're afraid to. "Don't be afraid," he'd say. "A person should have his own opinion on every subject. Fight for what you think is right."

And many times he told me, "I'm from the working class myself. The working class is the healthiest part of society. Yes, they can be crude and rough. But the working class always knows what's what. The intellectuals can vacillate, swing left, swing right, but the working class sees straight out what's good and what's bad. Always stick with the working class."

He was the greatest of papas, and so to be worthy of him Revekka had to be the best of daughters.

*

Ilya Jaffee had been a member of that working class since the age of thirteen, when the Whites beat his father so severely that Ilya himself had to go out and make the family's living. He had seen a lot. He had seen the Tsar three times, he had seen color photographs of ape and human hands, and he had seen executions performed by the roadside. And finally he saw the light.

In 1920 I joined the bakers' union as soon as I turned fourteen. You had to be fourteen to join under Soviet law. I started attending Young Communist League meetings. And that's where I got my political education. And what the agitators drilled into us was that communism wasn't philanthropy, it was a faith, a deep faith. And it was the making of a new society, one based on economic laws.

"Sign me up," I said.

There was nothing unusual about me. There were hundreds and thousands of others just like me. And we were as certain that world revolution was inevitable as we were that it's dark at 9:00 P.M. in Moscow.

Ilya Jaffee's deep need for certainty had been fulfilled. It was the world around him that still shifted and slid. Even the profession of baker, always one of the most secure in Russia, was suddenly itself in jeopardy, for famine struck the land and there was no grain for bread and no bread to eat.

Ruth Bonner, the "little terrorist," who had been forced to watch the revolution from the window of a "professor's house," got her chance to see some action and make her own contribution as a field nurse in the Red Army. Then, as a good Young Communist she threw herself into the battle against hunger.

I n 1921 I went to the Volga region where famine had broken out. And that was one of the chief grain-producing areas. The great Volga River with all that fertile soil around it, the largest harvests were always brought in there. And in 1921 there was outright famine. Drought, crop failure, horrifying famine.

A commission was sent to the area, followed by the American Relief Administration, who were bringing in an enormous amount of food. They were looking for strong young people to work there and I of course was one of the first to volunteer.

I ended up on a hospital train that had also been outfitted by the Americans. It had more than twenty cars and was especially for children. There were triple-decker plank beds, you could pack in as many you wanted. The staff was all

Russian but some of our food was American. But we weren't allowed even one taste of that food. We were given soldiers' rations, which were better than regular.

The train would stop and our job was to go out and around carrying stretchers, real ones or ones we'd just put together ourselves. We'd go around and pick up the people who could no longer walk by themselves. Most of them were children, that was our assignment. But of course sometimes we'd pick up the mother too.

Sometimes we'd bring back a corpse instead of a live one. You couldn't tell who was alive and who was dead, and every so often you'd make a mistake.

That was our day assignment, and at night we did the laundry. You didn't get regular sleep. One time I almost drowned. It was after a day of work, I was doing the laundry that night, washing it in the stream. I worked and I worked and then I just keeled over into the water. They had to pull me out by my feet.

That stream was the Volga. The Volga had dried up and turned into a little stream. Still, you could do laundry in it. Warm or boiling water was out of the question. We'd pulled down all the fences we could find. And everything else you could use for firewood had long since been pulled down and burned by the people who lived there.

The train made three trips, in '21 and '22. On the first one we went between Moscow and the town of Chekhov. Chekhov's family had voluntarily donated, absolutely free of charge, their house outside of town, which had a small piece of land with it. We seeded the land ourselves, and we harvested what came up. And we settled the children there. We carried the half-dead children right in from the train on stretchers.

Volunteer doctors and nurses, mostly still in medical school, would come out after classes and lend a hand. Nobody was paid any salary there. All you were given was soldiers' rations, enough to keep you alive.

We also made a trip to Central Asia. It was a thriving region, very warm and rich in grain, mainly corn. We brought a large contingent of children there. And to our great astonishment lots of people came running and offering to take the children into their families. Nobody was taking in any children in Russia. But in Central Asia people were well off, and they were Asiatics, they loved big families, lots of children. Right away we started noticing that they were taking mostly girls. But we didn't smell anything fishy and we let them have the children. But when we got back to Moscow they really let us have it—when those girls'd turn ten or twelve they'd be sold as wives.

And we thought they were such kind people for taking in girls!

Ruth Bonner laughs a black and complicated laughter, directed at herself, the high-minded suppositions of innocence and the twists introduced by the world as it was.

Hunger was everywhere, it even followed Ruth to school.

I went to school between trips and lived in a huge dormitory for students and workers. There was a huge, communal stove for everyone. The stove was fed with logs and it was enormous, it took up half the room. There were always wives, mothers, grandmothers around it. The stove was so huge you had to stand on a bench to cook at it.

Our group of girls had somehow gotten hold of a pot. One of us, Valka, a great girl with a real head on her shoulders, would do the cooking. And here's how. Valka would fill the pot with water, stand there all day stirring that plain boiling water.

I kept asking her, "What is it you're stirring?"

And she'd say, "That's the way I cook, you have to keep stirring all the time. That's how I'm used to cooking."

Meanwhile, if any of the people cooking beside her should so much as even yawn, Valka would snitch something from their pot—a hunk of meat, a piece of fish, a scrap of potato pie or bread. And that's how she cooked—little by little. One time she was caught and got a good beating.

Later on, I came down with pneumonia and spent a day or two in the hospital. They released me and gave me a mustard plaster to use at home. Valka takes one look at the mustard plaster, sniffs it, and announces, "I'm not going to let you use the mustard plaster. I'll make you a cold-water compress. Then we'll all get together and use the mustard plaster to spread on our bread, it'll make good eating."

Valka made me compresses of paper and water. And we ate the mustard plaster.

All of Russia was starving to death, and Natalya Viktorovna had gone on a hunger strike because her mother had placed her in a sanatorium. And by the time NEP started producing results and the markets were full again, Natalya still wasn't eating much because her mother's party salary was so meager, almost a vow of poverty. Her mother kept being transferred, sometimes at her own request, but more often by party command that took them to small villages in the Ukraine. There the peasants expressed their hatred for the communism her mother was preaching by refusing to loan her a horse when Natalya was bitten by a mad dog and by gang-raping a young woman in their home while they were walking the many miles to the hospital.

As Natalya saw in the seaport of Odessa, NEP brought corruption as well as plenty.

Odessa in those days was an absolutely unique place. Huge numbers of foreigners. Heavily made-up male and female prostitutes. Cocaine everywhere. And there was unemployment, too. And when some Russians see their neighbor prospering they don't try to work harder and do better but find it more natural to burn their neighbor's house down. The people who prospered under NEP were called NEPmen and they were disgusting. Of course I had class hatred for them, with their fat faces and fancy carriages.

I was a terrible hellion. I'd get the other girls into all kinds of trouble. One time I talked one friend into telling her parents, good bourgeois people, that when I was a little girl I

had seen my whole family hung and had gone out of my mind.
Afterwards, I'd got better but still had attacks. I went to her
house and feigned an attack right there. I ran over to the
cupboard and grabbed all the pastries, I was howling, my eyes
were wild, I was snarling. Then I ran off and later on she and I
ate all those pastries.

*

The famine passed, NEP took hold. There was food at the market
and goods in the stores. The sound of gunfire had disappeared
from the countryside and the city streets and could not be heard
from the brick execution cells.

Lenin was so positioned in the psyche politic of Russia that
a blood vessel bursting in his brain could alter the destinies of
millions. The first of what once were called "God's strokes" came
in May 1922, and the second came in December. He was transformed by them, smiling oddly at people as if only for the first time
seeing who they were, and he felt remorse for what his party had
done to the working people, whose forgiveness he now sought.
But even incapacitated and so transformed, Lenin remained thoroughly political. He fired missives from his sickbed, insisting that
the party's Central Committee be enlarged greatly, by at least a
hundred real workers. There were too many foreigners, Jews,
intellectuals among the Bolsheviks.

But that wasn't the real reason. Great assayer of power that
he was, Lenin had understood that the party was dividing and on
the verge of its own civil war. The two leading forces were clear,
Trotsky, the creator of the Red Army and a brilliant orator who
had always been prominent, and Stalin, whose preference for
working behind the scenes made it seem that he had come out of
nowhere. The most important political legacy Lenin could leave his
party now was to side with one or the other. No longer able to
write, he began dictating his thoughts on Trotsky and Stalin, order-
ing them placed in a sealed envelope to be opened only on his
personal instruction or, in the event of his death, by his widow,
Nadezhda Krupskaya.

As Lenin struggled with pain and politics, the Union of
Soviet Socialist Republics came officially into existence on Decem-

ber 30, 1922. Some of the territory of the old Russian Empire had been lost in the turmoil of war, revolution, and civil war, but the USSR was still the largest country in the world.

By early 1923 Lenin could feel Stalin making the first tentative feints, at him, Lenin! Stalin had insulted Krupskaya, just at a time when Lenin needed his wife to be concerned only with him, and not in some private pain of her own, caused by a crudeness that was calculated and all the more crude for being so. There was such a thing as loyalty, and Stalin had none. Described as a "grey blur" when he was an up-and-coming revolutionary, Stalin had finally shown himself.

As the months passed, Lenin recovered his vitality, though he had lost nearly all ability to speak and walking was stiff and difficult. His energies were focused on the 13th Party Congress, which would be held in January 1924. Of course, there had to be clashes when all the leading communists of the country assembled to debate the future, but this time there would be more than clashes, there would be the opening moves in the war for the succession.

The party congress lasted for three days, January 16–18, and was unique in being the first that neither Lenin nor Trotsky, both for reasons of health, had attended. A good time for Stalin to make his move.

Sides were chosen, fates were sealed. Ivan Vrachov had done many things—launched the revolution in Voronezh, helped shift the capital of Russia—but it was at the 13th Party Congress that Ivan was to have his finest hour.

Ostensibly, one of the floor fights was about a small but vital piece of party doctrine that Lenin had introduced three years earlier, when he was still the vigorous and iron-willed leader of his party. He saw that the party had splintered into various factions, a result of the trauma caused when the "Reddest" fighting men of them all, the sailors on Kronstadt, had risen up against the Bolsheviks. Not only had party unity been violated, but some of the factions seemed to be forming an opposition party within the party, which was intolerable.

"Lenin was very disturbed by this," says Ivan Vrachov,

never pronouncing the leader's name without respectfully lowering his voice. "And so, besides introducing legislation about NEP, he introduced a resolution on party unity. Given the situation, Lenin was forced to impose a certain constriction of the democratic rules existing within the party. He proposed that the resolution have a secret clause, one not to be published in the press. That clause would allow the Central Committee, in the event that an opposition arose, a power struggle among factions, to switch the membership status of individuals in the Central Committee from full membership to nonvoting or candidate status; and the secret resolution also allowed for those with candidate status to be expelled from the party."

The point was passed and came back to haunt the communists in January 1924, as Lenin lay in his sickbed, avid for news of what was happening at the 13th congress of his party. And what was happening was that Joseph Stalin had launched his attack, moving suddenly, swiftly, and on two flanks.

T he congress had been preceded by discord within the party, *says Vrachov.* A group of old Bolsheviks had submitted a statement to the Central Committee criticizing the country's economic condition and, most important, criticizing the alarming developments within the party, which was deviating from its own principles of party democracy.

Trotsky was among the signers of that resolution. And that gave Stalin a hook on which to hang a name on that group: the Trotskyite Opposition, as he called it when he took the floor.

But that wasn't enough for Stalin. He also wanted to publish the secret point about party unity, the power to transfer people out of the Central Committee. And under pressure from Stalin the 13th Party Congress passed a resolution to make the secret point public.

Stalin had made two canny moves. He had identified his enemy with "the opposition." And he had forced the sanctification of a procedural point whose value he saw with perfect clarity—if the

Central Committee could expel members in the minority, it was possible to pack the committee with his own people.

Few people rose to challenge Joseph Stalin that day, but one of those who fearlessly took the floor to address his fellow communists was Ivan Vrachov.

A nd I asked Stalin, and the Congress, why they wanted to vote in that secret piece of party procedure. "Are there really any fundamental disagreements about platform in our party? You know there are none. We may diverge on individual tactical points and on the party's internal structure, but why do you need this point? You need it to get even with all those who think differently than you!"

And then I asked Stalin point-blank, "Tell me what attitude you're going to take toward Comrade Trotsky. What's your approach going to be—will you cooperate with Trotsky or will you try to isolate him, and discharge him from all his posts in the leadership? Give us an answer, plain and clear! And then at the next party congress we'll see if you've kept your promise or not."

After an instant of stunned silence, one of Stalin's henchmen called out: "You won't be at that Congress."

"I probably won't," I shot back.

Ivan understood the threat, but he also understood that it was a fateful hour, with both Lenin's life and the life of the party hanging in the balance. Vrachov then called upon all the delegates, all those who had, like himself, come from the small towns, the poverty, who believed in the cause so much they would risk everything to preserve its vital integrity, democracy at least within the party itself. Vrachov's words live in the history of Russia's freedom and are repeated to this day.

"Comrades," he said, "we may only have a few hours of democracy left, so let us put those hours to good use!"

But they were not. Stalin had declared war and had won the first battle. His star was in its ascent. But perhaps Lenin could still influence events; his health was reported to be improving, though the latest developments would not do much to lift his spirits.

Five days after the end of the party congress all the communists in the land were instructed to hold meetings to mark a very important day, January 22, 1905, when unarmed workers had marched peacefully to petition the Tsar and had been cut down by Cossacks. Known as Bloody Sunday, it was a holy day in the Red calendar.

Among those solemnly filing into auditoriums across Soviet Russia that day was Ilya Jaffee, by then a member of the Young Communist League. His zeal was so great that it wasn't long after he entered the league that he was heading his local branch.

The party organization had a meeting scheduled for January 22, 1924, to mark the anniversary of Bloody Sunday, *says Ilya.*

Everyone had arrived, but nobody came out and opened the meeting. We sang Young Communist songs for a while but then we started getting tired of waiting.

All of a sudden the curtain on the stage opened—red flags and black bunting.

Lenin was dead.

There were no tears, no hysterics.

And on the day Lenin was buried, we all stood out in the freezing cold for four hours while all the factory whistles blew and artillery salutes were fired in honor of his memory.

*

At least one man was busy dishonoring that memory. In charge of Lenin's funeral, Stalin ordered the body mummified so that it could be placed in a glass case in a mausoleum on Red Square. Lenin's widow protested, knowing Lenin himself would be horrified by this garish Egyptian idolatry. Stalin prevailed.

When Lenin died, Trotsky was taking a rest cure on the Black Sea. Stalin telegrammed him, informing him of Lenin's death and that the funeral would take place the next day. Logistically, it would be impossible for Trotsky to attend the funeral—it was more than twenty-four hours by train from the Black Sea to Moscow.

Trotsky had been duped. The funeral would actually not be for several more days and Trotsky's absence would besmirch his honor ineradicably and reinforce in people's minds what they already disliked about him—his superiority, arrogance, aloofness, the self-absorption of the great, the intellectual's small, cool heart. Another victory for Stalin, for whom no victory was ever too small.

Stalin knew that Trotsky lacked suspicion, just as he lacked humor. Trotsky, as commissar of war, certainly could have availed himself of other channels to obtain correct information about the date of Lenin's funeral. This he did not do. And, in not doing so, he revealed himself as hopelessly unpolitical, hopelessly unprepared for the struggle to succeed Lenin, and hopelessly unequal to his opponent in that struggle, who may not have been the orator, author, and military man that Trotsky was but who bested him in patience, cunning, and determination.

Stalin won the skirmish of the funeral and gave the principal oration, one that was striking in its liturgical cadences, echoes of the young Stalin's years in a seminary. Phrases were balanced and repeated—"Leaving us, Comrade Lenin ordered us to keep the unity of the party like the apple of our eye. We vow to thee, Comrade Lenin, that we will honor this, thy commandment." Stalin understood the Russian need for liturgy, drama, magic spectacle, and legendary leader. Lenin was to be sanctified and his relics would become a sacred shrine. People would come from all ends of the country to stand in the bitter cold for hours for a glimpse of the great leader.

All this would have sickened Lenin. It went against his style, the Bolshevik style, brusque and plain, where the personal was always of the least importance. And it violated his every conception of politics. He was a man of some moral and aesthetic taste, especially at the end of his days, and the gaudiness of mummification would have repulsed him to the core. Only one thought might have been able to quell his disgust—that all this would help preserve the unity of his party.

But Lenin would fire one last political salvo from the grave. The envelope containing his testament was opened and brought to the Central Committee by his widow, Nadezhda Krupskaya. The members of the Central Committee saw how important the testament was—so important, they decided, that it must be kept secret, a matter for the innermost party only.

It was a choice that the Lenin of old would have approved. Nothing was more important than the unity of the party. If the party broke into factions, it would lose power because it no longer had any support among the people. The loss of power would mean the defeat and massacre of the communists.

The contents of Lenin's testament went off like a depth charge, but the decision to keep them within the party muted their effect. If honest communists like Ivan Vrachov had learned of them at once, the country might have taken a different turn, but by the time Vrachov learned of Lenin's wishes, it was late in the game.

Nevertheless, in the struggle for power between Trotsky and Stalin, Vrachov sided with Trotsky because that was what he understood Lenin's wishes to be, and he was ever loyal to Lenin. Besides, Trotsky was the obvious successor, for, as Vrachov says:

After Lenin, Trotsky was number one. It was that way during the revolution, and that way after the revolution. Trotsky was a member of the Politburo, and for more than six years he had been the commissar of war. He had played a dynamic role in the creation of the Red Army and in our victory in the Civil War. He was always delivering reports on behalf of the party at conferences and congresses. He wrote pamphlets, books.

The text of the letter was not made known to us delegates. Two of Stalin's supporters spoke, saying that Lenin had left a testament and made some comments about it. It was only three years later, in 1927, at the 15th Party Congress, that under pressure from the opposition, including Trotsky's supporters, Stalin was forced to make the testament's contents known to all the delegates.

As a communist whose honor is untainted and who has remained true to his leader and his party, Ivan Vrachov cannot bring himself to simply paraphrase Lenin's last directive. He must go and get the text and read it word for word:

> In my opinion, relations between Trotsky and Stalin constitute the chief danger of a split, one which could be avoided and whose avoidance, I believe can be achieved by increasing the Central Committee by fifty new members.
>
> As general secretary, Stalin had concentrated unlimited power in his hands, and I am not sure that he will always be able to use that power with sufficient carefulness. Trotsky is distinguished not only by his outstanding abilities but is probably the most able man on the Central Committee, but he suffers from excessive self-confidence and has a bias for the administrative side of things.

In a postscript, Lenin had added:

> Stalin is too coarse and this failing, entirely tolerable within our circle and in dealings with us communists becomes intolerable in his post as General Secretary. I propose that the comrades consider the issue of removing Stalin from this post and appointing to that post a person who in all respects differs from Comrade Stalin, to wit, is more tolerant, has a greater sense of loyalty, is more polite and considerate of his comrades, less capricious, etc. This may seem a trifle but I believe that from the point of view of preventing a split in the party . . . this is not trifle, or the sort of trifle that can be of decisive significance.

Lenin had understood that character would be the swing factor in the small, self-enclosed world of the party. But, as if absolving Lenin for a lack of foresight that only proved his humanity, Vrachov adds: "For Lenin it was unthinkable that once Stalin had fortified his position, he would begin to chip away at the party, slice away at it, expel people from the party. First expel them, then exile them or throw them into prison. And that wasn't enough for him either, he had to physically liquidate them too. A monstrosity of this sort would have been inadmissible to the mind of the great leader of our party, Vladimir Lenin.''

But what was an inadmissible thought to Lenin was an entirely admissible act for Stalin. But he still had to proceed slowly. At the congress Stalin read Lenin's testament aloud, accepted the criticisms and promised to change his ways. The congress voted that Lenin's testament be published as part of his collected works, but that decision never went into effect. Copies of the testament were passed from hand to hand among the opposition, some typed, some copied by hand on rolling papers. Anyone found in possession of a copy would be expelled from the party and then put at the disposition of the secret police.

"Lenin had proposed that Stalin be removed from his post as General Secretary of the Party,'' says Vrachov. "But had he proposed that Trotsky be removed as commissar of war? Nothing of the sort! To be crude about it, it had all come out ass end to.''

Stalin took one slice a year. Trotsky would be dismissed as commissar of war in 1925, expelled from the Politburo in 1926, expelled from the party in 1927, exiled to Alma-Ata in remote Soviet Central Asia in 1928, and exiled from the Soviet Union itself in 1929.

*

Ivan Vrachov was stunned and heartbroken by the turn events had taken. He sought solace and solidarity with his friend Mikhail Boguslavsky, who had also sided with Trotsky. Boguslavsky's enchanting, dark-eyed daughter Revekka, twelve years old now, still adored Ivan Vrachov, sometimes peeking at him from behind the piano, sometimes just running into his arms. Yet there was no one she adored as much as her father, and nothing she adored as much as ballet, and so nothing could be more perfect in all the world than to attend a ballet with Papa.

Papa was in the government and we had a ticket which gave us the right to attend the Bolshoi. Usually we sat in the government box, which used to be the Tsar's box. I was mad about ballet at the time.

I was twelve years old, it was 1926, when Papa took me to see one of my favorites, *The Little Humpbacked Horse.* For some reason, we didn't sit in the government box but the director's box. It was small, the chairs upholstered in dark red. We sat in the front row, four of us—Simashko—the minister of health—Papa, me, and Demian Bedny, the famous proletarian poet.

Suddenly, during the second act, the door to the box opened and someone came in. I turned around and my eyes met the heavy gaze of a man I had never seen before. He leaned his elbows on the back of a chair.

I couldn't tear my eyes away from him. I was dumbstruck by him. He had a low brow, black hair, a very powerful nose. His face was pockmarked, he had a moustache. He was a strong-looking man, short. His eyes were black and something—a glint of yellow, or of cruelty—flashed in them.

When comrades came into a box, I was used to them saying hello, and some of them would even make quiet little jokes. This man came in and said hello to no one. And no one said hello to him either. A foreign body.

He stayed about eight minutes, never once breaking his silence. Then he left without saying good-bye.

As soon as he was gone I turned to my father and asked, "Who was the man with the terrible eyes?"

And Papa said, "That was Stalin."

Part Two

As an ardent communist, Ruth Bonner was "forever being elected to something or other." This congress, that congress. "I'd go and sit there all day long and it couldn't have been more boring. I said, To hell with this. And I enrolled in a high school."

But there was one meeting she was dying to attend. In 1921 all the "luminaries" were going to speak at the 3rd Congress of the Communist International, including Alexandra Kollontai, who had electrified Russia's youth by declaring that sex was as natural as drinking a glass of water and was of about the same significance. Admission, however, was only to certified delegates.

There was a young man who was chasing after me. "I'll get you in," he said. He was the grandson of a very important official. And he did get me in.

But there I was in my high school skirt with a school notebook tucked under my arm. I couldn't have looked less

like a delegate. And no sooner had I taken my seat than a
soldier walked over to me and said, "One minute. Let's see
your pass."

"I don't have a pass."

"Come with me to the command post."

My first interrogation.

"Are you a delegate?"

"Yes, I'm a delegate."

"What's your name?"

I remembered that the young man had gotten me in
under the name of Mikhatsky. And so that's what I said my
name was.

They just laughed and laughed. Mikhatsky was a very
well-known figure.

Then the commandant slammed his fist against the table.
"Stop your fooling around here! Tell me who you are, and
what you are."

I told him my name and that I was a student. They
called the school and the school said, Yes, we do have a Ruth
Bonner. The commandant called a Red Army soldier over and
told him to bring me to Metropol Hotel and report to
Comrade Mikhatsky that this woman had in some way got into
the congress under his name, and to find out how that had
happened.

They brought me to a large room in the hotel. And
there was a handsome, middle-aged, Asiatic-looking man with a
grey beard, sitting at a table. There were fruit and nuts on the
table. First time in my life I'd seen either. I was from Siberia
where they didn't have any and by the time I came to Moscow
the fruit was long gone. But this man had grapes, apples, nuts.

The room was full of people. Mikhatsky asked me a few
questions and then started laughing. He told the soldier to go.
Then he asked me questions in more detail—who I was, what I
did, where I was from.

"Look at this, will you. She looks like a perfect
Georgian but she's from Siberia. And what a bold one she is
too. She snuck into the congress on my pass."

Then he asked who gave me the pass. I said I wouldn't tell.

And he said, "I know who it was. And I'm going to break that worthless kid's arms and legs. It couldn't be anybody but my grandson, he's the only one capable of anything like this. Please, please, have some fruit."

I was too bashful. So, he made up a little package and thrust it on me. Then he said to one of his men, "Show her out, so she doesn't end up in the wrong place again."

It turned out that his grandson traveled with Mikhatsky as a sort of secretary, an assistant, and always kept his grandfather's papers in his pocket so they wouldn't get lost. The old man's sight was failing. So, the grandson read to him and translated into Georgian. Russian, Georgian, and Armenian were among the thirteen languages the grandson spoke.

And the grandson had simply shown his grandfather's pass and of course they had let me right in.

The grandson was an Armenian, Gevork Alikhanov. He became my husband. That was how we first met.

Alikhanov had been born in Armenia, but after the Turkish Massacre of 1915 he had fled to Tbilisi, the capital of the neighboring republic of Georgia. Romantic, fiery, moustached, he became a prime mover in the Armenian communist movement, a comrade in arms of Anastas Mikoyan, who would rise to join Stalin's inner circle and remain there unscathed to the end.

It was considered bourgeois in those days to mark love with any sort of ceremony. People like Ruth and Gevork believed that it was love that made a man a husband and a woman a wife. The revolutionary high-mindedness of the times was reflected in Soviet law, which did not make the registration of marriage mandatory in the least. That would come later, as Stalin's empire grew at once more bourgeois and barbaric.

*

Ilya Jaffee burned with zeal. And for its reward zeal wished only greater scope for zealotry. Ilya Jaffee requested that he be allowed to work on Dneprostroi, which was to be the largest hydroelectric dam in Europe, second only to the Hoover in the United States.

As soon as it was officially announced on March 15, 1927, that construction on Dneprostroi was to begin, I was one of the first forty workers who walked the five miles to the site, all of us singing the whole way.

We had forty-two thousand men there. Meaning forty-two thousand shovels. We didn't get any earth-moving equipment until the third year.

The base of the dam had to be laid by a certain date. The Young Communists were asked to put in extra hours after our day's work was done. For the next three months, we each put in another five hours after a day's work, five days a week. We flattened the cement, by stomping it with our feet. No pay. For the cause. All they gave us was boots and canvas clothing.

Our pride was immense. Nothing can stain the purity of those memories!

Ilya Jaffee's voice is both tender and defiant. No one can understand communism's defilements without first understanding its purities.

It was also there at the construction sight that Ilya Jaffee, who had seen the Tsar, seen his father transformed into a cripple and a lecture stage turned into a tribunal, was to be granted another crucial vision.

When Trotsky was removed from his post as commissar of war, he was placed in charge of the country's entire electric power industry. And Dneprostroi was the country's number one hydroelectric project. So it was natural for Trotsky to go there and address our party organization.

Trotsky spoke for a few hours. He spoke exceptionally well, like a true Russian intellectual. Always the pince-nez, he was born with pince-nez.

He didn't seem to ever joke.

He spoke exceptionally well but what he said I found absolutely repulsive. He said, "It's the ninth year of Soviet power and we've only reached the economic level we were on in 1913, the last year before the war. But," he said, "the working class rose in revolution because the economic level of 1913 was one of utter poverty.

"To become as rich as the Europeans, we have to create industry. And that would also enlarge the size of the working class, the real supporters of the revolution. But you have to have consumers for the products of industry, there's no reason to produce anything if there's no one to buy it. Who are the consumers going to be? The peasants, ninety percent of whom are paupers? The peasants have to prosper and private farming is the road that leads to that prosperity."

Everything in me objected to this. What kind of socialism is that with all the peasants getting rich? It was clear to me that Trotsky had betrayed the cause of socialism.

After that, no matter how hard the Trotskyites tried to get me to come to their meetings, I'd never go. I'd tell them, Trotsky's a traitor, he wants private farms.

Ilya had good instincts, good reflexes, of vital importance in Darwinian Soviet Russia. He had chosen against Trotsky, no guarantee of survival but no death warrant either. His admiration for Trotsky was thin compared to an organic repulsion at both his manner and ideas. He was fond of saying that there were thousands of others just like him. So thousands of others across Russia must also have recoiled at the humorless man with the pince-nez and goatee.

*

Natalya Viktorovna was thirteen when Lenin died.

M y mother, the aristocrat who consciously sacrificed her entire life to the revolution and the party, forcing herself to believe, sobbed when Lenin died and I sobbed along with her. My mother was running a children's home then. One of the girls there, an orphan, and myself made a secret vow when Lenin died. We vowed not to toss our clothes on the floor but to fold them up neatly, and to try not to cry so much because girls that age cry so easily, one remark and we'd burst into tears.

By the time I was eleven I had read all the great Russian classics, Turgenev, Lermontov, Gogol, Pushkin. And when I was just about to turn twelve I had a meeting with a person, which changed my life.

We had moved so much and I had spent so little time in school that I was something of a wild child. For me life was just a flood with no distinctions between the beautiful and the ugly, the good and the bad.

And we were always moving. By then we were living in the little southern town of Ovidiopol, named in honor of Ovid, who had been exiled there. We were very poor and never had any possessions, all I ever owned was a little trunk and a folding bed. We never had a table or a chair of our own. The furniture was always either the landlord's or the state's.

In Ovidiopol we rented a room from a priest. My mother made so little money that the priest supplemented our diet with Communion wafers. My mother was always terrified that I'd say something about this to someone—the secretary of the party organization living with a priest and eating Communion wafers!

There was a teacher in the local school, a young man in his early twenties, Boris Gurevich, who used to come to our house and one time even said to my mother, "Your daughter is going to grow up to be an eccentric." I was very flattered, though I had no idea what the word meant.

On the day that changed my life, I came running in a T-shirt and shorts, all tanned, my hair very close-cropped. I was always out running and swimming and I'd throw a stone through your window if I didn't like you. That day, Boris came to visit my mother but she wasn't home. And I came running in all tanned and wild. "Sit down, Natalya," he said, and he was the first person ever to address me with the formal "you."

He touched my knee so I would be still and then he began reading poetry to me. It was Blok, Alexander Blok,

> She arose at dawn
> and blessed the children
> who dreamed in joy . . .

In that moment the world became a different place for me. All this—Boris, the poetry, not being addressed as a child—came as a revelation that made me a grown-up. At least I've never changed that much since then.

Stalin not only went after Trotsky but after all those who had sided with him. Revekka's father and Ivan Vrachov were expelled from the party. The two men she loved most were bereft. "For Papa there was no life outside the party." But her father and Vrachov were given a chance to redeem themselves. Appointed to high administrative positions in remote places, they were told that recanting and good service might yet win them reinstatement in the party.

Ivan Vrachov hadn't been afraid to defy Stalin to his face and he wasn't going down without a fight.

The opposition was in a tragic predicament. We had been scattered but we were still true to our principles. We believed we had been treated unjustly. We were pained by the state of our party and our country, and considered it necessary to fight for Stalin's dismissal.

But what could we do, people who had essentially been deprived of all their rights? We corresponded with each other, we received letters from Trotsky in Alma-Ata. And anyone with access to a typewriter made copies of those letters and distributed them. Of course, exiles weren't allowed to have typewriters.

Stalin wasn't satisfied. He decided to exile Trotsky from the country. A treacherous move. When I found out about it I told the other people I knew from the opposition, "This is a devilish move, and soon we'll all be renouncing Trotsky and condemning him."

They told me, "You're out of your mind!"

I told them, "Wait and see!"

And us people in the opposition, rejected by the party, driven from its ranks, were faced with the problem of what we should do next. We could not continue our struggle by political means, and to just become ordinary citizens—we weren't cut out for that. There was only one path open to us—to capitulate, to get back into the party at any cost.

There was a lot of haggling over terms in Moscow. Finally, one of the comrades, Karl Radek, called me and read me a draft of a statement that would appear in the papers. I sighed as I listened. And Radek said, "Ivan, don't sigh. We stuck to our principles but nothing's coming of it. There's no other way we can get back into the party. Sign the telegram with us."

I signed. And in July 1929 *Pravda* printed a statement saying that we were leaving the opposition and breaking with Trotsky. And among the signatures was mine.

I returned to Moscow and was given a very good reception. I had to wait six months to see if I was reinstated in the party. Nevertheless, even though officially I was not in the party, I was sent out by the Moscow Party Committee to speak at mass meetings of workers. The party treated me like one of its own. I wrote for the newspapers and even published a few pamphlets. Everything seemed just fine.

But then they started going for us on the sly. There would be party meetings at which various issues were discussed—linguistics, philosophy, and so forth. What was I supposed to do? Not say what I thought? But then they'd say—Vrachov's not saying anything, that means he's got something to be quiet about. It wasn't enough that we'd capitulated, that we'd been beaten, they had to kick a man when he was down. We'd fallen into a trap.

Under the tsars, exiles were allowed to hunt for food, even with rifles if the district were sufficiently remote. In his several Siberian exiles, which he always took as his true school, Stalin mastered the art of trapping. A subtle skill that requires a sensitivity to the prey, it was also easily transferable to the affairs of men.

1929 was Stalin's year. Trotsky had been physically removed from the Soviet Union in February. Stalin had smashed the opposition. Some, like Vrachov, were not allowed back into the party; some, like Revekka's father, Mikhail Boguslavsky, were briefly reinstated.

On December 21, 1929, Stalin's fiftieth birthday was celebrated with maniacal, Byzantine splendor. Except for a few columns at the back of the paper, all eight pages of that day's edition of *Pravda* were devoted to Stalin's greater glory. Before the year was out, Stalin announced that the NEP was over, and he would now move the country in a new direction. ALL POWER TO THE SOVIETS had become ALL POWER TO THE BOLSHEVIKS and, now, finally, was ALL POWER TO STALIN.

Collectivization

The women have not been fighting lately in the kitchen of the communal apartment at 6 Sretensky Boulevard. A tense civility prevails. To her surprise, Lusya finds herself enjoying it, almost a form of privacy. But it is not the privacy she craves, not the zone of sanctity called home. The summer of 1988 has passed, the school year and the bad weather have started, and they are all still stuck there sharing the kitchen, bathroom, and hall with strangers, still stepping out of their bedroom into "Red Square."

As she does every day, Praskovya, the hefty country woman, shuffles to the kitchen, teapot in hand. But today is special, for Praskovya has a guest. Her friend Alexandra, who lives in another part of that vast, block-long building, has taken the elevator, still damp with urine, still marked DEATH TO KIKES AND TARTARS, to the fifth floor to pay a call.

Alexandra waits in Praskovya's room, which contains a wardrobe, an iron bed, a few odd chairs. Even inside, Alexandra does not remove her coat or her kerchief, the traditional black, green, and rose red. She sits at the very edge of the bed as if to take up as little space as possible. She herself is miniature, a village woman shrunken in a brine of grief.

Her grey eyes have the terrifying coolness of those who no longer believe in anything.

In many ways, Alexandra is just like her friend Praskovya. They were both born at the beginning of the century in poor peasant families, in villages that no city-dwelling Russian had ever heard of. They were both driven to Moscow by the famine of the early thirties, which took place when Stalin forced the peasants from their own farms into giant agri-galleys known as collective farms. And they both ended up working as waitresses, washer-women, cleaning-women, maids. Neither learned to read, and for them the ornate Cyrillic language was forever decoration, like the raised patterns on the wallpaper in Praskovya's room.

Alyosha, Lusya's husband, has brought a plate of sweet pastries as a present to Praskovya, whom both he and Lusya love. And how could anyone help but love that simple country woman without a bad bone in her whole, big, soft body. And who had displayed the natural courage of the good when she stepped be-tween the two women about to commit violence in the kitchen. And who still loved a good laugh, though it was death she would have preferred.

Praskovya makes tea for her guest Alexandra, for Alyosha, and for herself, coming in when Alexandra is speaking about the one thing that makes her different from her friend—when she was thirty-nine she married a man twice her age. And for good reasons.

He didn't drink or smoke tobacco. He had two jobs, a watchman at a factory, a doorman at a restaurant. And he was handsome too. And I was sick of working as a maid, I worked for Jews, I worked for Tartars, I worked for Russians, I liked working for Armenians best. But I was thirty-nine then and sick of being a maid.

We had one child, he died young, pneumonia.

I took care of my husband when he fell sick. He was blind for nine years and on his sickbed for five.

Now my life is hell. There's this woman, an alcoholic, she does whatever she wants to me. She's not afraid of anybody or anything.

Last night she came into my room.

She broke in my door.

And she came in with a drunken man. Take the icons, she says to him. And then to me she says "Time to free up this room, old woman, time for you to be dying."

Alexandra seems stunned into silence by what she has just said, by what the end of her life has now become. Shriveled, doll-like, hunched at the edge of the bed, she begins to weep with clear and inconsolable bitterness.

A big tear rolls down Praskovya's cheek and she lifts her glasses up to wipe her eyes. Alyosha reaches over and puts his hand on Alexandra's trembling shoulders.

"I'll talk to that woman, don't worry," he says to Alexandra.

She nods to indicate she understands and believes him, but also to say that the threat may be removed but not the insult.

Later that evening Alyosha tells Lusya the story Alexandra had told him. Perhaps since both Praskovya and Alexandra were driven to the city by collectivization, Lusya thinks of her great-grandfather Vassily, the busy peasant, whom she cannot recall without smiling:

Great-grandfather Vassily was a hard-working Russian peasant, so hard-working that he sometimes made foolish mistakes. When their tenth child was born, yet another daughter, Vassily went into the village to register the birth. He didn't even consult with his wife on what to name the child. When he came back from the village, his wife asked him, "What did you name the child?"

"Maria," he said.

"What do you mean—Maria? We already have one Maria."

"Too late now. We'll call one of them Marusia and the other one Manya."

And that wasn't the first time either, there were already two Tanyas in the family.

They were a very hard-working family and had a decent life. Enough to eat, clothes to wear. They owned a horse, a cow, a little land. And they were such simple, naïve people that when the propaganda team came and told them they had to join the collective farm, they just submitted—If they say we have to then we have to.

They weren't rich peasants, kulaks, they were middle peasants. When they agreed to join the collective farm, everything they owned was taken from them—the horse, the cow, even their sheepskin winter coats.

Then they were told to report to the village soviet the next day to sign up for the collective farm. But when they got there they were told, "You people are kulaks, get out of here before we arrest you."

They were left with nothing. No food, no money, no flour, no plough. Vassily took the older children to the city to look for work but he died right away, probably typhus.

One of the propaganda teams dashing about the Ukraine was led by Ilya Jaffee, who never used threats but always relied on a greater force, passionate sincerity. "I believed that if the peasants pooled all their ploughs and wagons, we'd have paradise on earth in no time flat."

Ilya had been repulsed by Trotsky's vision of rich peasants supporting urban industry, and lucky for him that he had. Initially, he had become a Stalinist out of repulsion for Trotsky, but now as the thirties began he was a Stalinist out of conviction. His candidacy for membership in the communist party was officially accepted in 1929, the year of Stalin's triumph. The boy who had studied Torah and was converted by Darwin and violence was now, as he put it, a "typical rank and file member of the Stalinist intelligentsia." He shared the belief that the peasants were a reactionary class by nature, and the richer the peasant, the more conservative. The richest class, the kulaks, were the enemy and must be treated as such. Ilya was now a devoted communist who believed that history was Darwinian, that communism, as he had been taught, "was not philanthropy but a faith, a way to build society according to economic laws." And he was by nature so ardently zealous that he not only believed in collectivization but that its implementation would bring "paradise on earth in no time flat."

*

Ivan Vrachov, who cannot speak of Lenin without lowering his voice, cannot say Stalin's name without furious disgust:

S talin, if I may say so, robbed the opposition of its ideas, then perverted them. Collectivization is a classic example. When it came to agriculture, the opposition was in favor of carrying out Lenin's behest—rely heavily on the poor peasants, be on good terms with the middle peasants, and fight the rich peasants, the kulaks. There was to be an all-out effort to develop agricultural co-ops, to make it advantageous to work collectively, to do so when the time was ripe, the principle of voluntary joining to be observed at all times.

Stalin launched a new theory—the liquidation of the kulaks as a class. Where did he take that from? Can you find anything of the sort in the works of Marx, Engels, or Lenin? No, you cannot! The destruction of the kulaks as a class was a Stalin original.

Ivan Vrachov frowns as he catches himself in a contradiction. Either Stalin stole the idea of collectivization or else it was an original. Or did he so pervert the idea as to make it his own? In any case, for Vrachov, a dedicated Leninist, the name of Lenin must be kept apart from all the horrors that are concealed by that greyest of words, collectivization.

Original, stolen, or perverted, the idea was something new in history—the obliteration of a certain layer of the population, sociological murder. It was also the transformation of society by decree, the thousands of years of Russian farming traditions to be smelted down and rebuilt into gigantic collective enterprises.

To the young people aflame with enthusiasm for communism, collectivization meant justice, plenty, and modernity, and they raced to the countryside to serve their nation. One of the volunteers was Veniamin, who was twenty-two in 1930. Working in a Moscow textile factory by day and taking evening classes at the university, he was proud to be a member both of the proletariat and the intelligentsia, a new fusion, but he was willing to sacrifice all that to help the country modernize its agriculture. When he volunteered, he was offered a propaganda job in the district of Ryazan.

But Ryazan was just a stone's throw from Moscow, *says Veniamin.* That didn't interest me in the least—if you're going to go somewhere, go somewhere far away. That's what I requested and that's what I got—Kazakhstan, which isn't far from China.

When I arrived in the Kazakh town of Chimkent, I reported to the party committee for my assignment. They said to me, "You're from Moscow, a student? Wonderful. We're making you chairman of the 'Start' collective farm."

I nearly went out of my mind! Me, a twenty-year-old kid, the chairman of a collective farm?

But to be from the capital and to have studied at a university carried tremendous weight in those parts. Veniamin had asked for an adventurous assignment, and for a good communist the more exacting the challenge the better. He accepted.

It was late in the winter of 1930. The snow drifts there were something fearsome. They wrapped me up in a fur coat and put me in a sleigh. There were no trucks there, no cars. They drove me to the village, where the snow was so deep people had to dig passageways to walk through.

It was a well-to-do village of Russians and Ukrainians, no Kazakhs there. A little collective farm had been set up there eight years before. It had been a struggle but now the farm was on its feet.

The party had nominated me to be the chairman of the "Start" collective farm, but I had to be approved by the members. The whole collective farm met in a building that had once been a church before being turned into a club. It was a large building and many people came, not only the collective farmers but the farmers who had still kept their private farms.

I got up and told them that I grew up in the city, had worked at the "Red Textile Worker" factory, attended university, and didn't know the first thing about farming.

Then an old, grey-haired saddle maker got up and said, "How are you going to lead us if you don't know the first thing about farming?"

I said, "I don't intend to teach you about farming. I'm sure you know that very well. All I can do is tell you about my experience of working with a large collective at my factory, and point out the advantages of everyone pulling together. I have no intention of issuing any orders or instructions about farming. That's all up to you."

They liked me—a young kid but calm and cool. And they approved me as chairman of the "Start" collective farm.

There was a mass drive on for collectivization. In those parts the peasants weren't being forced to join. It was a campaign of persuasion. There were about 450 farm households in that large village and about a hundred of them had already joined.

There was one peasant by the name of Tverdokhlebov who was very typical. A middle peasant, a simple muzhik. Every evening he'd come to see me and ask my advice—should he join or not?

First he'd list all the reasons he should join and then I'd say, "Fine, so join."

"Yes," he'd say, "but on the other hand . . ." Then he'd list all the reasons against joining.

"Fine," I'd say, "so don't join."

Tverdokhlebov kept coming, day after day after day. I never lost my temper. And I had a certain authority for those peasants because I wasn't one of them but from the city, someone who'd been to a university. To them that all sounded very grand. Finally, in the end, Tverdokhlebov joined.

An innocent heart and gentle persuasion had won the day in Kazakhstan, but the peasants of the Ukraine needed more convincing. There, communists were being murdered with pitchforks and shotguns. Rebellious regions were bombed from the skies and attacked through the fields by tanks, another historical first.

One of the people on the attack was Natalya Viktorovna's mother, the former aristocrat who willed herself to believe.

They gave my mother a pistol and sent her out to the Ukrainian countryside to combat the peasant uprisings against collectivization. And it was collectivization that set the two of us at odds.

By then we were living in the Ukrainian town of Zhitomir. As a party member there were two seats reserved for mother at the local theater, which she never used because she was always too busy, always away. But I was glad to go. One time a traveling company staged the opera *Aida* and some of those provincial troupes had quite good singing voices. But this was an *Aida* like no other. At the end of the opera Aida and Radames are walled up. But in the version I saw the people rise up, tear down the wall, and free Aida and Radames, handing him a red banner which he carried as they all went off to storm the palace. That was the first time I'd seen *Aida* and I thought that was how the opera ended.

But I was seeing other things too. There was a wagon which went around Zhitomir three times a day picking up corpses. The person walking in front of you on the sidewalk could just fall down and die. If you went out in the morning before the wagon had come round, you'd see corpses with their buttocks cut off, the meatiest part.

Veniamin was ignorant of the crimes taking place in the Ukraine and innocent of any such violations on his own collective farm. He had won the peasants' confidence, but the day-to-day running of the farm was another matter entirely. Yet he proved a natural executive, able to delegate authority, to let processes take their natural course, and to recognize an opportunity when it came his way.

The local branch of the national meat-packing association had built up a huge backlog of cattle, but no one had given any thought to finding fodder for them. The cattle started dying. I was being pressured to care for the cattle on our collective farm. They said to me, "Take the cattle from us. We won't count them by the number of head but by total weight. If there's any increase in the total weight, the money goes to you."

I called a board meeting. All issues were discussed by the board and anyone wishing to could attend any meeting of the board. The people on the board had good heads on their shoulders and they agreed when I said, "We can't let this opportunity slip us by."

We took in 250 head of cattle. They weren't in great shape but we put them in barns and fed them good fodder. By the time spring planting came, all the cattle were nice and fat. And with the money we made we were able to buy more plows and plant another twenty-five hundred acres of land.

The peasants were impressed. The young man was not only sincere but correct as proven by their increased prosperity, the only measure.

*

Lusya's story of Vassily the Very Busy began with a smile and ended in tragedy as she told of her great-grandfather succumbing to typhus in the city. But by then a quick death from disease could seem a blessing, as her great-grandmother's fate proved.

My grandmother was also one of the peasants who went to the city. After a year she went back to the village where she'd left her mother and her little children. Her mother was in bed, all skin and bones. For a whole year she'd had practically nothing to eat. She and the children were all just lying there dying.

My grandmother had brought some food with her. She walked over to her mother and said, "Look, mother, I have food, some cucumbers and bread. Here, take them."

But her mother said, "Those aren't cucumbers."

She'd gone insane with hunger and could no longer recognize cucumbers.

And so my grandmother said, "Mother, can I bring you some water?"

And her mother said, "There's no more water. All the rivers and wells are full of blood."

She died a short while later.

Lusya's great-grandmother had the misfortune to live in a part of the Ukraine that Stalin had sentenced to death by artificial famine, real hunger. The method was simple. Armed squads confiscated all food, armed squads patrolled all roads, forcing the peasants to remain in their villages with nothing to eat. When the winter was over, other squads would be sent in to clear out the corpses, and new people would resettle the villages, still perfectly intact. Starvation was the neutron bomb of the early 1930s in Russia.

And all the while, Veniamin the young collective farm chairman was winning victory after victory for Stalin by using tact and intelligence and daring, if need be.

Right from the start I could see that a peasant didn't like it if he saw one of us administration people out galloping on a horse that had once been his. Even though all the horses belonged to the collective farm now, to him it was still his horse.

So, I issued orders that horses only be used for working the fields. If any administration people needed to go out to the fields for any reason, they were to hitch a ride on a grain wagon. No horses under saddle!

But that was to cost me later on. Toward the end of the

planting season I learned that a group of about twenty private farmers had gone off to where one group was sowing the land and was trying to convince them to quit the collective farm. I knew that this particular group of ours was among the most volatile, and I was afraid they'd be talked into quitting.

But the place they were planting was twelve miles away and there wasn't a horse to be found anywhere! And all because of the orders I'd given.

We had a special stable for breed horses. They led a life of luxury with plenty to eat and nothing to do, but they were still wild, never broken for work.

"Give me a horse!" I said to the stableman, who gave me a young stallion. He helped me into the saddle and off I went. The horse was trouble the whole way. It'd chase after every other horse it saw and once almost collided with a telegraph pole. The reins were rubbing my hands raw.

I didn't know the way and asked directions, but I still kept getting lost. When I finally reached their camp around dinnertime, I was on the wrong side of the river. They were all just getting ready to hold a meeting and so no damage had been done yet.

But that idiotic horse of mine would only go into the water up to its shoulders then get scared and bolt back. No matter how hard I pulled the reins, I couldn't make it cross the river.

But there was another young communist on the other side of the river, a fellow by the name of Andrusha. He grabs a mare and fords the river. "Your horse is a young stallion," he says, "it'll chase after the mare."

All the peasants had lined up on the other side of the river to watch.

He was a better rider so we decided to switch horses. When we had each dismounted, I turned my back to the stallion to get up on the mare. Just then the stallion kicked me with everything it had. The pain was horrible. But I had to show the peasants I could take it. I gritted my teeth and didn't make a single sound. I mounted the mare and set off back across the river. By then Andrusha was on the stallion, which bolted right after the mare just like he said it would.

The peasants lined up along the river loved it—two smart young Russian lads harnessing the oldest force in the world, a stallion's lust for a mare. It was a folk tale in itself and well worth the retelling. And who would want to leave a collective farm run by a young man like that? Once again Veniamin had won the day.

*

Ilya Jaffee had dashed through the Ukraine preaching "heaven on earth" through the pooling of resources. He was traveling even faster than consequences, so he had no idea how many kulaks were being slain or deported en masse in cattle cars to Siberia, where they would be thrown into a wilderness of chest-deep snow to either survive or perish. Besides, he was not involved in collectivization for very long. He was needed elsewhere.

"Just when the campaign for collectivization was reaching its hottest, the party suddenly comes out with a new slogan—MASTER TECHNOLOGY, COMMUNISTS FIRST! There was a competition which I did well in and was sent straight from collectivization to an institute in Leningrad, where I was to study engineering and economics. And, to be honest, there in Leningrad, I had no idea about the terrible famine that followed in the Ukraine."

And if he had, he might have ascribed it to "sabotage by the rich peasants," as Natalya Viktorovna's mother did. He certainly would not have blamed Stalin but, like Stalin himself, would have placed the full onus on the overzealousness of certain cadres in the field.

So there would be no doubts on the subject, Stalin himself picked up his pen and wrote an article, "Dizzy with Success," which was printed in *Pravda* on March 2, 1930. Enthusiasm is a good thing, of course, chided Stalin, but some people get carried away. The article was to shift blame from leader and policy to isolated individuals, the bad exceptions to the good rule.

Stalin's article brought some temporary relief to the places where the suffering was greatest, but it only caused trouble on Veniamin's farm, where everything had been going quite well.

No sooner had Stalin's article "Dizzy with Success" appeared than rumors started going around the village: Stalin said to leave the collective farms. That's how they interpreted the article.

A meeting was called. Many of the people who were against collectivization attended. My biggest problem as chairman was keeping the peace between the poor and middle peasants, there were no real kulaks in our village. The poor and middle peasants were always clashing and I was forever trying to make peace between them. They all liked me but couldn't stand each other.

I was well prepared for the meeting. I answered all questions to everyone's satisfaction. But then some stranger took the floor and said that collective farms were for the poor peasants, lazy bastards who'd never made anything out of themselves and who wouldn't do any better on a collective farm either. Naturally, the poor peasants replied to that attack by calling the middle peasants bloodsuckers.

Then, to make matters worse, an official from the party's district committee sided with the poor peasants, which only fueled the flames. It turned into such a shouting match that it was impossible to go on with the meeting. A total breakdown, everyone went home.

Then that official from the district committee became very frightened and said to me, "You don't know the people around here, you don't know what these kulaks are like. They all have weapons and all we've got is two pistols."

He was right about that—we had only two revolvers. But I said, "What do we need weapons for? Nothing's gotten out of hand. People argued, but what's unusual about that? People have to talk things through . . ."

At first he demanded that we write to the district committee and request an armed detachment be sent here. I fought him tooth and nail on that, saying that would make more trouble. What I proposed was to meet separately with each of the five work brigades and give them a close, detailed reading of Stalin's article and the resolution passed by the government on the basis of the article. The resolution said that people should not be forced back onto the collective farms, that churches should not be forcibly closed, and that chickens and other domestic livestock should not be collectivized.

We hadn't had any of those problems. Everything had been voluntary on our collective farm. People just needed things explained to them, you had to talk to them like human beings, that's all.

I called the first meeting with the brigade I knew was spoiling for trouble. The meeting was in one of the peasants' huts. It was packed, not a breath of air, and everyone smoking too! I read them Stalin's article, dwelling on every line. I not only gave them the opportunity to ask questions but to take the floor and speak as long as they wished. No time limits, absolutely none.

And then I said, "Farming operates on a yearly cycle. The cycle we're in now ends in the fall. We can't shake things up before the fall. If you want to leave the collective farm in the fall, feel free to do so. But you'll only receive your share of land in the fall. Each household will receive twenty-five acres. But will you be able to work that much land by yourselves? Of course you won't, and it's not realistic to think otherwise. Leaving the collective farm would not only be wrong but foolish. Think it over."

Then we moved on to the question of the village church. I said that as far as I knew the church had not been forcibly closed and turned into a club. But then one woman took the floor and said, "It wasn't that way at all. We were intimidated. It wasn't fair. We didn't want to give up the church."

One woman after another took the floor. The men weren't saying anything. I said, "What do the men have to say?" The men only grinned and didn't say a word.

And so I said, "Doesn't matter. Women make up half the population of the village. There should be a meeting of all the village women, not just the women who belong to the collective farm. And if they decide that the club should be turned back into a church, we'll raise the issue at the general meeting."

The women met a few days later. All the village women attended and they didn't let any men in. They only allowed the chairman of the village soviet and myself to attend, but without the right to speak. It was purely a women's meeting. They elected their own chair and observed all the rules of procedure. They debated the point—some felt that the club should be turned back into a church but others said, They show movies once a week in the club and the Young Communist Theater Group meets there.

Finally, when the issue was put to a vote, the majority was in favor of keeping the club as it was.

It was all absolutely and completely democratic.

But Stalin's article was only a ruse and a respite. "That article was typical of Stalin's way of doing things," says Natalya Viktorovna. "First he'd do something, then blame somebody else for it, so that he came out looking good and wise and concerned. Some of the farmers did indeed leave the collective farms which they had joined in 'voluntary coercion.' That was the term used then— 'voluntary coercion.' But none of their equipment was returned to the farmers who left. They were given some land to work with their bare hands and a crushing tax to pay. It was impossible to pay it but, if they didn't, they were considered criminals, saboteurs, allies of the kulaks, and exiled or sent to the camps."

It was only a breather between horrors, as Natalya was to see for herself:

There was a wealthy man who lived across from us in Zhitomir. He kept pigs. Now there were hordes of starving people trying to get into the cities, peasants from whom everything had been taken. They weren't allowed into the cities but some of them would slip in anyway. One day one of them went into that rich man's yard and began rummaging through his garbage for something to eat. Suddenly he started shouting—he had come across a huge number of human fingers. A crowd formed at once. It turned out that our neighbor had been luring people into his home promising them a place to spend the night and some food. Those were all country people, no one knew them in the city. He'd kill them and then chop off their fingers. He'd make cutlets out of their flesh and his wife would sell those cutlets of human flesh at the market. He'd also feed his pigs with human flesh then sell those pigs.

You couldn't go out in the street alone. Otherwise people would lasso you, drag you off and eat you. Cannibalism was very widespread. My mother was now giving political instruction to the local police. One policeman and his wife killed their own son and pickled his flesh in a barrel.

Now I began clashing with my mother, who said all the problems were due to sabotage by the peasants. She always tried to stick to the official line. The newspapers of the time had headlines about the "flourishing Ukraine." But the contrast with the reality was so great that I ceased believing in communism once and for all. I believed that it was a historical necessity, inevitable, but that it was horrible and repellent.

"But collective farming could have worked," says Veniamin. "It worked in Israel, the kibbutzes are collective farms. But it couldn't be done by force and decree. And there are people who are simply not cut out to work in a group. They have to do everything by themselves. Why force someone to join a collective farm if he can produce twenty times more working by himself?"

Though Stalin was perfectly willing to reap the benefits of collective farms that worked as well as Veniamin's, his real interest lay in control. And Stalin's real people were not the Veniamins but the strangers at the collective farm meeting who pitted the poor peasants against the middle peasants and the party official who could not distinguish between disagreement and treason and

wanted to call the troops in at once. Veniamin did not last long on
the "Start" collective farm. Someone—maybe the stranger, maybe
the party official—made a call, and Veniamin was transferred to the
army. Veniamin was wrong for the times, had the wrong outlook:
"Everything had to be done slowly, humanely. The process should
have taken several decades. Maybe fifty years, maybe seventy."

But Stalin, though admirably patient, could not wait fifty or seventy
years. His name might be immortal but his bones were not. Everything had to be done quickly, at what Russians then called the
"American pace." Speed was the essence of the times. Everything
moved at a greater tempo—vehicles, progress. And if war came,
as war always comes, then the nations that were left behind would
be devoured. Besides, every true communist could feel in his heart
the same certainty that burned in Ilya Jaffee's, that pooling resources and pulling together would lead to "heaven on earth in no
time flat."

  "We didn't know anything about the terrible famine that
followed in the Ukraine after we had gone through speaking to
people, trying to convince them to join collective farms," says Ilya.
"By then I was in Leningrad, studying engineering and economics.
I got my food at a closed party store. We communists were fed very
well. Almost two pounds of bread a day. But that also put a certain
crack in our integrity. That was the beginning of our fall from
grace, our Original Sin."

  Ilya falls silent and the corners of his lips crinkle. He knows
that he has not told the whole truth. The fall from grace had come
earlier, when he was still out racing through the Ukrainian countryside. Ilya's original sin was not that of eating well while Russia
starved.

  His eyes, usually flashing with mischief, passion, or defi-
ance, now grow vacant behind the wraparound glasses as he withdraws into himself to decide whether or not to make Stalinist
confession. The decision is reached and put at once into effect:

One day during collectivization I talked to the peasants of a
village called Razumovka. After the meeting I was given a

paper to sign. It was the list of people being deported as
kulaks. I signed the paper and went on to the next village.

A few days later on my way back through Razumovka, I
heard a terrible wailing. It was coming from a crowd of people,
young women, children, and men, two of them tied up.

"What's all that?" I said.

"It's just the Polyakovs, they're all upset about being
resettled."

The Polyakovs were taken away.

Then I started asking some questions.

"Don't worry, they're kulaks. You saw the list," I was
told.

"But how come there's so many of them?"

"It's the whole family."

When it hit me, it knocked me for a loop. I
remembered the list said that the Polyakovs had fourteen
horses and nineteen cows, so there could be no doubt that they
were kulaks. But now when I checked, it turned out that the
Polyakovs weren't one family but five!

My heart was racing! What had I done?!

It was ten miles to the city and late at night by the time
I got there. And the next day was a Sunday. Monday I got in
to see the official in charge of resettling kulaks.

"Listen," I tell him, "there's been a mistake. The
Polyakovs aren't kulaks. They're what Lenin calls middle
peasants."

Cool as can be the official says, "How am I supposed to
find them for you? Their train's been gone three days."

I didn't blow my brains out. But for something like the
next forty years, there'd be nights when I'd wake up in a cold
sweat. And even though I didn't know it at the time, I am
guilty of consigning those people to their doom.

And that has left a bitter taste in my mouth. A bitter
taste.

The Terror

Kirov

That somewhere near or far people are dying hideously has never kept the young from falling in love. At the age of eighteen Revekka fell in love for the first time, though this was hardly her first love. Her first love was, and remained, her father, Mikhail Boguslavsky, who had the face of a poet and the body of a hunchbacked tailor; her father, the virtuous communist who scolded her for tardiness by saying, "Vladimir Ilich Lenin is a little bit busier than you but he's never late"; her father, to whose side she had instinctively drawn after the stranger had left their box at the Bolshoi Ballet; her father, who had told her the stranger's name: Stalin.

There had been another man to whom Revekka's heart had flown singing, her father's friend Ivan Vrachov, who had defied Stalin to his face, calling on his comrades to act at once, since there were "only hours of democracy left" in Russia. Like her father, he had been expelled from the party for belonging to the Trotskyite Opposition; but they both had fared reasonably well, being as-

signed to important positions where their abilities could be put to
good use. The locations, however, were remote. They were far
from the center of power and that was the true punishment for a
communist—to bar him from participating in the making of history.

In time, Revekka's girlish infatuation with Ivan did not so
much cool as come to a deep and respectful stop. Suddenly the
seventeen years between them became a gulf, even though when
she was six that same span of years had been no more difficult to
cross than the living room floor as she ran to throw herself in his
arms.

And so Alexei Merkulov was Revekka's third love, though
every love is the first.

I was a Young Communist by 1932 and I became very close
with Alexei Merkulov. He was seven years older than I, a
member of the party. He was in charge of a division at his
factory and was also head of the party committee there. Two
years later, he proposed.

I didn't give him an answer. I knew that first I should
get Papa's permission. When my father had been expelled from
the party, he had been sent to Novosibirsk in Siberia to serve
as chairman of the Five Year Plan Commission and direct the
construction of a large factory that produced mining equipment.

And so, all on my own, I took a train to Siberia, to
Novosibirsk, to ask my father's blessing.

Papa took me to the construction site. I was so proud of
the way the workers said hello to him. How they smiled at
him, not groveling, which humiliates a person, but with real
respect. And it made me happy to see the way Papa went over
to the workers and spoke with them. It was all simple, direct,
to the point.

Papa and I had very good talks, we went walking in the
woods. I told Papa about coming to know Alexei and said that
he had proposed to me. "But I won't give him an answer
without first hearing what you have to say."

And Papa said, "Being a wife is a big job. You have to

run the house and run it well. If you love this person, the choice is yours. I would have preferred you to start the university first and then . . ."

Papa promised to come to the wedding. I turned twenty in October 1934 and in November I was married. And Papa did indeed come to the wedding, where his jokes and joie de vivre made him the center of attention.

In those days you didn't get three days off if you got married, like people get now. The next morning after the wedding I went off to school and Alexei went off to work.

Then we moved in with Alexei's family and I got to know my father-in-law. In one corner of the living room there were icons with candles burning in front of them. And to one side of the room there was also a pedestal with a large bust of Karl Marx. But I had some problems there, it was very hard for me to call my father-in-law "Papa" since there was no comparing anyone to my father.

After turning twenty in October 1934, Revekka married in November, severe times when the honeymoon lasted exactly one night. But the honeymoon wouldn't have lasted long in any case, for on December 1, 1934, Sergei Kirov, the popular head of the Leningrad communist party, was assassinated, a pistol shot that would reverberate through all eleven of Russia's time zones.

Kirov had both Bolshevik steel and Russian good-guy charisma. Big, blonde, blue-eyed, Kirov represented both a Russian genetic ideal and the image of heroic manliness, as would become apparent in the posters of World War II. Kirov had been a frequent guest at the Stalin household, picnicking with the family on radiant summer days.

Stalin liked Kirov, but affection was the least of obstacles for him. Stalin would have been glad to see Kirov removed as a rival while genuinely mourning the loss of a friend. In a rare foray into public, Stalin dashed to Leningrad and attended Kirov's funeral, kissing him farewell while the coffin was still open. Streets, squares, bridges, factories, whole cities were named for Kirov, and the Marinsky Ballet took his name as well, the Kirov.

Stalin also personally supervised the investigation into the murder. Whether he had also personally supervised the elaborate assassination carried out by a deranged communist is not entirely certain, but Stalin had the best motive and the most ample of opportunities for murder.

The newspapers and radios announced what the investigation personally overseen by Stalin had uncovered. Kirov had died a victim of a fiendish plot by the Trotskyites, though it went beyond them as well. The roots of this conspiracy ran very deep, but the Great Uprooter in the Kremlin would yank out every last tendril.

People would be phoned at work or home and asked to come in to clear up a few small points, and they would never be heard from again. Or, if a search was required, the police came to people's homes. Some, not trusting themselves to act pragmatically in the confusion of arrest, kept a bag packed with warm clothing. By two o'clock in the morning most people figured they could safely fall asleep. The police were being worked very hard and they needed their rest too.

*

I n 1933, when I was nineteen, I married the most immoral man. *Natalya Viktorovna smiles with the smile of a woman with no regrets.* He was in the army, a machine gunner, he could sign his name with his machine gun. That was considered quite dashing. A very charming man, intelligent, capable, but absolutely perverted. One time he told me to go home and that he'd meet me there. I waited and waited and he never came home until the next evening. "What happened?" I said. "I was with some women drinking in a bar. I told you to go home but I already knew what I'd be doing that night. But what I needed was to know I had a pure, loving wife at home waiting for me while I was there with those sluts . . ."

He never hid it from me. After a while I got tired of it all and left him. But without any pain at all and no hard feelings whatsoever.

I went to see my mother in Zhitomir. It was after the Kirov murder, and there had been a wave of arrests there too in the Ukraine. Her consolation was that Khrushchev, the boss

of the Ukraine, said that the people who were being arrested
were enemies of the people, Stalin's line. My mother and I
clashed even more now. If someone she had worked with a
long time and whom she knew to be a devoted communist was
arrested, I'd say to her, "Alright, Mama, you've said it yourself
many times, the man's an excellent communist, a good
comrade." And her reply would be, "You don't understand.
The enemy can disguise himself so well that not even his
mother, his children, and his friends can see who he really is."

At the time, my mother was working as a political
instructor for the secret police. One day she was called in and
shown a list of communists in Zhitomir that were to be
executed. Her name was on the list. A new party directive had
arrived before the Zhitomir secret police had gotten around to
executing her.

Even Stalinists weren't safe. Not even "typical rank and file members of the Stalinist intelligentsia" like Ilya Jaffee. He may have had
his deep regrets about consigning five peasant families to their
doom during collectivization, and he may have been gnawed by
the worm of doubt while eating well at the party canteen, but Ilya
Jaffee was still with Stalin. The byword of the day—When forests
are cut, chips will fly—appealed to Ilya Jaffee, who had read Darwin and seen his father crippled by political violence.

Ilya Jaffee was living in Leningrad when Kirov was assassinated there. Still studying engineering and economics at an institute, he was married and the father of a young son. Then his wife
learned that an old friend of hers by the name of Shumsky was
studying at Ilya's institute and was now herself married, with a
young child of her own. Naturally, she asked Ilya to put them back
in touch. Nothing could have been easier for a dynamic man like
him, and it wasn't long before the two women were sitting beside
each other on a bench, talking as they watched their children play.

Ilya was a man of instinct, and there seemed to be no danger
in helping reunite two old friends. Everything in him had been
repelled by Trotsky—his ideas, his lack of humor, his pince-nez—
and thus Ilya had the good luck to be both timely and sincere in

his loathing for Trotskyites. With his excellent recall for dates, Ilya says:

On November 7, 1934, the seventeenth anniversary of the revolution, some of the students threw a party. I stayed away because I knew there'd be Trotskyites there.

The students did a little drinking and then started singing songs. Then a woman named Shumsky broke in in a loud voice and said those weren't the songs people used to sing back in the twenties, she ought to know, she'd been in the party before being kicked out as a member of the Trotskyite Opposition.

Immediately after Kirov was murdered, we were all called in, in groups and individually, and requested in the name of the party to inform them of anyone who was in any way, shape, or fashion a Trotskyite, or close to the opposition, for those were the very people behind Kirov's murder.

A good many people did in fact inform and with the best of intentions too.

Kirov was killed on December 1, 1934. I was called in by the party committee on January 8. No sooner had I opened the door than the party secretary said to me, "Hand over your party card."

"You weren't the one who gave it to me," I said. "I'm not handing you anything."

The next day I received an official warrant from the party. I went back and they took my party card away. I was expelled from the party for having a family connection with Enemy of the People Shumsky. For the next eight months I wrote everyone I knew and did everything I could, but nothing helped. The other students were afraid to sit near me.

I hadn't been expelled from the institute. Later, I was sent to the Caucasus for training and I started getting letters from my wife. In the first one, she said: You had some visitors. They were awfully interested in you and your books. Of course, I understood what she meant—they'd come with a search warrant and one for my arrest. Later on, she wrote that

I'd started getting postcards summoning me to the Big House, police headquarters in Leningrad.

I wrote and asked my wife to send me a little money so I could buy a return ticket to Leningrad via Moscow. In Moscow I'd go straight to the Central Committee and find out what the real story was.

I arrived in Moscow. I had two brothers there, both party members, but I was afraid to go see them. I sat hungry and waited for the Central Committee to open. I didn't have any money or cigarettes. I could only bring myself to ask someone for a cigarette.

Finally, at ten o'clock the building opened and I went right to the pass office. As soon as I told them my name, they said, "They've been looking for you."

I was told to go up to the second floor. I entered a long, narrow office. There was a man at a desk, and the first thing he said to me was, "How come you married such an old woman?"

I said, "What do you mean, she's only three months older than me."

And he said, "But if she was born in 1906 too, how could she have a friend who's been a member of the party since 1907?"

Then I remembered my wife mentioning that her friend Shumsky had four sisters. Her friend was the youngest, there was around twenty years between her and the oldest, who was the one in question.

I said I had never laid eyes on that sister.

It turned out that he had already reported my case to Yaroslavsky, Stalin's number one man on party affairs. And that's what saved me! Yaroslavsky had looked at the file and said—"How could a twenty-eight-year-old student know Shumsky? I was in exile with her in Yakutsk. Go get this cleared up."

And so they had been looking for me. The man at the desk said Yaroslavsky wasn't in yet, wait, he'll be back, they'll give you a pass. I said I'd be glad to wait if they could give me some breakfast, because I didn't have a kopeck to my name. He gave me three rubles and said, "Here, go have a good breakfast and be back here at two o'clock."

I went back and he showed me the paper they were sending to the Central Committee in Leningrad.

Comrade Bogdanov:
Comrade Jaffee cannot be connected with the Trotskyite Shumsky. His case must be reviewed and closed.

Emelyan Yaroslavsky.

When I got to Leningrad, Bogdanov said, "Yes, I received the paper. We'll be reviewing the case."

"No! You've got to review it right now. I was expelled for no reason. I'm being summoned by the Big House. What proof do you want, that paper was signed by Stalin's number one aide, and it says I wasn't mixed up in anything."

They wrote me out a paper right there on the spot, reinstating me in the party. But with a strict reprimand for my lack of party vigilance. After all, I had been friends with one of the Shumskys.

I was summoned to the Big House the next day. A lieutenant informed me that since I had taken so long to respond to their summonses, I had to leave Leningrad at once.

"The party doesn't trust you to live in Leningrad, the decision was made by a three-man tribunal."

Now I lost all control. "What do you mean the party doesn't trust me? Who told you I wasn't a member of the party?" I pulled out the paper and showed it to him.

His tone changed immediately. "Please have a seat. You're the first case like this we've seen. You certainly are a lucky man. You can go back and get your degree."

I went back and graduated with honors.

*

A rrests were something that happened to other people, *says Natalya Viktorovna.* That's how people thought about it. In any case the terror died down in the middle thirties, which was a relatively good period. Many people, many intellectuals joined the party then. The worst seemed behind us. One man I knew was arrested then released. He made a good joke about the Boss, as Stalin was called. He said, "The Boss got confused for a minute. He thought I was the one who murdered Kirov. But the Boss is an honorable man and when he remembered that he was the one who killed Kirov, he had me released."

The middle thirties were a time of hope. The Stalin Constitution was adopted in 1936 and was a pretty good constitution at that. The stores were full and, unlike NEP, which had great unemployment, now there was plenty of work. It was a brief moment of prosperity and peace, a breathing spell.

That's just how Ilya Jaffee figured it. It was clear to him that the more prominent the head, the more likely it was to be lopped off. And he had just graduated with honors!

Ilya was for Stalin and the party, but he was for Ilya too. Now his instincts told him to move away from the center, from Leningrad, which had been hardest hit by the first wave of terror. Experience had already taught him that a person could be ground under by a farcical, clerical snafu, and so what if later on someone tried to unravel the error, as he had tried to in the case of the peasants wrongly consigned to their doom by his signature.

"I knew they could assign me to some important post. So I said to myself—Don't accept it. Face facts.

"I went to personnel and insisted I be sent to work as an ordinary foreman on a power station that was being built in Murmansk."

Ilya prevailed. He was transferred to Murmansk, one of the northernmost cities of European Russia, close to the point where the USSR meets Norway above Sweden and Finland, the perfect place to be lying low when the terror returned, as it inevitably would.

Spain

Something in Starinov's nature drew him to combat and detonation.

When the Civil War broke out in 1918, he had already been swept by the revolution to a post so high—supplying boots to an entire army—that he qualified for an exemption. For some men the relief would have outweighed any shame. But Starinov was young, pugnacious, Red. Instead of sitting in an office drinking tea, he went running across open fields into a horizontal rain of bullets.

But his first wound had come from the racing, random surgeries of shrapnel. There was no sense of being wounded. One second you're fine, the next you're bleeding.

For true soldiers every scar is a medal, every wound a lesson. Starinov saw it clearly—in modern war explosive power would count most, the ability to blast and obliterate.

And it was that first wound, forever special, like first love, that brought him to his explosive calling.

He had served as a machine gunner's assistant for a time during the Civil War. Feeding the belt during battle, Starinov liked what the job had absolutely required—a pit-of-the-stomach calm. But what he liked best of all was the shock waves from dynamite reverberating in his rib cage.

When the Civil War ended Starinov had of course remained in the army. Even his skin felt more at ease in his uniform—leather strap across the chest to the belt—than in clownish civilian shortsleeves. He went to the military academies, where he distinguished himself more by ardor than academics. He majored in partisan demolition, disabling transport systems behind enemy lines. War was big numbers, an engineering problem, but it was also small sudden raids.

Two of the great generals of the Civil War, Tukhachevsky and Yakir, were firmly convinced that the partisan experience of the Civil War would prove more than useful in the next war. To Starinov those two were true heroes, true patriots, true men. Something to aspire to. And they shared Starinov's own belief that the next war—whatever war it was, but you could smell it coming—would be largely decided by the best placement of explosive power. At the academies they studied chemistry, built explosives, and sought to learn the lessons of the Civil War.

But the Civil War had other lessons that were not on the academy's curriculum as Starinov was soon to learn:

The world came crashing down on my head in the fall of 1935. A check on party documents was being run. I was summoned into the political section for the special troops of the Leningrad garrison.

The head of the department spent a long time studying my party card. I knew the man fairly well but that day he was a changed person.

"Is my party card in order?"

"I'll ask the questions. Did you vote with the Trotskyite Opposition!?"

"No!"

"Did the Whites take you prisoner during the Civil War?"

"Yes. I've indicated that in all the questionnaires and personal statements. After one night I escaped and went back to my regiment, the 20th infantry!"

"That's what you say. But who knows how you were taken prisoner and how you got your freedom. Where's the proof that you escaped?"

The political officer stopped and thought for a minute and looked like his old, good-hearted self again. Then he says, "You've got to be able to prove it. Collect signed affidavits. In the meantime leave your party card here."

I must have looked totally stunned because he spat out some quick advice: "Don't lose your head. Go get the papers."

Bulldoglike in both physique and tenacity, Starinov went and got the papers. He tracked down men who had served with him and were all quick to swear that Starinov was a good soldier who had taken the very first chance to escape, as a good soldier must.

It was still a time when the truth could matter. But it took weeks for his file to be examined, a decision to be reached. And in that interim, Starinov knew the emptiness known by every exile.

"Finally, I was called in by the political officer, the one I'd spoken to before, and he gave me my new party card. He was basically a good person and now he was ashamed of himself. I couldn't wait to get out of there."

His party card was back where it belonged, left breast pocket, over the heart.

The army had given Starinov the dignity of calling but had exacted its price. He was away on assignment when his mother died. After the revolution she had gone back to her village, but the hard Russian land sapped her strength. And he was away on assignment when his father died. It was bitter not to stand by that grave and say that most final of good-byes, a handful of dirt striking the wood of a coffin.

They had been so close, not only in feeling but in who they

were and the way their fates were bound by rails. The father who had inspected track, the son who had exploded track, tie, and rails; the father who had brought trains to a halt with his red lantern, and the son who blew trains sky high with the sudden red lantern of dynamite.

But it was all so theoretical, even the detonations on the range seemed insubstantial, papery. The desire to test his knowledge under real conditions was only part of what made Starinov volunteer to fight in Spain when Franco's Fascists attacked the Republican government in 1936. Starinov was drawn by the din of battle, Starinov wanted another war. And what better war than one where you were on the side of the angels.

For a year or two Spain was the world's great adventure and it drew the hardiest souls—Hemingway from America, Orwell from England, Starinov from the USSR. But being drawn is one thing, getting sent is another. His written requests to serve as a volunteer in Spain did not meet with refusal, only silence.

Then one day by chance Starinov ran into a friend at a railway station who turned out to have a say in who went to Spain. Starinov seized on that and would not let go.

T hree days later I was called in and told I was being sent to Spain.

But then the officer in charge said to me, "But what about the language?"

"Maybe I can study up," I said timidly.

"There won't be time. We'll try to find you an interpreter."

"Fine," I say, "but he has to be familiar with demolition terms."

They found one, but it wasn't a he.

I was speechless when the officer introduced me to a tall, young, good-looking woman with large, light-blue eyes and close-cropped blond hair.

"Comrade Starinov, this is your interpreter, Anna Obrucheva. She's a volunteer too."

I was so embarrassed by the whole thing, I couldn't look her in the eye.

We left for Spain the evening of that same day. Friends saw us off at the station. There was one thing I didn't like about it, the way some of them hinted that in case anything happened we shouldn't worry about them forgetting our families. That didn't concern me, I was a bachelor, but Anna was leaving an eight-year-old daughter in Moscow to go fight in Spain!

For the purposes of the Spanish expedition, Starinov's nom de guerre was Comrade Rudolph. And he'd grown a little moustache just in case any intelligence agency had a photo of him on file; the Poles in particular would be glad to interdict a Soviet on his way to Spain to fight for revolution, and Poland was the first country he would have to pass through on his way out of the Soviet Union. That anxiety was so severe that it kept him from enjoying the mahogany and polished brass of the international train, not to mention his brave and beautiful companion.

Starinov was dark-haired, and his broad, open face had the sort of homeliness some women find more attractive than good looks. He was capable of embarrassment but of quickly overcoming it, a man who could back his bluff.

Europe's air was evil with the coming war. Even Paris seemed Fascist-infested. The mood never lifted until they arrived in the Spanish town of Port Bou during a golden dawn in the Spanish spring, the flowers suddenly bright and dramatic. They were met by crowds throwing flowers at them, women holding little children up for a look, cries of "Viva Rusia!"

Then on to Barcelona and a confusion of flags. The flag of republican Spain, the flag of Catalonia, the red of the communists, and the red and black of the anarchists. Those were still the great days of the Spanish Revolution when all the parties were allied for the good fight, when working men were king, and bootblacks would not accept tips. The elation of camaraderie was in the air, wonderful Spanish spring air scented with oranges and the singed-metal smell of war.

No sooner had Comrade Rudolph and Anna arrived in Valencia, the capital of republican Spain, than Franco's planes bombed the city. The damage was slight. The republic was on the offensive and winning. Comrade Rudolph had not, as he had feared, come "too late."

His first battle was to convince the Republican Command to allocate funds, equipment, and personnel for the training of partisan demolition units. He was given an audience, a chance to make his case. With Anna beside him interpreting, he spoke with passionate conviction:

"Mines are the best offensive weapon! Sometimes an artillery shell hits its target, sometimes it doesn't. But a mine never misses. And it packs more explosive power too. You can't destroy an enemy battalion with a shell, but a mine exploding under a train will destroy a whole battalion and all its equipment. How could anybody disregard a weapon like that?"

He paused to let the tall, blond woman beside him repeat his words in Spanish, watching the Spanish commander's face out of the corner of his eye. It was Comrade Rudolph and Anna's first victory together. He was given a school in a beautiful house on the outskirts of Valencia and twelve willing students led by Capitan Domingo.

"Domingo was a lean man with black hair who looked a little like an Uzbek. For a man of thirty-five he was very quick and nimble. Sometimes he seemed a bit unbalanced but he wasn't crazy, just very temperamental."

Comrade Rudolph initiated the thirteen Spaniards into the mysteries of detonation. The ways of dynamite, the habits of fuses, how to knock out a stretch of track, and how to take a whole train with it. He revealed the weakness of walls and the vulnerability of bridges. He instructed them in the calculation of time, time which is never more keenly real than when you are running from a burning fuse behind enemy lines.

As in any art, what counts the most cannot be taught. And what counts the most in the art of demolition is the calm at the pit of the stomach, the sheer nerve to work with explosives, some of which, if dropped or jolted, could blow a man up so completely that no button or bone could ever be found, while others would just tear off the arms. This could happen at any second; courage was tranquillity.

Comrade Rudolph had no illusions. His group was an experiment. Success might bring them recognition; failure would certainly doom any further outlays of men, money, or matériel. By December 1936 he had taken his students from the classroom to the testing range. Now, he decided, they were ready for the field and reported that fact to his superiors.

The strategic city of Teruel was under Fascist control. Comrade Ruldolph's partisan unit received their assignment—to cut all links to the city—road, rail, and telegraph. But he had only a moment to savor that pleasure, for he was immediately thrown into a quandary.

S hould I go with them or not? I didn't have to go. I was their instructor, not their leader. Capitan Domingo was their leader. It was a tough one.

Then Anna asks me, "Are you going out with them?"

"Yes, I have to."

"Why, wasn't their training good enough?"

"That's not the point. What would the fighting men think of me if I stayed here?"

"And am I supposed to stay here?"

"It doesn't have to be here."

"I'm sorry but I can't accept that," she says. "I'm your interpreter. I'll be right there at your side."

Her tone of voice was so absolute you couldn't argue.

Capitan Domingo threw up his arms in despair when I told him. He yelled, "Women don't go behind enemy lines!"

"Oh yes they do," I said.

We left under cover of dark, twelve of us, wearing rope sandals for the mountains. Each of us was armed with a pistol and a knife, and we had one submachine gun.

It's an eerie feeling crossing enemy lines at night. It's like crossing a chasm on a narrow footbridge, one wrong step and it's all over.

But once they were behind enemy lines they were also beyond fear. And Comrade Rudolph knew that in the end it had only been fear that made him hesitate about going. And he had gone not only because of what the men would think of him but because of what he would think of himself if he had taken that exemption.

The first outing brought Comrade Rudolph the disappointment of small success. His team set charges, the charges went off, the objectives were destroyed. But some of the objectives were poorly chosen—a small bridge over a dry creek, what kind of impediment was that to a truck or a tank? And the course of battle had not been in the least affected by their efforts. Teruel remained in Fascist hands.

Subsequent raids did nothing to prove Comrade Rudolph's thesis that explosives were central to the equation of victory. Morale plummeted dramatically. And, since they were all close now, they all shared the gloom of failure. But Comrade Rudolph didn't know Spain yet.

One day I stopped by Capitan Domingo's house. Everything was in a total tizzy. Clouds of steam, women ironing, their little boy getting whacked each time he ran by, Domingo's wife shouting—"I wish I was never born!"

Then between ten and eleven, it all quiets down. And out comes the senora wearing a black lace mantilla and holding a fan. Domingo's wearing a bright tie, a snow-white shirt, and pants with razor-sharp creases.

I thought—Franco's butchers are outside Madrid, hundreds of soldiers were lost at Teruel, enemy bombers are hitting Valencia day after day, the streets are full of hungry refugees, doesn't matter—there's a bullfight today, a corrida!

Comrade Rudolph declined Domingo's invitation. He'd already seen a corrida and it hadn't been to his liking—the matador was gored. For a man whose every instant was a potential explosion, watching a bullfighter make a fatal error was hardly a form of relaxation. You had to be Spanish for that.

Deciding that additional manpower would make them

more effective, Comrade Rudolph began searching for people who understood Russian. He inquired among the International Brigade, which was made up of volunteers from many lands. He found twenty who were so eager to join up he couldn't refuse them, even though not at all of them spoke Russian.

"There were Czechs and Slovaks, Poles and Hungarians, French and Italian, and one American, Alex. A Jew, an American Jew, and a great fighter. Alex fought wonderfully until he was killed. What's his name, Hemingway, wrote about Alex in *For Whom the Bell Tolls,* but he changed his name."

The new, enlarged group was better and bolder. They moved freely behind enemy lines, inflicting real damage now, but the odds also started catching up with them. They began taking casualties; and Miguel, one of the original twelve apostles of demolition, was killed, a particularly painful loss.

And it was also painful that their work still had not been given the recognition it deserved—more units, more dynamite, more of an active role in prosecuting the war. Then they were given a tricky assignment outside Córdoba—to destroy the troop train that would be following close behind a passenger train. If they destroyed the troop train they could win the glory that had so long eluded them, but if there were civilian casualties they were through.

The passenger train passed at nine in the evening, right on time. We waited a few minutes to make sure there were no enemy in the area. We did our work calmly. If you go about setting explosives calmly, everything will be just fine.

We could see the lights of Córdoba from there and hear the sound of Italian bombers taking off to bomb cities and civilians. We set two mines on the tracks and used all the detonators we had on them.

Then the rails started to hum. The enemy train was coming. We couldn't see its lights yet, but it was coming. We only saw its lights when we were a few hundred yards from the tracks.

Then Juan shouts in horror—"Look!!"

It's another passenger train!

And when it blew, for some reason it flashed through my mind that there were no men on the train, only women.

All the lights went out in Córdoba.

I knew I was finished in Spain. But the next morning they wake me up and there's Capitan Domingo sitting under an olive tree with a fat old man.

And that fat old man tells me that it wasn't a passenger train after all. It had been transferred to military use and was full of Italian soldiers, officers, and aviation specialists.

Then the press gets wind of it. And the famous Russian writer Ilya Ehrenburg visits our unit and writes us up for *Izvestiya.* All of a sudden we're famous. Now the Republican High Command recognizes our value and makes us into a special battalion, the 14th Partisan Corps.

Equipped, financed, respected, they began operating in several theaters and always with greater success. Then it happened.

I t was a time of moonlit nights. The moon kept rising higher and staying longer in the cloudless night sky. We cursed the moon for helping the enemy.

It was on one of those moonlit nights. I was looking through a sack of explosives that had been dropped by a badly wounded man and I made a careless move. Only the electrodetonator went off but it almost cost me my right hand. The doctor who dug out the shrapnel made a good joke, he said, "And I heard you guys only get one mistake!"

His second wound taught him that whatever luck he possessed had been used up, there could be no second error. The fact that the explosion they had all been waiting for had happened proved nothing. It could always happen again, at any second.

Now Comrade Rudolph's group was not only striking at various points across the country but manufacturing explosives as well. This too went exceedingly well, even though the Spaniards had a maddening tendency to bravado, enjoying nothing more than a smoke on a case of dynamite. But he also understood their need to flaunt their bravery, for it only made them calmer in action. He had seen that first with Domingo, always emotional except in battle, when he had the peace of stone.

His workshop produced excellent grenades, some of which may have ended up in George Orwell's hands. Orwell had gone to Spain with the idea of writing articles but was drawn into the fight by that atmosphere that made it seem criminal not to take up arms. At one point, huddled in wet trenches rank as cesspools, Orwell noticed a dramatic improvement in the quality of the hand grenades they were being issued. And Orwell used them to good advantage during a night raid that erupted into fierce fighting, taking pleasure in seeing the grenades he lobbed hit their target. A short while later, a bullet through the throat took him out of the war.

Those were great and heady days for Comrade Rudolph and his men. No obstacle was too great for them, not even the monastery called La Virgen de la Cabeza. His eyes are merry as he says:

The republicans had made several attempts to clear the Fascists out of the monastery but with no success. Nothing worked, not artillery, not even aerial bombardment. The walls of the monastery were too thick, the cellars too deep to do any real damage to it. Then someone thought of using Capitan Domingo's men.

But Domingo was against it—any group large enough to carry the explosives we'd need would be wiped out on the way. And any group small enough to approach the walls couldn't carry enough explosives to make it worthwhile.

Then the head of the mine workshop came up with an idea, one, as he put it, that was "based exclusively on the Fascists' complete ignorance of the classics."

A week later a man riding a mule appears on the road by the monastery. The mule is loaded with two cases of bullets. The Fascists open fire, the rider jumps off and runs. Now the mule is left without a rider and he starts nibbling on the grass.

But there's not much by the road, it's much greener over by the monastery.

The next morning the mule's gone. The Fascists had taken him, glad to get a work animal and two free cases of ammunition.

Two days later another man goes riding a mule down that same road and this mule is also carrying two cases of ammunition. But this was a special mule, one that had been captured from the Fascists. And the peasants had told us that this mule had been reared in the monastery.

One of the cases on the mule was filled with useless ammunition, and the other with forty-five pounds of dynamite, nails, and scrap metal. The case was designed to detonate on opening.

This rider had the same bad luck as the other one and he too had to abandon his mule under fire. The mule of course saw where he was and ambled over to the gates of the monastery.

There was a battalion waiting to attack and they rushed the walls as soon as they heard the explosion. Two days later the white flag came up over the monastery.

Domingo had a huge grin on his face when he said, "Goddamit to hell, an Andalusian mule's as good as any Trojan horse!"

That was the last of the good laughs. Returning from the field in June 1937, Comrade Rudolph learned that the leading generals of the Red Army, including two he knew well and respected deeply, Tukhachevsky and Yakir, had been exposed as Bonapartist traitors, tried, and immediately executed by firing squad. He couldn't believe it. But he had to believe it.

I couldn't understand it. Tukhachevsky fought against the Whites. The Whites had even put a price on his head. He had everything he could want, he was a general in the Red Army. Could he have gotten himself blind drunk and then

gone and done something stupid? It didn't make
sense.

After that our luck went bad. One night we were
storing our dynamite under Anna's bed. A kerosene stove in
the next room tipped over and the burning fuel went streaming
across the floor toward Anna's bed. And it was almost there
before Anna stamped the fire out with her blanket.

We'd almost lost Anna, who was going back with me to
Russia as my wife.

And then on an operation outside Saragossa a stray
bullet hit a knapsack full of dynamite on one of the men's
backs. He was blown to bits and three others were seriously
wounded.

It was over now, the Spain of bravado and camaraderie. There were
two wars now in Spain, one against the Fascists and one between the
Stalinists and all their many enemies. Stalin had not been averse to
drawing France and England into a world war in Spain. War was
coming, and better that it break out as far from Russia as possible.
And there would have been good propaganda value in dealing the
Fascists a defeat, a boost to morale. But a communist government in
Spain could never have been one of Stalin's objectives. Socialism
was to be built in one country, socialism was to have only one
capital. And a second capital of communism would inevitably accept
Trotsky as a resident, if not a leader. To have Trotsky waiting on
Spanish soil to begin a triumphant return march was every bit as
dangerous as having bold generals who might be tempted to Bona-
partism by the proximity of such an alternative. No one is indispens-
able, that was one of the Bolsheviks' mottoes. The generals were
sacrificed, Spain was sacrificed.

Comrade Rudolph accepted the party line that the "Spanish
Republic had been betrayed by the bourgeois countries of the West,
and strangled by the Fascists." But it was exceedingly difficult to
accept the party line that those great generals with whom he'd
worked had betrayed their country. And even supposing they had,
what had Russia become that such honorable men would betray it?

'37

Natalya Viktorovna married again during the merciful pause in the mid-thirties. Or, as she saw it, married for the first time—whatever she'd had with that corrupt and charming young soldier who could sign his name with his machine gun, it wasn't a marriage.

I t was really just an affair, and it left no trace on me, no scars. Neither the relationship nor leaving him meant anything to me. An absurd bit of childishness that I am now even inclined to treat with some humor.

My real husband, David, was a brilliant, witty, and eccentric man, twenty-five years older than I was. He was forty-six, I was twenty-one. Before the revolution he had graduated from Petersburg University with two degrees, one in law, one in mathematics. In 1929 he was arrested and held for two and a half years under investigation until he was finally released. The way he formulated it was: arrested to determine the cause of arrest. He said that he couldn't practice law in a lawless land and devoted himself to mathematics. He also taught Latin for a time, one of the ten languages he knew, and he played chess with masters and grand masters.

We had two children in those years and lived in one room of an enormous eight-room communal apartment in Leningrad where people knew how to keep the peace.

We couldn't have seen the world more differently. One time he came home from the store with some sausage. "The bastards," I said, "they didn't remove the string when they weighed the meat!"

"Natalya," he says to me, "we're so different. When I saw the salesgirl doing that I thought, Oh good, she's throwing in some string."

But that sense of merciful pause was only the general tone and did not at all affect those who were caught in the terror, which had not ceased, only subsided. Once again the terror began to spread until it was everywhere, in knees, larynxes.

According to Stalin's reading of the Russian people, what they wanted was a leader who would spare them nothing, as Ivan the Terrible had spared them nothing when reforging Russia from a land shattered by two centuries of Mongol domination, as Peter the Great had spared them nothing when wresting Russia from the ages into modernity. Both Ivan and Peter had killed their own sons, why should they be any gentler with the people? In Stalin's reading, what the Russians wanted was him.

Ivan Vrachov was a natural candidate for extinction. He had defied Stalin to his face in front of others at a party congress. He had called on those other party members to use "Russia's last hours of democracy" against Stalin. He had sided with Trotsky because he had understood this to be Lenin's wish, and he knew no greater honor than to carry out Lenin's wishes. Any one of these reasons was sufficient cause for a quick bullet behind the right ear. And killing Vrachov would be no mistake. He was Stalin's enemy to the core.

For a time, the terror respected certain territorialities. In

1934 it was not yet quite possible to simply snatch away Ivan Vrachov. He was then the number one aide of Anastas Mikoyan, the dapper Armenian in charge of consumer production whose political nimbleness inspired the joke: Mikoyan, you can't go out without an umbrella, it's pouring! And Mikoyan says, I'll just dodge the raindrops.

They started persecuting the members of the opposition, exiling them, after Kirov's murder in December 1934, *says Vrachov.* They tried to exile me from Moscow too, but at that time I was working with Mikoyan, working directly under him. To his honor I must say that Mikoyan stood up for me. Back then he still could. Later on, he couldn't stand up for a single soul.

But he saved me from exile and I continued working in Moscow until 1936.

In 1936 a new measure was introduced—a covert purge of the party. Officially, the campaign was called the "exchange of party documents." They summon a party member and he has to report to his party committee and place his party card on the table.

When I placed mine on the table, I wasn't given a new one back. On what grounds? I was shown the official memo: "Vrachov, as an active member of the Trotskyite Opposition in the past, to be expelled from party."

Ten years ago Vrachov was a member of the opposition, *says Ivan, slipping into the third person,* and therefore he is now being expelled from the party! But he's not being accused of anything now.

And that was how I became a pariah, an outcast.

He was cast out from the party, from Moscow, from history. He no longer had the right to think of himself in the third person, as "Vrachov." All that was left were small towns, little jobs, rented rooms. But Ivan Vrachov was not in the least defeated. He was a Bolshevik, he was a Leninist and absolutely loyal to Lenin and the party of Lenin. And he had the Russian peasant's terrifying patience. He dug in his heels and prepared to outlast them all.

Revekka knew that Ivan Vrachov was no longer in Moscow but there was nothing unusual in that, people were being shifted about the country all the time. Hadn't her father been dispatched to Novosibirsk in Central Siberia? The workers there respected her father; that, and the distance from Moscow, would keep him safe.

Revekka could not help but believe in the future, for now she was a young wife, a young mother, a Young Communist. The worst was behind the country, everyone said so. Worrying did no good and there was no time to worry. She was a student at the university, she had a baby son, and she was also a daughter-in-law at pains not to let her husband's father see how much it cost her to call him "Papa." There was so much to do, there was barely a minute to sit down for a cup of tea and do a little reading.

Revekka had bought a copy of the party magazine called *The Communist,* but she hadn't so much as opened it. It was an important magazine, one that any true communist should read and read promptly, the kind of magazine that emanates a silent reproach from the table or desk. Finally, one day late in the summer of 1936, Revekka found the time.

I picked up the magazine *The Communist* and read that in Siberia a certain Trotskyite had been exposed and arrested, Mikhail Boguslavsky, my father.

I was stunned.

When my husband, Alexei, came home from work, I showed him the article.

"I should go to the party and report this," he said. "And you should go to the Young Communists. It's party rules."

The next day I went to the Young Communist League and was immediately expelled as the daughter of an Enemy of the People, a traitor to our country. Alexei was expelled from the party a few days later, on September 27, which happened to be his birthday.

The system seemed to be having some problems with information flow. *The Communist* had been informed that Revekka's father had been arrested but the local branches of the party had not, otherwise Revekka and Alexei would have been called in. But that wasn't really necessary. As good communists, aware of the party regulation that family members of people under arrest must report that fact to their organization, Revekka and Alexei did not delay in doing so. It was as impossible for her to break the party's rules as it was for her to believe that her father was capable of doing the party any harm whatsoever.

Party members, even after being expelled from the party, would still report of their own volition if summoned by the police, which saved the state the expense of sending out men and a vehicle. Alexei was summoned first. More important than Revekka, he was a full-fledged party member, head of an electric motor shop in a factory. But when Alexei was summoned, he could not bring himself to tell Revekka. Instead, he told her that he had some business in a store on Kirov Street, and never came home that night.

"I was out of my mind with suffering. I screamed, 'I'm a widow at twenty-two!' My mother called and said, 'Come over here, we'll cry together.'"

When he finally returned home the next morning, Alexei jauntily explained that the store had been robbed while he was there and everyone had been dragged in for questioning. The police said they'd call her and let her know, but hadn't. Revekka didn't believe a word of it.

One morning a few days later Alexei got up, calm as can be, and said, "Your shoe has a hole in it. I'll get it fixed on the way to work. Otherwise, water will get in and you'll catch cold."

He wrapped up the shoe and left for work.

Alexei wasn't home when I got back, and I went to my mother's. She was taking care of our son, who was a little over a year old. At my mother's I got a phone call from the woman who usually took care of the baby. She said, "Your husband's been arrested. Come home fast as you can. People are waiting for you here."

"Who's waiting for me?"

"I can't say."

I took my baby and went home. When I got there I saw the shoe my husband had taken that morning.

I said to the man in charge of the search, "Where have you taken my husband?"

"We didn't take him anywhere. He came in by himself."

"What's that supposed to mean? He left here this morning to get my shoe repaired and now that shoe's back here."

"He asked us to give it back to you."

It was all as clear and horribly ordinary as the hole in her shoe. When she felt her own fear being communicated to the child in her arms, Revekka came to a realization. "I understood that I had to take myself in hand, as Papa had taught me. To be guided by reason, and not give in to emotion."

And like all of her father's advice, it held instantly true. No sooner had she mastered her emotion than she noticed that the police, oafishly sticking to the letter of their instructions, were displaying no interest in her father's books and papers, some of which she was keeping for him.

She knew exactly what to do. When she was certain they were gone, Revekka set about hiding what she could hide and destroying what she could not. Her instincts were good. The wrong marginalia could cost a person ten years.

That's what they cost Boris Yampolsky, and maybe the best ten at that—his twenties. Boris had grown up in Saratov and Astrakhan, old cities on the lower Volga where in his youth the patriarchal ways of old Russia were still observed. The men had beards down to their chests, they wore their shirts outside their pants and their pants stuffed in high boots. Turbaned Asiatics still rode camels to market. What Boris loved most in the world was reading; he was one of those readers who cannot help but respond to what they read by grabbing a pencil and scribbling a comment in the margins. And though heretical marginalia may have cost him his youth, it never cost him his youthfulness, for all is youth and freshness in the home of Boris Yampolsky.

"Look at Paika!" cries his five-year-old daughter, Sanya, squealing with glee as she stands back to admire her handiwork— she has covered Paika, the family's long, lean-faced borzoi, with a blanket and put a pillow under its head. After a moment of looking around, Paika has settled its head into the pillow.

As Sanya laughs, her mother, a Slavic Rubens, looks from her daughter to her husband, her glance uniting them into a family—a five-year-old girl, a woman in her early forties, and a veteran of the Gulag, a Zek, now pushing seventy.

His eyes still flashing with amusement, Boris slips out yet another cigarette. He would never smoke anything but the old-fashioned Russian cigarettes—a hollow cardboard mouthpiece, an inch of potent, brown-black tobacco. Boris pinches the cardboard tube twice in the same place but at opposite angles to give it the properly raffish shape. One Mephistophelian puff of smoke and Boris is a Zek again, light-hearted, dashing, infinitely sarcastic.

Perhaps it was his daughter calling out the dog's name that had reminded him of the camps. In camp slang, *paika* means the daily ration, the daily bread of the Lord's Prayer. Boris has granted the dog a high Zek honor in bestowing it with that name, for no word was ever pronounced with more reverence. But whether it was the mention of Paika or not, the camps are always close to mind. The stories come easily. Every Zek is a Dante.

Now Sanya moves to her mother's side, rests her head against her warm, firm arm and looks up at her father's face, the bushy, grey sideburns and moustache, the flashing glasses, the lips speaking smoke. Though nothing has been said yet, she is already listening. In a minute, Daddy is going to tell how he was arrested.

I t was around one o'clock in the morning. I was reading in bed, afraid that my mother might come out of her room. She'd see I was reading and make me turn off my light. She was always worried I'd strain my eyes.

When the doorbell rang, I hopped right out of bed to answer it before it woke Mama up.

I asked who was there and I heard the building manager stammer, "Boris, it's me, open up."

I opened the door and in came two men, followed by the building manager. They walked right past me and into the front room. I had no idea what was going on.

The first question they asked was, "Are your parents home?"

"They are."

"Where are they?"

"Sleeping."

They showed me some piece of paper but I didn't even look at it. I went straight into my parents' room. They were already up. They'd heard the bell and of course knew what was happening. But they thought they'd come for my father, not me. My mother was combing her hair in a rush and my father was nervously tying his shoelaces.

But he didn't show the slightest sign of being nervous when he went out into the front room. They handed him the paper. He read it and then he knew.

Then the two men asked my parents, and quite politely too, to take a seat off to one side, so that they could make their search. The building manager stood in the doorway, probably there as the official witness.

They spent most of their time searching through my books. I wasn't afraid. I found it all terribly interesting, even flattering. I thought it was just a search.

It lasted until four in the morning. Then they packed up a whole huge suitcase full of books and took it and me away. As they were leading me away, my father followed me with his eyes, his gaze imploring me not to play any games with them. But for me it was all still a game.

Twelve people were arrested with me on the same charges: Article 58, point 10, anti-Soviet agitation, and point 11, belonging to an anti-Soviet organization. Needless to say there was never any such organization. And I had never even laid eyes on half of the twelve other people arrested in the case. And when I said that to my investigator, he replied, "Come on now, that's typical of any conspiracy, people not knowing the identity of the others."

They didn't have any real peg to hang anything on. I had a lot of friends and since we had a large apartment they used to come to my house. That must have brought me to the attention of the police. Later on, when they need to pick someone up, they think of you.

About a year before they arrested me, a girl—I won't mention any names, old habits die hard—a girl who was my age and still in school herself came to me and said she was being called in and asked questions about me. I didn't attach any importance to this even though two of my uncles had been arrested. They were grown-ups and I was just a kid of nineteen who still lived at home.

I may also have been denounced by a false witness. There was a man named Prozorovsky, he worked for a newspaper. He'd been to see me about two years before to borrow a collection of poems by Lebedev-Kumach.

I couldn't bear Lebedev-Kumach. To me he was a Soviet hack of the worst sort. And I had said so on the margins. When I was interrogated, I caught a glimpse of some photocopies of those pages with my marginalia.

My remarks really were scathing, but they weren't about the poems' contents. I just questioned whether the man was even a poet.

I told my investigator that I knew nearly all of Mayakovsky's long, revolutionary, avant-garde poems by heart. That he found no proof that I was pro-Soviet. But rejecting Lebedev-Kumach proved I was anti-Soviet. That was really all they had on me.

There was a joke in those years. A new man arrives in the cell. "How long did you get?" everyone asks.

"Fifteen years," he says.

"For what?"

"For nothing."

"Couldn't be. For nothing they give ten."

Boris got ten. He also got a lesson in literature; it was a matter of vital significance, if only because the police subscribed to the theory: Tell me what you read and I'll tell you who you are.

*

Ruth Bonner was not arrested for suspect marginalia. She had married the nervy Armenian who had smuggled her into the party meeting on his grandfather's ID. In the meantime, he had risen even higher in the party, heading the Balkans section of the Comintern, an organization that dealt with the communist parties in countries outside the Soviet Union. Ruth Bonner was now the mother of two children—a son and a daughter, Elena.

Ruth was arrested because her husband was arrested. The girl who at a very tender age had begun visiting aunts in prison, the girl who had been born in the easternmost section of Siberia to which her ancestors had been "sent on foot, under the lash" in the eighteenth century, must have always suspected that prison and exile would not forever remain solely a part of her past.

She and her husband were arrested in the worst year, 1937, and it is enough for a Russian to say " '37" to conjure the terror again—any adjective would only dilute the effect. And she would be in prison and exile for the next seventeen years.

She too has the Zek sense of humor, blacker than noir, withering. She laughs as she remembers one of those revolutionary aunts of hers. "In 1905, she organized a mutiny among soldiers and was sentenced to death for treason. But because she was a minor the sentence was commuted to life. She was in prison from 1905 to 1917. Twelve years. A little less than I got. And I didn't start any mutinies." This is too funny, and Ruth cannot contain her laughter, which racks her fragile body and her lungs, ruined by smoking.

Anyone who served time in prison or a camp knows their date of arrest like a soldier knows his serial number, and Ruth rattles hers off with the same staccato blur: "My husband was arrested on May 27, '37, and on December 9, '37, they arrested me."

The category into which Ruth Bonner fell was Family Member of an Enemy of the People. It was not so much a crime as a condition. Still, it made perfect sense according to the laws of vengeance.

A member of a traitor's family, especially a female member, had some chance of surviving. The "traitor" himself had practically none. He would vanish so utterly that even the year of his death could never be determined.

I n the six months between my husband's arrest and my own, I brought money and packages to Lubyanka. That's where you had to bring them. But what prison he was actually in, that I didn't know. I didn't hear a single word from him, there wasn't a single note, and I was not allowed to meet with him even once, *says Ruth.*

After my husband was arrested, I was notified to move out of our apartment and into a room in the basement. I sent the children to live with relatives. I had a lot of books and was afraid the mice would get at them. I called a library and said, "If you want them, come get them."

Everyone in the building who was going to be arrested had been moved down into the basement, myself included. There were a lot of rooms down there, they'd probably been for the servants. There were two or three people to a room. And after they had everyone down there, they started coming and arresting them, a few at a time. I saw what was going on and I knew the only way out of there led to prison.

But out of sheer obstinacy I refused to go into hiding. Why should I hide if I'm not guilty of anything? And I did have somewhere I could hide. A room in a place in a forest outside Moscow, where even the devil himself wouldn't have found me.

But to hide meant to admit you were guilty. And I was not guilty of anything.

One fine day they came for me. They said, "Get your things and let's go."

I had no things. I just put on my coat and left.

Straight to Lubyanka. It was like a small, modest hotel. Except that the rooms were packed tight as herrings in a barrel. Until they figured out what prison to send you to next—Lefortovo, Taganka, Butyrka. Butyrka was my alma mater.

There were gradations even there. First, I was with the wives of other Comintern people and we received rather privileged treatment. We were given blankets. But then they switched us to regular cells where you were given nothing but bare plank beds. And they packed those planks too, you had to sleep spoon-style.

They'd give you the command to turn over. We were in a huge room but it was so crammed that we had to sleep in three shifts. Sixteen hours on your feet, eight sleeping.

Lubyanka, headquarters of the secret police and the most infamous prison in Moscow, is located a short distance from Red Square. The "sword and the shield," as the secret police called themselves, should be near the red heart, the Kremlin. But Lubyanka was an elite institution and did not have the capacity to serve as anything but a central clearinghouse. Prisoners were then shipped off to other Moscow prisons until the paperwork was done. The usual route lay to the famous prisons Lefortovo and Butyrka, though some people were rumored to go to special prisons in the woods outside Moscow. Their families would be notified that they had died of heart failure or pneumonia, but they would not be dead. One to a cell, never even seeing the guard who slipped the food through the slot, they were entombed in eternal solitude.

*

At twenty-three Revekka was suddenly alone with a two-year-old child, her father in prison in Siberia, her husband being held somewhere in Moscow. It was all up to her now. The virtuous daughter was about to have her virtue tested to its very molecules.

M oscow's prisons were overpacked, they were holding prisoners at the railroad stations. My husband, Alexei, was being held at Kazan station, *says Revekka.*

As soon as Alexei was arrested, I understood—a counterrevolutionary coup was happening in the Soviet Union. It started with the murder of Kirov. If they were arresting people like my husband and my father and Lenin's old guard, what else could it be but a counterrevolutionary coup?

Now that she understood, she could act. And, as a good daughter and a good communist, she had to act. Revekka did what every Russian woman in that situation did—she brought money and packages of food and clothing to the receiving window at Lubyanka and used whatever connections she had to gain—if not mercy, then at least a scrap of information. But Revekka did more than that. She went on the offensive and soon found the rules of conspiracy were logical, natural, even oddly familiar.

Guileless, she proved guileful. Her specialty was wheedling information out of guards. Who could resist the innocence of that voice, that pretty, dark-eyed young woman who made you want to put your arm around her. First, she determined that her husband was being held at Kazan railroad station; then, before a KGB official quite knew what had happened, she had gotten him to tell her to what part of the station the prisoners were taken for exercise.

I went to that part of the station. I saw trucks driving up and I knew that meant the prisoners were being given their packages. There was a guard standing next to a locomotive. He had a fire going in a barrel. It was February and freezing cold.

I walked over to the soldier thinking to strike up a conversation with him. "I heard they're holding prisoners here."

"Yes, down in the basement."

I decided to egg him on. "The basement's not deep enough in the ground for the likes of them. Do they let them out for exercise?"

"If they're in solitary, they bring them out one at a time, if it's the main cell, the whole cell comes out."

But guile can only take you so far. Now Revekka decided to risk all.

L isten, my husband's in there, I have to see him no matter
what the cost. What time does the main cell come out?"
"Around seven o'clock."
"I'll be back at seven. Will you be here?"
"I will."

Revekka ran home and changed her clothes to look good for her
husband and to seem to anyone else no more than a pretty young
woman enjoying a flirtatious chat with a Russian soldier. She ate
and, on her mother's advice, drank a glass of vodka as protection
against the cold. She took her mother's advice but did not include
her in her counsel. Revekka was on her own now.

W hen I returned to the station, the soldier tried to sidle
away from me. I said, "Listen, friend, don't pull away
from me. You and I have already both been spotted, there's no
doubt about that."
    When they brought the prisoners out for exercise I
spotted Alexei and he caught sight of me too. His face showed
joy and fear and bafflement as to how I could even be there.
We didn't say anything to each other but what I did do was
give him a little quick wink and start for the exit so that he'd
know I was free to go.

Now Revekka had proven to herself that she was capable of suc-
cessful action and that the system was not all rivets and steel plate,
there were little rust holes a person could slip through. And her
foray into the train station also produced unforeseen and immedi-
ate consequences. That same evening the secret police called.

T his is Investigator Chachenko speaking. I'm in charge of
your husband's case."
    "That's not true. Somebody else is in charge," I said.
    "As of today, I'm in charge."
    They must have spotted me, I thought.
    "Do you want a meeting with your husband? Come
here and there'll be a pass waiting for you."

I went. And there really was a pass waiting for me. I was taken to Chachenko's office. He paced back and forth.

"You're so young and you've been through so much," he said.

And I replied abruptly, "I thought I was invited here to meet with my husband."

Chachenko picked up the phone and said, "Bring in the prisoner."

When Alexei came through the door I jumped up and all the food and clothing on my lap went flying. I threw my arms around his neck.

"Alexei, I saw you today."

"I saw you too. Just don't ever do it again."

Chachenko, the investigator in charge of Alexei's case, was a very decent person. He was raising a Spanish child who had been orphaned during the Spanish Civil War. Chachenko arranged for several other meetings before he was arrested himself.

"Yes, yes," says Boris, pausing to light another cigarette and squinting from the match's acrid smoke. "Today's investigator was tomorrow's prisoner. It was a phantasmagoria, a danse macabre."

Boris watches as his wife, Alla, takes his daughter Sanya off to bed. But sleepy as she is, Sanya doesn't want to go—one more kiss, one more story. A kiss alright, but no story. Enough of these Russian bedtime stories.

After arrest and interrogation, Boris had been sent to Bogoslovlag, which means God's Word Camp, no doubt named for a nearby town. The irony was not lost on the Zeks, on whom no irony was ever lost.

God's Word was a feared camp because its business was logging. After weeks of felling trees, prisoners would just fall dead, their emaciated bodies hardly making any sound as they hit the snow. "Of the twelve arrested in my case, five did not make it through the first winter," says Boris, pausing to hear the silence of the dead, the background hum to every Gulag story.

Two things kept a person from death in the camps. One was

luck and the other the ability to extract maximal sustenance from any scrap of bread or beauty. Boris had that ability, but his luck didn't seem to be clicking in. He was transferred from felling trees but only to breaking stone in a quarry, which was "not one fucking bit easier," he said. "My legs were swollen, creaking with pus. One day I looked in a barrack window and saw a Zek with a puffy face and teeth dangling from his blue gums. It took me a few seconds to realize that it was my reflection."

It was in those critical weeks, when Boris was being inexorably nudged toward a mass grave, that his luck finally changed. His parents learned his whereabouts and began sending him three or four food packages a month. That kept him alive and allowed for chance to come into play. As usual, it came in the form of orders from above. An aluminum plant was under construction near the camp and the prisoners were to supply the labor. The new director needed a more productive labor force and accordingly doubled the bread ration, the *paika,* from one pound to two. Groats appeared in the watery gruel. And there was even an occasional omelet made of American powdered eggs, siphoned off from Lend-Lease.

But the survival dream of every Zek was a cushy job in a warm place. That dream came true for Boris when he was made a medic in the camp infirmary, which had a wood-burning stove. Instead of being worked to death, he was alone in a warm place where he could read to his heart's content. In the evening other prisoners would gather by the wood stove, drink tea, smoke, and speculate endlessly on Russia's past and future, or tell their own stories, savoring the shapes fate could assume. It was, in a very Russian sort of way, heaven.

But then all of a sudden this "patriarchal idyll" of ours was in danger. Word went around that the camp was getting a new security chief. You get used to one chief, you know his ways. How to act with him. When to show your face, and when not to.

But what the hell can you know about a new one? There were also reports of what he looked like—a short guy who wore an American-style jacket and had a little moustache.

One fine day I'm in the infirmary and there's a knock at the door. None of the guards ever knocked. I open the door and there he is, the new security chief. He says hello like anyone else, apologizes for the intrusion, and asks if he could warm himself up a little by our stove.

Meanwhile, there's a woman from the women's labor camp in the room. She'd brought over some women prisoners who were sick and, while waiting for their X rays, had stopped by to see me. All and any contact between men and women was forbidden. And for the chief of security to find a woman with a man—at the very least, she wouldn't be allowed to escort patients there any more and it might even land her in an isolation cell. But all he said was, "I'll just sit in here a little while, otherwise I'll get too warm to go back out in the cold."

Then he noticed a book of poems by Pasternak on the table and he struck up a conversation about Pasternak. We talked for fifteen or twenty minutes, feeling each other out. It was clear to me that Pasternak really meant something to him.

He came in to warm up the next day and we picked up where we'd left off.

In the end we became friends, and it was Pasternak who brought us together. I would recite one poem by heart and he would recite another. He'd come by after lights-out, I slept right there in the office. Or sometimes I'd go see him.

He told me his story. He had graduated from a university with a degree in literature. Then he was drafted and sent to the front, where he was wounded. After being released from the hospital, he was declared physically unfit for combat and transferred to Security. When he came to our camp and saw what went on there, his eyes nearly popped out of his head.

Once he said to me, and this I remember word for word, "You're a prisoner in a camp jacket and I'm a prisoner in a KGB coat."

The new security chief had proved he was a decent human being that first day when he hadn't said anything about the woman there. Men weren't allowed to go into the women's camp and the women weren't allowed into the men's camp. But that didn't stop anyone. There were checkpoints between the camps but they didn't count for much because they were usually run by prisoners. But if a guard caught a man in a women's camp or vice versa, it'd mean a punishment cell—an ice-cold box, no bed, a stone floor.

The presence of a women's camp had a positive effect on the male prisoners' manners. If the women were moved away, the men would go right to pot. They'd take a leak wherever they happened to be, which they would never do if there were even one or two women around.

Life didn't stop in the camps. On the contrary, life was more intense in the camps than anywhere else. And sex was too.

One of the professional criminals once told me about another camp where he had worked in the stables. It was a closed camp with no women for miles around. The stables where he worked weren't guarded and, to make a long story short, he became romantically involved with one of the mares. Her name was Little Star, and he even came to prefer her to women. He'd get up on a wagon shaft and grasp Little Star by the tail. After a while, she'd get into the swing of it and give as good as she got.

One day he was caught in the act. The mare was taken away and replaced with a gelding. After a few days he started up with the gelding. But it was nowhere near as good as Little Star.

A girl of fourteen or fifteen would sleep with someone for his bread ration, his *paika*. But it had to be done fairly quick—around the corner, behind the barracks, inside the barracks at night.

We had a special word, *zanachka*, which meant a secret place where a man and a woman could be alone together. The toolmaker had a huge chest where he kept shovels and crowbars. He had made a false bottom for the chest, which had just enough room for a couple to crawl into during the lunch break. There were some grimy prison jackets for them to lie on. The toolmaker charged half a bread ration for that.

But there were also romances on a very high level, that sometimes even led to suicide. But it would be disgusting to speak of them in the same breath, *says Boris with a grin of sarcastic nostalgia at having fled again into that vast, grimy cloud of quilted jackets, mud, death, and snow, Pasternak, tea by the wood stove, the Mystery Play of the Gulag.*

*

Ruth Bonner was now in one of those women's camps, and what she soon learned was that life in the camps was only possible if you found friends.

But there's friends and there's friends. I had a close friend who was a close friend of Stalin. His name was Grisha. He was a lot older than I but we were friends. He knew Stalin when they both were young during the Civil War and he even called Stalin by his revolutionary nickname of Koba. They were friends and their families were close.

One day Grisha gets a call from the police to come in for a little talk.

His wife's very frightened. "I'm afraid to let you go. People who go there don't come back."

Grisha picks up the receiver on his personal line to the Kremlin and calls up Stalin. He says to Stalin, "Listen, Koba, I got called in, what am I supposed to do? I'm afraid once I'm in there, there won't be any getting out."

"Don't talk nonsense! Who would dare arrest you?" said Stalin. "Drop by, help them straighten it out. They probably screwed something up over there, the fools. Go help them straighten it out. And tell your wife not to worry."

And Grisha says to his wife, "See, and you were worried."

So, Grisha went. And that was the end of him.

Grisha trusted Stalin, and the women in Ruth's work crew trusted the guards.

In the beginning we were all the wives of enemies of the people, no common criminals or others. For the first six months the women worked with a will because they'd been led to believe that hard work would knock time off their sentence. It was all just a trick and a swindle of course.

One woman said to her investigator, "Why are you asking me what my husband thinks about one Soviet policy or another. I slept with him, I gave birth to his children, I cooked for him, I washed his clothes, I took care of him. As far as politics goes, that was something he did with you, not me."

They beat her senseless for that one, *says Ruth with a laugh this time, for nothing is ever quite so funny as that first encounter between innocence and evil, especially to those who have experienced it themselves.*

There were women who had never done a day's work in their lives, had never washed a dish or rinsed out a tea cup. Some of them had been involved in their arts, singers, and there was an actress who was worried that the camp might ruin her nails . . .

There were many women who were certain they'd be pardoned by the authorities. And there was a certain percentage who'd say, Good Lord, what did that husband of mine go and do that they're punishing me so severely for it?

Most women helped each other. You couldn't survive without friends. But some women cozied up to the authorities and some became informers. People were afraid of them and they had no friends. But the authorities looked out for them. And to some extent that helped them survive.

But the worst women of all were the ones who ran the camp. You practically never saw a guard, it was prisoners who were responsible for getting the work done. And the prisoners in charge of other prisoners were the most terrible of all.

The black light of the camps took an exact X ray of a person's character. Some women squealed, some became bullies, some slept with men for half a day's bread ration. Some would sooner die than surrender their humanity, and many of them did just that.

Revekka had no intention of surrendering anything—her humanity, her life, or the lives of those she loved. She was still actively fighting against the silent coup that had taken place behind the red brick walls and dwarf evergreens of the Kremlin. What else but a coup could explain the fact that the best people in the land were being arrested. The best person in the world, her father, was being held in prison in Siberia. Or so she thought until the secret police called, using the telephone like everyone else.

Hello, this is Serafim Pavlovich Popov calling. I am the investigator in charge of Mikhail Boguslavsky's case."

"That's strange. My father is in Novosibirsk."

"He was in Novosibirsk, now he's in Moscow. Would you like to visit your father? Give it some thought before you answer."

"There's nothing to think about."

"Then come to Lubyanka tomorrow."

I went to Lubyanka the next day, got my pass, and went to see Popov. He was the chief inspector. "You're going to see your father," said Popov. "But you mustn't talk about anything but people's health. In no way are you to mention that your husband was arrested. If you do, you'll be punished."

I was horrified by the sight of my father. His eyes were always so full of life and humor, and now they were like slits. He couldn't sit still and kept putting one hand or the other under him. I didn't understand why sitting was so uncomfortable for him. I was so green I didn't even realize they'd been torturing him.

"How are you?" he said. "But where's Alexei?"

"He's home. Everything's fine. Don't worry."

I was afraid that if I said anything I wasn't supposed to, it would mean trouble for Papa. And for me too, because then they wouldn't allow me to see him again either.

Later on, he asked again, "Where's Alexei?"

I had never lied to my father in my life. I looked at the investigator, who was standing right there, then I looked at Papa and lowered my eyes. "He's home."

Papa understood.

When our time was almost up, Papa asked the investigator in a humiliating way, "Allow me to meet with my daughter again. Please, allow me. I implore you."

Seventeen days later another another call at work, the police again, Popov again.

"Do you want to meet with your father again? Don't forget, you can refuse to meet him."

"I would never refuse."

The papers were already running stories of wives who had renounced their husbands and children who had renounced their fathers. And the papers were also running stories about Trotskyites exposed as saboteurs and spies, who were going to betray the Soviet Far East to the Japanese and the Ukraine to the Nazis.

I asked Investigator Popov, "How much danger is my father in?"

"They'll put him on trial and convict him. He'll go to prison or a camp. You'll be able to write him letters and send him packages."

There was a store near Lubyanka that was selling Spanish oranges. We'd never seen them before. Each one individually wrapped in a piece of white paper. I bought two pounds for Papa. I was on my way to see him for the second time and I had decided to tell him everything—that he would be put on trial.

And when they opened the door of the room where Papa was waiting, I couldn't believe my eyes. He looked so young and ruddy!

"You look wonderful," I said, kissing him again and again.

"I was just out in the cold," he said.

I told him I had brought him a letter from my brother Adolph in which he said that he still believed in Pushkin's line that "the dawn of fascinating happiness will yet arise."

And when I told Papa that I had brought him some oranges, he said, "You shouldn't have. I just finished eating some. I was even going to save some for you, but my friends said, You eat them yourself, your daughter's free, she can buy her own."

He looked so good I had to believe he was eating oranges. I'd already figured out that they'd fatten them up before the trial.

Then I told him what the newspapers had been saying about the trial and about people renouncing their husbands and fathers. He got so worked up that he jumped to his feet and said, "Renounce me, if you think I have brought shame on us, renounce me."

I jumped up too. "Papa, under no circumstance would I ever do that."

He kissed each of my fingers and covered my face with kisses.

"Meeting's over," said the investigator, a minute later.

I left, and on the way out it came to me all of a sudden—what if that was the last time I'll ever see Papa. It was such a heart-wrenching feeling that I had to go back, even though my pass was marked that I was supposed to be leaving, I turned around and went back.

I opened the door abruptly. Papa was looking right at me but he could not see me. He had unseeing eyes, he looked absolutely hypnotized. I stood there and looked. The investigator didn't say a word. Papa did not react in the slightest to me.

He had been drugged.

I wanted to scream, to call for help, but I kept myself in hand and went back out.

That was January 22, 1937. The trial started five days later.

Now the "dawn of fascinating happiness" had become a much more limited and specific dream than it had been a century before, in Pushkin's day. Revekka's dream was that Chief Investigator Popov had told her the truth. That her father would be convicted and sentenced to a prison or a camp where he would have the right to receive letters and packages. Everyone knew that chief investigators were always informed as to the sentences well before the trial, and the only people who were deceived by the outward form of due process were the foreigners, the writers, the correspondents, who flocked to Moscow for the great trials of 1937 and 1938. And the sentence that the chief investigator had indicated was a sentence that was commonly passed out. And hadn't she asked him the question in the same innocent way that she had used before, to secure information from guards and even from other KGB officials like himself? And hadn't he rattled off the sentence with comforting banality?

Revekka had firm grounds for hope. But the Zek knows there is no hope and nothing to believe in. There is only revelation after revelation of reality, only the rare instants of beauty and kindness.

That's just what makes the camps so interesting, *says Boris.* A person reveals himself more quickly there because there's danger at every step and nowhere to hide.

In our cell we had a man from Moscow who had once been very high up, on the ministerial level. His jacket still had traces of all the medals he'd once had. I won't mention his name.

One day, everyone had gone out for latrine call, everyone but him. And me. I was still on my bunk, a top bunk. I watched as he turned his back to the peephole in the door and began slipping the other prisoners' bread rations inside his shirt. His fellow prisoners' *paika! exclaims Boris with a snort of contempt.*

Paika the borzoi hears her name called and raises her head but then, seeing she is not wanted, lowers it back. She is used to hearing her name called when she isn't wanted because the word *paika* is inevitably used so often in that home.

But there were other sorts of surprises too, *continues Boris.* One evening I was out for a walk by the camp garbage dump. And in a Gulag garbage dump there is absolutely nothing a person would eat, no matter how hungry he was. All of a sudden I hear poetry being recited. I go closer and I see—two stubbly faced guys sitting on top of the garbage, the both of them hungry as dogs, their jackets belted with a piece of wire. And they're sitting there reciting the poetry of Igor Severyanin:

> It was by the sea and the surf in filagree,
> Where town carriages are but rarely seen;
> In the castle tower, the Queen played Chopin
> and with each note her page fell deeper in love.

You hold things dearer in there. Hearing music in there is not like hearing music out here. I would not have missed it for the world.

*

Revekka's father, Mikhail Boguslavsky, had been on trial for five days, a trial important enough to be broadcast on the radio.

On February 1, I decided to spend the night at my mother's. I could feel that the trial was coming to a close. At six o'clock in the morning they broadcast the sentences on the radio. Among those to be executed—Boguslavsky.

I ran into the little room where my mother and brother were. My mother fainted. And I said to my brother, "We've been left without a father. They lied to me again."

Not a single ray of Pushkin's "dawn of fascinating happiness" had shone upon Revekka. It was only early February, but 1937 was already the worst year for Russia, and for her.

*

Boris was still just a young man in his early twenties, and he had a young man's taste in poetry. He was especially fond of the nineteenth-century Romantic, Mikhail Lermontov, killed in a duel at twenty-seven, but not before writing poems that were so vivid and rhythmic that to read them twice was to know them by heart.

I was in quarantine with a high temperature. I had gotten hold of a volume of Lermontov in the labor camp. Half the pages had already been used to roll cigarettes of course.

I was lying there in the bunk reading when all of a sudden from the row above comes a woman's voice, a cultured voice, saying, "Good morning."

We asked all the usual questions—who are you, where are you from, what's your sentence. I thought at first she was one of those ex-prisoners who stayed on to work at the camp, but then it turned out she was in for being a "Member of a Traitor's Family."

"What are you doing," she said. "Reading?"

"That's right, I'm doing a little reading."

"You won't get much reading done in here."

I shrugged my shoulders.

A year and a half later I'm doing heavy work, logging. At midday they bring out a pot of gruel. I was standing by a bonfire trying to warm up a little. I've got the book of Lermontov stuck in my belt. Even though I knew all the poems by heart, I still like the feel of the book in my hands.

Someone calls me from behind, I turn around, and it's her. By then I'm unrecognizable of course.

"Is that you?" she says.

"It's me."

"Still reading?"

"Still reading."

Then she smiles and walks over to me, and says, "Wait till everyone else gets theirs, then grab a mess tin and come over. I'll tell them to give you a good helping."

"I'd feel funny about taking it just for myself."

"So grab a kit for someone else too."

They really did give us the thick stuff from the bottom of the pot.

I didn't see her again for what must have been eight years. By then I was working in the infirmary. One day I was on duty and sitting there reading Pasternak when there's a knock at the door and in she comes. She'd been released but she'd stayed on in the camp.

"Wouldn't you know it," she said.

"Still reading," I said.

"I can see I was wrong, Boris. You did get a lot of reading done. You'll be reading as long as you're alive and you'll stay alive as long as you're reading."

And whoever that woman was, so ruined by fate that she chose to remain in the camp even after she was free, she had understood Boris as well as any wife could, and he loves her for that to this day.

*

As Boris says, a person's nature could not be concealed in the camps, and Ruth Bonner was by nature impertinent. She may have been a revolutionary as much out of impertinence as out of conviction. In any case, her outspokenness cost her what every prisoner feared most—a spell on a penal brigade, where you're worked till you drop and it's only the last reserves in the marrow that give you the strength even to wake.

What you're supposed to say to anyone on camp staff is, Yes, sir! But one day that's not how I answered.

"Listen to this one," says the guard. "She thinks she's Countess Trubetskaya."

And then I have to go and say, "Trubetskaya wasn't a countess, but a princess."

"Now she's correcting me!"

Ruth laughs her smoke-blackened bitter laugh, venting all her scorn and merriment, free to do so this time since she herself is the butt of the joke.

The penal brigade could have killed her, but she found friends, corners that could be cut, work that could be faked. And she also learned what Dostoyevsky had learned before her—that beauty saves.

The women were lined up in the subzero darkness for a

head count before the day's work began. This was even worse than the hard labor, because at least work allowed you to keep moving or to find a place to hide from the wind.

A huge, red sun rose over Kazakhstan.

"Look how beautiful it is," said Ruth.

The other prisoners stared at her as if she had gone mad. But Ruth did not respond to any of those looks of alarm and compassion. The red sun rising over Kazakhstan had her full attention.

*

Great as the loss of Revekka's father was, it was also his final gift to her. Now she knew her mission in life. Of course, her goal was to survive, and to help her son, mother, husband, and brother to survive. But her mission was to clear her father's name of that final indignity, that such a great human being, Papa, had been executed by traitors as a traitor.

But this was the year 1937, and there was barely time to gather her strength before the next blow fell. "On March 18, 1937, they arrested my brother. They didn't even allow him to graduate and get his degree. He just vanished. Everyone just vanished.

"My husband, Alexei, had been transferred from the Kazan railroad station to Butyrka Prison. I was able to visit him there several times. On his birthday, September 27, 1937, I went to the prison window where they took the money for prisoners. I had fifty rubles for Alexei. They wouldn't accept my money."

The Soviet state was above any petty chicanery—they would not accept money for a man who was dead. This also served as a semiofficial death notice. The departments in charge of issuing such certificates were swamped, backlogged for years. That may explain why two certificates for Alexei's death were eventually issued, one to Revekka, saying he died in 1942 of pneumonia, and one to Alexei's sister, saying he died in 1937. That might have been just a clerical error, or it might have been deliberate policy. In Stalin's Russia you could never tell.

*

The poetry of Pasternak had helped Boris make human contact with the camp's new security chief, and a volume of Lermontov, half the pages used for rolling cigarettes, had won him the friendship of a woman and a lucky, thick portion of gruel. Art—even a cheap reproduction of a painting depicting the Battle of Kulikovo Field, Russia's first victory in arms against the Mongol Horde, which had overrun the country in 1240—had an amazing power to leap the vast spaces between human beings, even that between a "political" like Boris and a hardened criminal from the Leningrad underworld.

One day I went into the mess hall. There was a stage in the mess hall and up on that stage there's a guy sitting and copying a black-and-white print of the painting *The Battle of Kulikovo Field* from an old magazine. But he was copying it in color, even the monks' robes.

"What are you doing, man?" I said. "Monks' robes are black."

He gave me an evil look and told me where to go. I saw who I was dealing with and got out of there fast.

Two or three days later, all of a sudden my door opens and in he comes. He's embarrassed. He apologizes. "I'm sorry I flew off the handle. Can you tell me what the monks were doing at the battle?"

After that he started coming around to see me. His name was Volodka and he was from a working-class family in Leningrad. A repeat offender, he'd done time before. He'd started by stealing potatoes and worked his way up.

I shared what I knew with Volodka. I gave him dictations, taught him how to write grammatical Russian. He started asking good questions—You say use a comma, so how come Gorky uses a dash?

After the war started, Volodka volunteered for the front. On the way to the front his unit stopped in Sverdlovsk for some training. He wrote me letters from Sverdlovsk. Not only that, he used to go to the library and use a razor to slice pages from magazines he knew would interest me. Then he wrote that they were being shipped to the front, and that was the last I heard of him.

Until thirty years later, when he tracked me down. As soon as I got his letter, I sent him a telegram, and he telegrammed back to meet him at the airport in ten days.

I was worried I wouldn't recognize him. I'm standing right at the barrier at the airport staring at everyone that comes out. That's not him, that's not him. That's an Armenian or a Georgian. Finally, out comes this very impressive-looking personage wearing a fancy coat and huge, tinted glasses and carrying a briefcase. He's looking around too. I look very hard and I can just barely tell that it's Volodka.

Needless to say, we threw our arms around each other. I had a taxi waiting but he said, "No, let's sit here a while."

There were lilac bushes and flower beds outside and we sat down there. He pulled a bottle of cognac and some appetizers from his briefcase. We drank the whole bottle right then and there and it was just as if we were back in the camps swearing a blue streak.

But later on when I introduced Volodka to my wife, she was taken completely by surprise—I'd told her she'd be meeting with a professional criminal, a ringleader, and Volodka was gallant as could be with her. And why not, in the meantime Volodka had become the conductor of a symphony orchestra!

To avoid being sent to fight at the front, Volodka had wangled his way into the army band. It turned out he had an excellent ear and could play nearly every instrument and play well. Some criminals are very gifted people. Later on, he even became the bandleader.

When he was discharged from the army, he started writing popular tunes, became a conductor, and was even invited to join the Composers' Union. His orchestra was always on tour and he showed me the posters. But now he was quitting conducting, his legs had started giving him trouble. He was married and his daughter was studying at a conservatory.

He stayed with us a week, and one day when my wife

was at work, I said to him, "Volodka, tell me, are you happy?"

"I'll tell you. I've got everything, a television, a piano.
It's a peaceful life. But it's boring. Boring! No kicks. But I've
got a plan. As soon as my daughter graduates from the
conservatory, I know just the fucking job I'm going to pull!"

*

There were only two months left in '37. Revekka's father had been
tried in January and executed in February. Her brother had been
arrested in March. Her husband had died in Butyrka Prison in
September. She still had her mother and her son, who was about
to turn three. October passed without incident. And so did the first
of November.

On November 2 they came and arrested me at work, *says
Revekka.* Just as I was, in the fashionable clothes I wore to
work—a kimono-style coat, patent leather shoes, a little hat
with a ribbon on it—I was taken to Butyrka Prison, Cell
Number 6.

The door opened. I had never seen anything like it in
my life. Though it was November and cold, the women were
all in their underwear, about one hundred of them in a space
that normally held about twelve. The stench was awful. I was
seized by terror and huddled by the door. These women had to
be criminals, thieves.

Then suddenly one of them walked over to me and asks
very politely, "Could you please tell us your name?"

"Revekka Mikhailovna Boguslavsky."

It went around the whole cell in a minute—Mikhail
Boguslavsky's daughter, Boguslavsky's daughter . . .

And she was Boguslavsky's daughter when they called her in for
interrogation.

What do you know about Boguslavsky's
counterrevolutionary activities?"

"I know that if all of you were communists like
Boguslavsky, I wouldn't be sitting here now."

"And what do you have to say about your husband's counterrevolutionary activities?"

"The same."

The women in Cell Number 6 proved not to be criminals but people with more or less the same social position as Revekka. The wives of the more important people, like generals, were sent to a special camp where they received special treatment before they were executed.

Revekka quickly learned the same lesson that every other prisoner learned—you must survive, and you cannot survive without friends. Short of torture and murder, the camps were the worst that human beings can inflict on one another. It was only one degree from intolerable, and friends were that one degree.

A joke, a sunrise, a line of poetry, the touch of a hand, not only helped keep body and soul together but helped keep the soul itself alive. There was no point in surviving it all just to become one of those people who walk the streets of Russian cities with horrifyingly empty eyes.

There was a Frenchwoman in our cell, a ballerina. An enchanting, statuesque beauty, *remembers Revekka.* We closed up some of the plank beds and crammed ourselves into one corner so she could dance for us. She didn't want to at all but we kept trying to talk her into it. She just wasn't up to it. We understood. But you had to go on living, you had to survive.

And she danced for us.

While she was dancing, the cell door opened and in came the warden of Butyrka Prison, a tall, strapping man with a big moustache. And this cockroach says, "Holding a meeting, are you? Not tough enough for you here, is it?"

Revekka knew that there was only one explanation for people like that warden and for the fact that women of that moral caliber were locked one hundred to a cell. "Our party must have gone into hiding now. The Fascists had usurped the revolution. And after all we had gone through for the revolution. But that didn't matter. Only surviving mattered."

A prisoner was only out of the cell for interrogation or for further transport down the line that ended in the wilderness, in which case there would be the terse command: Take your things.

Everything was the same for everybody. From the cell to the train in a Black Maria. On the train for days, nineteen for Revekka. The same food for everybody—bread, water, herring. And everyone suffered the same terrible thirst from the salty herring, never enough water to quench that salty-herring thirst.

After two months in Butyrka, Revekka was shipped east.

"There were two hundred women in the car. The inside walls were covered with ice. There was a little cast-iron stove in the middle. We took turns standing by the stove. And we slept in three shifts."

It had been the same for Ruth Bonner, who also passed through Butyrka. The same for everyone.

And everyone had moments of perfect despair. Even the memory of her child's face was sometimes not enough to make a woman want to live another second. There was a point beyond the reach of love or beauty, an infinite dimness where suicide was the only star.

Three times Revekka tried to take her own life, and three times she was dragged back—by friends, by chance, by some ultimate insincerity.

What Revekka could not bear was being endlessly shifted from one camp to another so that even there, in the land of endless snow, there was not even one wooden plank you could call home:

There was a column of about four hundred women being herded through the snow on foot from one camp to another. German shepherds kept the column in line. Stragglers were shot.

I was walking with a young woman, a friend, Ira. She was an engineer from Baku, a beautiful Azerbaijani. I said to her, "Ira, let's help the old people walk. They can lean on us."

We'd been walking through the snow since eleven

o'clock that morning and it was already twilight by then.

We helped the old women walk. Then, all of a sudden, Ira couldn't take it any more and she dropped to the snow. "I'm dying of thirst." She started scooping snow into her mouth.

"Get up at once," I said. "Why are you on your knees, why are you humiliating yourself in front of the guard?"

I started pulling her up by the collar and beating her with my fists. I looked around and saw that we'd fallen behind. And the guard was slowly reaching into his pocket.

Now Ira was hysterical. She wouldn't get up. I used the vilest curses on her. I screamed, "Any second the guard's going to shoot us!"

Now he was pulling his hand slowly back out of his pocket, as if he still hadn't made up his mind.

I was in horror. I had a mother, I had a son. I had to live!

Ira wasn't moving. Slowly, slowly the guard's hand came out of his pocket.

And then I saw what he had—a roll of white bread.

"Here," he said. "Share with her."

War

Those who trust are tempted to betray, and those who betray are tempted to trust. Stalin, who trusted no one, trusted Hitler.

They came to terms in the still-poisonous Molotov-Ribbentrop Pact of August 1939—nonaggression, economic mutual aid. A series of secret clauses worked out how they would share all the territory between them when they went to war the following month. For Hitler this may have been no more than a way of advancing on Russia, and with Russia's connivance. The Soviet Union would think it was acquiring territory, while in fact Germany was thrusting its own border hundreds of miles to the east. The Soviet Union supplied Germany with food and raw materials, while Germany reciprocated with machinery that did not, however, always arrive with fabled German precision. Stalin was also gaining that forever-priceless commodity, time. Sooner or later there'd be war with Hitler; Stalin never trusted him that much.

The smell is never too pretty when two devils make a deal, and it was especially hard for the Russians to swallow, at least until

they realized what it really meant—not the dishonoring of socialism, but the absolute gravity that precedes war.

On September 1, 1939, nine days after the pact was signed,
the Germans invaded Poland. Their new invention—lightning
war, blitzkrieg—sounded not only modern but rang of Wotan and
Valhalla as well. The blitzkrieg was designed for a victory both
quick and total. It was overweening pride made military doctrine.

Poland fought gallantly, no greater honor than gallantry
maintained in defeat, but Nazi armor cut the country to shreds in
two weeks. Then, as agreed, on September 17 the Red Army
attacked from the east, occupying its half of Poland. The fighting
was light, only one thousand Red Army lost. The Soviets took a
large number of prisoners, which included some twenty thousand
Polish officers. Poland, which had been off the map of Europe from
1793 to 1918, had vanished again. Once and for all this time, as
Hitler put it.

It was the age of dirty deals. Later that same fall the Soviet
Union offered Finland a deal. To better protect Leningrad from
invasion, the Soviets wanted some Finnish land in exchange for
which they offered a rather considerable chunk of Soviet territory.
At least it was an offer, not an invasion. The Finns, however, didn't
see it that way. Sovereignty was not real estate. And those were also
the fairest and most Finnish of lands, Karelia.

The necessary incident occurred, and on November 30,
1939 the Soviet Union went to war against Finland.

In a Finnish cartoon of the time, two Finnish soldiers look
out across the snow at a horde of Red Army soldiers on the horizon. One Finn says to the other: Look at all those Russians!
Where're we going to bury them all?

Stalin's Red Army, decapitated in the thirties, was slashed
by the Finns, who had better weapons and better spirit, skiing out
of a white nowhere, guns blazing. And there were many snipers
with telescopic lenses high in the snow-covered pines.

In the supernaturally clear cylinder of vision that a lens
creates, a group of Soviet soldiers appeared, led by a barrel-chested
officer with a broad, open face. The unit was clearing mines and

moving slowly. The officer was compact and made a good target, and it was always better to knock out the officer than a simple soldier.

He got off two rounds from his submachine gun, *says Starinov,* and he got me twice through the right forearm, front to back.

I started losing blood. Losing consciousness.

The medics got there fast with tourniquets and bandages, but I was still losing blood. It was practically impossible to get out of that area because of the fighting. Friends of mine were worried because I kept losing blood, and they called headquarters in Leningrad. Headquarters sent out a plane for me. Unfortunately, the plane crashed when landing on a lake in the forest and the pilot was injured. Now they had to send another plane for the two of us. I blacked out.

When I finally came to I was still seeing stars. But then I looked up and saw the white ceiling, the white hospital ceiling.

I was there for a little over two months, and that was the end of the Finnish War for me. By the time I got out of the hospital, the war was over.

It had ended on March 12, 1940, with the Soviet Union being ceded the territory it had originally requested. But it had been an expensive purchase—fifty thousand Soviet soldiers had been killed.

Done with the Finns, Stalin turned his attention to the Polish officers and found no compelling reason why they should remain alive. On the contrary, they could be of great use dead. Half of Poland was already his. But Poland always rebelled against Moscow's domination, and these Polish officers were just the energetic, patriotic, able types to lead such a rebellion. As it often did, Stalin's logic led to execution. Nearly five thousand Polish officers were shot in the woods outside Katyn, the others are said to have been placed on barges that were set adrift, then sunk by artillery.

Britain and France were bound by treaty to declare war on any country attacking their ally Poland. Germany attacked both, finding Britain as unyielding as France was resigned to humiliation, falling by June 1940. A man himself very conscious of history and humiliation, Adolph Hitler insisted that the peace between victorious Germany and subjugated France be signed in the same railroad car in which the treaty ending World War I with Germany's defeat had been formalized.

The Nazis goose-stepped through the Arc de Triomphe. Hitler visited Napoleon's tomb. Resting his hands on the railing, Hitler gazed down on the tombs within tombs that hold the last great conqueror's body. Hitler had taken France at a cost of twenty-five thousand; the Soviet Union had won a small stretch of Finland and paid twice that for it. The math was clear.

While the Germans were invading France, the Soviet Army occupied the Baltic states of Lithuania, Estonia, and Latvia. By early August, those three countries were made constituent republics of Stalin's Soviet Union. Two weeks later, in a villa outside Mexico City, a Spanish assassin, Ramón Mercader, who had entered Trotsky's entourage by winning the heart of the sister of Trotsky's secretary, drove an alpine ice ax into the back of Trotsky's skull. If there were war, there would be no political hero or great general for the nation to rally around. Stalin had no rivals now.

Russia entered its last winter of dirty peace. And it was politics that was making the times so dirty, as Starinov knew. But the worst of it was what it did to a person. In Spain when Comrade Rudolph, as Starinov was known there, had learned that generals Tukhachevsky and Yakir had been executed as traitors, part of him wanted to believe the accusations just might be true. Who knew the temptations of highest position?

Back in Russia, he saw that it was far worse than he had feared:

One of my closest friends had died of a heart attck. He lived in such fear of being arrested that one night there was a knock at his door, and he dropped dead of a heart attack. And it turned out it was only a telegram.

Another friend wouldn't see me. "You understand, you

understand," he said. And then I heard that my best and oldest friend from the army had been arrested as a traitor. I couldn't believe it. But then my conscience asked me why I was able to doubt the generals' innocence and not my friend's. It had to be both or neither. I told myself, Stay as far away from the whole thing as you can.

Then I was called in by Marshal Voroshilov, the commander of the Red Army, and reported to him on Spain.

"You deserve a big reward," said Voroshilov. "A promotion and a major assignment."

I wasn't being investigated, I was being thanked for my services. That made me feel good, and feeling good made me forget about my friends. And that made me feel bad again. My brain was in a whirl.

Then I was summoned by the KGB. It was the usual routine—the light glaring in my eyes and the investigator's face in the dark.

"Don't worry," he says, "you're here as a witness."

"To what?"

"You can't guess?"

"No."

"Alright. We'll help you out. Why did you set up secret partisan bases twenty to fifty miles from the border?"

I had heard what the people who had been involved in preparing for partisan war were being accused of—not believing in the power of the Soviet state and Soviet forces, and, worse, stockpiling weapons with hostile intent. They wanted to get me to say the whole thing was wrong from the start. But I wouldn't.

I said, "That's right, we did set up bases fifty miles from the border. But fortified areas were also being built at that same distance, and even further in, and they must have cost millions or billions of rubles!"

"Forget about fortifications, they don't have anything to do with it."

"What do you mean, they don't? Those fortifications

were made on the assumption that the enemy might penetrate fifty miles. And, in that case, it's logical to prepare for partisan warfare in the area between the border and those fortifications. I trained the partisans to fight the enemy. Everything that was done was done for the good of the country."

The investigator wasn't happy, but he must not have had an order for my arrest. "That's all for right now," he said. "We're not touching you, because of all your military distinctions. But, who knows, we may meet again. In the meantime I advise you to tell me in writing everything you know about those generals, that whole crew. Don't hide anything. It'll make life simpler for you."

I went right to see Marshal Voroshilov. This time he was more closed and severe.

Still, he made a call for me. To Ezhov, the head of the KGB.

Voroshilov said, "I've a got a soldier by the name of Starinov in here with me. He's just back from Spain. And he's been called in for questioning for carrying out orders to stockpile weapons for anti-Soviet partisans."

The very high voice at the other end of the line said something and then Voroshilov said, "Of course, he performed treasonous acts, but he was a little guy, he might not have known what was really going on."

Ezhov, the head of the secret police, said something, then Voroshilov said, "But he distinguished himself in Spain and that redeemed him. Leave him alone. We'll deal with him."

A few days later I was made a colonel and offered a big assignment. I turned the assignment down, I wanted to work as far from the center as possible.

After that little talk with the KGB and then with Voroshilov, I had understood something. The partisan detachments and bases we had prepared so carefully in case of war had all been wiped out.

And that put a fear in me the likes of which I'd never felt before, not at the front, not behind enemy lines.

Hitler was the enemy, Hitler was an ally. General Tukhachevsky was a hero, General Tukhachevsky was a traitor. The Red Army's partisan detachments were in fact the enemy's fifth column. It was very bad and could not be understood. Starinov did what a soldier could do, his duty.

By June 1941 Germany had taken Greece, Yugoslavia, and Bulgaria. Now the border of Germany and the Soviet Union touched at every point from the Baltic Sea in the north to the Black Sea in the south. On June 19 Starinov arrived at an army camp near that border in Belorussia to run a training exercise. Most of the officers to whom he was to report could barely spare him a minute—they were deluged with reports of a German buildup of troops and equipment along the borders and of mounting German violations of Soviet airspace. But there were strict orders from the "Boss," Stalin, not to shoot those planes down.

Knowing that war was inevitable but hoping to put it off for one more year to finish rebuilding the army, Stalin now would do anything to prevent giving the Germans a cause for hostilities. Supplies according to the terms of the pact were now being pumped from Russia to Germany at an accelerated pace. Stalin's strange blind spot prevented him from seeing what was apparent to any reconnaissance unit near the border—the Nazis were preparing to attack. But that would mean that Hitler had bested Stalin in deceit.

*

After divorcing the debauched soldier who could sign his name in a wall with a machine gun, Natalya Viktorovna had remarried and known four years of love and family happiness before her bone tuberculosis flared up again. In June 1938 she entered a sanatorium that was then on Romanian territory and which, in all the shuffles, had become Soviet by June 1941. Her leg had been in a cast for a year.

O n June 19, all the dogs started howling and they kept it up day and night, *says Natalya.* On the same day, the nineteenth, I insisted that the cast be removed. People who spend three months in a cast usually have to learn to walk all over again. And I'd been in the cast a year. I just got up and started walking. All the doctors came running over to see it. I could barely put one foot in front of the other, but I was moving. It felt like walking on knives. Except that the knives weren't outside your feet but inside them, the points piercing out through your heels.

But if you can't overcome that, you'll just never walk again.

I wanted to be back in Russia. By June 21, the dogs had been howling for three days and nights.

June 21 was a Saturday. The evening was quite warm, people were out and around. Starinov strolled the town of Kobrin with his friend Kolesnikov—two officers in uniform doing the town, pausing to watch a pretty girl cold-shoulder a young man's attentions. Soldiers were carrying suitcases on their way home on leave; the atmosphere was relaxed, even somewhat festive. The special TASS government bulletin of June 14 had created a sense of security, though the reports continued to come in of German divisions massed at the border and German violations of Soviet airspace. Soviet officers knew that this was how an army preparing to attack behaves, though who knew? It might just be more dirty politics.

At the end of the evening Starinov and Kolesnikov returned to the engineering company office, where they were temporarily billeted. Soon they were fast asleep with the pleasant weariness that comes of a Saturday night in a strange town.

All of a sudden I woke up, *says Starinov.* I thought I'd heard an explosion through my sleep. But everything was quiet, except for the drone of airplane motors. It was just starting to get light. I checked my watch. It was 4:20. Now Kolesnikov was up and looking for his watch too.

Then we heard something strike hard not far away, followed by an explosion. The building shook, and the windows made a whining sound.

"Are they testing mines?" I said.

"Sounds like bombs to me," said Kolesnikov.

I was about to ask what our pilots would be doing dropping bombs, when we were drowned out by a series of deafening explosions.

Everything got quiet again. The only thing I could hear were the planes droning closer, then moving away. All of a sudden I remembered that sound from Spain—German Junkers.

Someone ran in and yelled for everybody to clear out at once. We yanked on our boots and ran out buttoning our clothes just as a squadron of planes came flying up right over headquarters.

We dashed across the square, jumped a ditch, and ran into an orchard. On the way, I glanced back and caught a glimpse of the bombs under the fuselage. The bombs were narrow and looked very small.

They made a piercing whistle as they fell. A direct hit on headquarters where we'd just been sleeping! Nothing left but smoke and dust. The air had been so shocked by the power of the explosions that my ears were ringing. And then another squadron appeared and started its dive.

As soon as the attack was over, we grabbed a ride into Kobrin. You could smell the buildings burning, that smell. Everyone had gathered on the square in front of a loudspeaker on a telegraph pole, one of those black, dish-shaped speakers used for public address.

We're all standing around waiting for the 6:00 A.M. news, the girl beside me was even up on tiptoe. The news comes on and it's all upbeat. Soviet success in industry, the good harvest coming in this year. And the foreign news is about English ships being sunk, German raids on Scottish cities, and the fighting in Syria. And that's it. Then they go right into morning calisthenics. The announcer says, "Arms out to the side, and a deep knee bend. Put some oomph into it. That's good, one–two, one–two."

The city is on fire, and it's one–two, one–two!

The government finally came on the radio at 12:30 that day and was heard by everyone except those already fighting and dying in large numbers. Molotov, Minister of Foreign Affairs, the man who had put his name to the Molotov-Ribbentrop Pact allying Germany and the Soviet Union, informed the nation that it had been "perfidiously attacked" by the Nazis. Molotov struck the note that would give the war its dominant tone—like the war against Napoleon in 1812, this was a war for the land of Russia. The cynicism of the Politburo permitted no illusions.

By the time Molotov came on the air, most of the Soviet Air Force had been destroyed, twelve hundred planes gone in eight hours, and eight hundred of them had never left the ground.

The Germans were attacking along the whole border with an army of 4.6 million soldiers supported by 5,000 planes and 3,700 tanks. Now the blitzkrieg had been turned against Russia. An armored trident was seeking to skewer Leningrad, Moscow, and Kiev. These three were the main plexus—Leningrad in the north, with its heavy industry; Moscow, with government and industry; and Kiev, the capital of the grain- and energy-rich Ukraine.

The entire operation was predicated on success. A leader who was already being compared to Napoleon by his enemies could not, by his very nature, plan for anything but triumph. Greatness requires every ounce of nerve and confidence, not a drop can be sacrificed to doubt. All the violations of Soviet airspace clearly indicated that the Red Army was not in a state of war readiness. Their air force could be destroyed on the ground; they were weak in tanks and antitank weapons, all they had was troops and artillery. In the case of a blitzkrieg, speed and success are synonyms. Leningrad, Moscow, and Kiev had to be taken before the roads turned to mud in October and to ice in November. But those months seemed far away on that first lovely June morning of the war.

*

Though he had been expelled from the party and the capital, Ivan Vrachov had not vanished like his dear friends Mikhail and Revekka had—the father lost in the limbo of the executed, the daughter sent to a labor camp almost to the Chinese border. Ivan Vrachov, the young man with three years of parochial school who had risen to assist Vladimir Ilich Lenin, on whose orders he had helped shift the capital of Russia from Petrograd to Moscow, had now fallen even lower than he had been when poverty had forced him to work at the age of eleven. But Vrachov was unchanged. If anything, he was more devoted to Lenin than ever—to Lenin's party, Lenin's revolution. He fully intended to outlast the gang that had seized control of the party, the Kremlin, the country. But Molotov's announcement superseded everything for Ivan Vrachov.

On the first day of the war I reported to the Central Committee. I said, "I am at the disposal of the Central Committee. Send me to the front."

Like all people who had already served in the army, I had my papers, which stated that in the event of war I was to be called up with the rank of Chief Political Officer. But since I'd been expelled from the party I could not of course hope for any such rank. *But certainly Ivan Vrachov could be allowed to fight for his country and for socialism, the Stalinist sickness didn't run deep enough to prevent that. Or did it?*

Starinov and his friend Kolesnikov headed away from the front toward Minsk to be reassigned, as they were only temporarily in Kobrin to run a training exercise. On the way they stopped in Pinsk.

In Pinsk the local authorities asked our advice on building bomb shelters. Their town was located sixty miles from the border, and they were certain enemy forces would never make it there. But still there might be air raids, and you had to prepare for that.

That's how we were all thinking! We thought it was only right where we happened to be that the enemy had caught our troops by surprise. Elsewhere, our planes had to be bombing the hell out of them!

Starinov spent the night in a village, but he could not provide the curious villagers any real information. He had no idea how bad the first day had been, not realizing that what he had seen was not an evil exception but rather a benign one.

The first day of the war, a Sunday in June, was over.

On the second day of the war, Starinov and Kolesnikov entered the outskirts of Minsk and saw cattle killed by bombs along the roadside. Minsk too was burning. At headquarters in Minsk they received their orders—return to Moscow at once. They covered the 450 miles between Minsk and Moscow in two days. There Starinov was given his assignment—to head up a newly created engineer corps charged with obstructing enemy progress on the Western Front.

"The officer giving me my assignment says, 'You'll get four specialists in demolition, three sapper battalions, six thousand antitank mines, and twenty-five tons of explosives.

" 'Twenty-five tons! You'll pardon me but that's not enough even for one day!' "

On June 27 Colonel Starinov headed back for the front with enough explosives for one day of war. He had feared that his country was unprepared but hadn't known how badly. Now he knew.

*

Natalya could walk, but not without crutches. The crutches took both hands, which meant she couldn't carry her bag. But good people were found, and money, as always, helped. A bird on sticks, she began hobbling home to Russia.

It took several days to reach the Romanian port of Ackerman on the Black Sea, where she could get a boat for Odessa.

Everything was very orderly in Ackerman, very tidy, very calm. And everyone was unusually polite. When I got to the pier for the ferry that went the five miles across the Black Sea to Odessa, there was a mob there of I don't know how many thousands. But the Romanian ferry captain picked out the old women, and the mothers with children, and me on my crutches, and let us board first.

On the way across, German planes strafed us with

machine-gun fire. It looked like they were going to try to sink us, but they were just having a little fun and flew off.

Finally, we pulled into Odessa. Everything had been so orderly in Ackerman, but in Odessa it was total pandemonium. Everyone was cursing a blue streak—your mother this, your mother that, people were going wild, fights were breaking out. Was I ever happy to be home!

It was the end of June and the end of the white nights in Leningrad, when twilight lasts till dawn. That city of stone, water, and sky becomes even more fluid, as if time itself had dissolved into a grey-white shimmer. But Leningrad also becomes a city of night carnival, with droves of young people out with bottles and guitars, fishermen angling for a bite, lovers disappearing under the shade of trees, the city cut into dozens of islands by the raised bridges, the great flow of ocean traffic always moving by night there.

The magical restlessness of the white nights caught everyone, including Ilya Jaffee, who was back in Leningrad. He was too zealous to remain long unnoticed in Murmansk, where he had taken refuge from the Terror in a small job and a distant locale. Soon he had been retransferred to Leningrad with an important party and technical assignment at the Kirov Plant, a major munitions factory. The former imperial capital had now become an industrial center, but it was also the city where Kirov had been assassinated, a nest of treason. The Terror had abated, not ceased. Ilya, who had seen the Tsar three times, had seen the Terror up close once. He came out unscathed, his reputation as a communist endorsed by Stalin's number one aide. Ilya felt out of danger, if not unafraid. His voice is grave with shame as he says:

The Terror gradually enveloped us, and deprived us of will and the ability to act. The Terror penetrated into people's marrow. One wrong word and I'd disappear. Just disappear. Only one thing was certain in those times and that was that the country wasn't ready for war.

The war started on June 22, 1941, and on June 29 the

director of the Kirov Plant called me and told me to come by his place that evening. It was a hot night. He was in his slippers, wearing a T-shirt.

There were a few other people there as well. I was given a special form to sign. Then the director made a speech to us—"What I'm about to tell you is something only sixteen other people in Leningrad know. If there's any leakage before Thursday, some of us will pay for it with our lives. This is a state secret—We're being given ten days to prepare to relocate our factory."

The factory was to be relocated to Sverdlovsk on the far side of the Ural Mountains, which separate European Russia from Siberia and Asia. And they had ten days to do it. Which could only mean that someone had decided that in two weeks it might be too late. But now at least there was something worth fighting for—the country and life itself.

Russia had space and track. Soviet industry began rolling east on miles of freight cars. Factories were dismantled and reassembled in Siberia, fifteen hundred in all. They were back at work while the timber walls were still going up around them.

*

It was of course not only Russia that drew Natalya Viktorovna back, but her family as well.

W hen I had entered the sanatorium, I sent my children to live with my mother in Zhitomir, which is west of Kiev. I also knew that my husband was there in Zhitomir, visiting the children. And so I gathered the nerve to travel from Odessa to Kiev, figuring if I could get to Kiev I could somehow cover the eighty miles to Zhitomir, even if it meant hiring a horse and driver, one of those big strong men known as "red Jews" because they all had red hair.

As always, Odessa was full of color and life. People had brought their primus stoves outside and were cooking in the street. Odessa was preparing to defend itself, but in very

Odessa style, which means people were also making jam
because the apricots had just ripened.

It was June 29, a week after the start of the war.
Nothing was running on schedule anymore but I did get a train
going to Kiev without much problem, though it was a freight
train, not a passenger train.

But the train to Kiev never went anywhere near Kiev. It
went all over the Ukraine, all over Russia. We practically didn't
even stop at the stations. They wouldn't let us off for a minute.
It was scorching hot, there was no food, no water. People
started getting sick. Typhus, dysentery. Children and grown-ups
too. And the sick people were just put off the train, in the
empty steppe, and left there to die. They were absolutely
merciless with them.

Once in a great while they'd give us water, but,
relatively speaking, I didn't suffer from the thirst. All my life I
never drank much and so it was easier for me to bear.

Ten days we were on that freight train and finally on the
ninth of July, the most idiotic thing of all, we pull into
Moscow. Probably for no other reason than it was possible to
go there. Typical Russian muddleheadedness!

The more Starinov discovered, the lower his spirits fell. The best
generals had been executed, the partisan bases wiped out, and he
had been issued enough explosives for one day of war, the rest to
come "right away," an expression that never had any meaning in
Russia except when said by a frightened subordinate.

And officers were still being arrested. It made Starinov
queasy to see his fellow Red Army officers quake at the green band
of a secret police hat coming through the tent door.

Starinov knew that they had good reason to quake, though
he could have no idea that the number of officers arrested and
executed ran into the tens of thousands. Stalin had said: "One
death is a tragedy; a million is a statistic." But the opening days and
months of the war proved that tyrant's aphorism wrong—the loss
of those officers was indeed a tragedy, for Russia. The Germans

had taken Kobrin, town of the idiotic calisthenics, on the first day of the war, an advance of thirty miles. The Germans suffered heavy casualties but inflicted worse. It was impossible to know just how bad things were, yet it was essential for officers at the front to have the most realistic picture possible of their situation. But another sign of complacence, if that was the word, was that units were in contact not by radio but by phone lines, which had to be strung in the battlefield. The technology of communication was not up to the technology of war. Cities were burning and nobody knew what was really going on. And, if Stalin knew, he wasn't saying.

A s soon as I got to the front, *says Starinov,* I was arrested and handed over to the secret police. In Moscow, with all the confusion, they had issued me my orders on the wrong form. Just the sort of little thing a German spy parachuted in might not know.

But I was a colonel in an army at war, and I demanded that this error be cleared up at once! It took about an hour.

It was one of those hours, empty and heavy at the same time, the way time had felt in '36 when Starinov had been ordered to turn in his party card until he could prove that he actually was who he said he was.

T he supplemental matériel promised me in Moscow was not arriving. But then I started thinking about how we'd done things in Spain. I remembered Rubio, who was a master at making grenades out of ordinary tin cans; I thought about Capitan Domingo, and the land mines we'd laid outside Córdoba and Granada. And so I put our group to work making homemade mines and delayed-action grenades.

We made fuses out of the cotton wicks for kerosene lamps. When there's no wind, that wicking burns at the rate of one centimeter every two minutes. So, by varying the length of the fuse, we could get anything from a five- to a thirty-minute fuse. We planted those charges in the roadway so that they would also hurl stone up at the vehicles. Those mines were particularly effective against motorcycles.

They had another nice little feature too. The mines weren't all that hard to find because of the smell the burning fuse gave off. But nobody could disarm them. The slightest attempt to remove the payload set it off just like that! Ba-boom!

So, Spain came in handy. One night we were sitting around a fire drinking tea when one of the men asked if it was true that I'd been in Spain. I ended up telling them about blowing trains and bridges. At the end, one of them asks, "So why don't we go strike behind Nazi lines?"

"Everything in its own time," I said. But I was thinking the same thing myself. The enemy was primarily advancing along roads and rail lines. He did not control the huge forests, the marshes, and the fields by the roads, and he *couldn't* control them. Right now the enemy's weak spot was behind the lines.

It certainly wasn't in front of them, where Russian troops melted into death by the tens of thousands.

But tens of thousands more were volunteering, the turnout heaviest in Leningrad, very strong in Moscow, lighter in Kiev. And the country was losing so much blood that nearly every volunteer, except the most laughably unfit, was accepted for active service, with the additional exception of those few who bore the stigma, like Ivan Vrachov.

Since Ivan Vrachov had defied Stalin to his face at a party meeting, he assumed that Stalin had not forgotten him.

I wrote to Stalin twice, he knew me. I asked to be sent to the front. But that produced no results either.

I appealed to the Central Committee again—Send me to the most dangerous sector, use me for partisan warfare.

I was called in to see Ponomarenko, first deputy to Voroshilov, the commander of the Red Army. Ponomarenko received me warmly, he treated me as a person worthy of trust.

He took me over to a map and showed me the displacement of our partisan troops.

"What do you think?" he said. "We're going to throw you out of a plane and have you go crawling around down there? No, you're a veteran political officer and that's what we're going to use you as. I'm 100 percent in favor of having you work right here with us."

Ponomarenko's office had a door that led into Voroshilov's. Voroshilov knew I was there. He called Ponomarenko in a few times but didn't come out to see me. Not a good sign.

I had a few more talks with Ponomarenko, all of them nice and polite, but in the end he said, "Consider yourself in the reserves."

He put it like that to sweeten the pill.

What choice did I have now? I went to a recruiting office.

"Where's your draft card?"

"I lost it."

"Your rank?"

"Private."

They needed soldiers, and they took me.

And so I went to war, a private in the army.

Vrachov had acted like a good party member, a disciplined Leninist. He had taken his appeal to the Central Committee, then up to the highest authority, Stalin. But Stalin was not speaking to Russia or Vrachov.

*

Stalin's silence lasted thirteen days. Whatever he had been in those thirteen days—drunk, humiliated, terrified, infuriated—he was calm as he addressed the nation on July 3, 1941. He spoke with his thick, Georgian accent but with a bare concision and turn of phrase which Russians liked. When he sipped water the click of his glass was heard from Moscow to Siberia. Most staggering, most frightening, most touching, he called his listeners "brothers and sisters."

"Comrades, citizens, brothers and sisters, fighters of our Red Army and Navy! I am speaking to you, my friends!

"All production must immediately be put on a war footing, everything must be at the disposal of the front. . . . The Red Army and Navy and the whole Soviet people must fight for every inch of Soviet soil, fight to the last drop of blood for our towns and villages.

"The enemy must not be left . . . a pound of bread, nor a pint of oil.

"In the occupied territories partisan units must be formed. . . . There must be diversionist groups for fighting enemy units, for blowing up and destroying roads and bridges and telegraph wires . . ."

It took exactly ten days for Stalin's general command to become specific orders for Colonel Starinov. On July 13 he was appointed head of the first partisan school at the front, which was officially called the West Front Tactical Training Center.

That put heart in Starinov, but the news was worse all the time. The Germans continued to advance, their superiority in tanks, airplanes, and experienced troops continuing to take victory over the Red Army, which was strong only in numbers and artillery. At least the artillery was functioning, mashing units of German armor and infantry, slowing the advance—but only that, slowing it.

There was one good sign in the heavens—a rain of red comets, hundreds of the new Katyusha launchers firing a dozen flaming rockets a minute. The Germans were thrown by this murderous, almost biblical wrath from the skies. But only for a time. The Katyushas opened fire on July 15, but six days later the first Nazi bombs fell on Moscow, some of them even cratering the stout cobbles of Red Square.

The Germans' fortunes were greatest in the south, in their drive for Kiev and the riches of the Ukraine. Finland was now in the war on the side of Germany, not only taking back what the USSR had seized from Finland but helping close the ring around Leningrad, which was almost cut off now. But the Soviet antiaircraft and artillery were very strong around Leningrad and Moscow.

The cities would have to be taken on the ground.

And it was on the ground that the Red Army was going to have to stop the invasion, if only because the air force had been essentially obliterated on the first day of the war. There were instances of Soviet pilots running out of bullets and simply ramming German planes with their own, the kind of action that becomes immediately legendary and makes the due impression on the enemy's assessment of morale. And equipment.

But no invasion of Russia could result in victory if Moscow were not taken. The old Russian city of Smolensk stood as the last great barrier between the border and the capital. The Soviet High Command decided to make Smolensk the decisive battle of the war at that stage. For the rest of July and August both sides concentrated their fire in the area around Smolensk. The Red Army not only stopped the Germans but even recovered some territory, only a small amount but still a first.

On August 23 Hitler turned down his generals' advice to make a concentrated drive on Moscow. When Napoleon had taken Moscow, he had found a deserted city that soon burst into flames. From the Kremlin Napoleon had watched his victory turn to smoke and ashes. Hadn't the Russians already evacuated industry to the Urals, hadn't the Russians already transferred many important government functions to Kuibishev? Even Lenin's mummy had been relocated there.

The attack on Moscow was to be continued, of course, and pressed hard. All three cities would fall.

And once again Hitler's star showed the brightest. By late August the Germans had driven the Red Army out of Smolensk. By September 8, the land blockade of Leningrad was complete. And on September 17, Kiev fell to German hands.

And it was also on September 17, two years to the day since the USSR had invaded Poland as part of its deal with Germany, that the USSR took Tehran, having invaded Iran along with its new British ally. Russia now had what it always dreamed of—warm-weather ports, good the year-round. And it wouldn't be long before massive American aid would be flowing in through those ports.

The Nazis had met less resistance in the Ukraine than in Russia proper. A portion of the population—those who remembered collectivization, the famine Stalin had created, the cannibalism, madness, and mass death—greeted the Germans as liberators, on the assumption that no one could be worse than the communists.

But German strength was German weakness. The towering self-confidence that allowed them to launch their vast enterprise would never allow them to treat the "subhuman" Slavs as equals. And they had spent too many precious days on the taking of Kiev. There were only two weeks left in September before the October rains and the October mud. And Moscow had not yet fallen.

But it would, for Germany was invincible. By September 30, 1941, two weeks after the fall of Kiev, the Germans launched their concerted drive to take Moscow. A blitzkrieg within a blitzkrieg, the strategy was to encircle the Russians with infantry, thus freeing the armor for a lightning dash at Moscow.

The fighting had been fierce for all three months of the war, but now it mounted to crescendo.

*

Some people die in the first minute, some go through the whole campaign without a scratch. The fates that war deals are always on time to the second.

The German drive on Moscow went through the part of Russia where Raisa Danilovna lived. Later in life she would become the mother of Mark whose Uncle Ilya saw the Tsar three times, but back then she was just a simple country girl of twenty.

I immediately volunteered to be an army nurse. I was a true patriot. A true patriot of the Soviet Union. We all were in those days.

I joined the army nurses in early October. I was immediately caught in the heaviest fighting. The Germans had several of our armies surrounded.

A few days after I'd joined, on October 13, I was in a peasant hut, treating the wounded. I went outside, a shell landed nearby and the shrapnel wounded me in the arm and the leg. I couldn't walk or move my right arm.

A civilian girl brought me to the village where my aunt lived. My aunt was very smart and full of energy. She brought me out to the big highway that runs between Moscow and Minsk. She went up to the Germans and asked them to take me the fifty miles to Smolensk. Of course, she didn't say a word about my being in the army. Just a girl, a civilian, wounded, that's all.

The Germans were perfectly decent toward me and took me to a Soviet civilian hospital in Smolensk. In the hospital Soviet doctors operated on me to remove the shrapnel. I was there a month but my recovery wasn't going too well because the hospital had no medicine at all.

After a month my aunt came to visit me. And the doctors just said to her, "Take the girl. This isn't her home."

And what they really meant was that I didn't have long to live.

My aunt took me back to her village. It took me six months, but one way or the other I got my strength back.

Then I had to leave my aunt's and take care of myself. To earn my own bread. I had to work where there was work. The Germans had work. They paid you in food. And so I went to work doing road clearance on the Moscow–Minsk highway.

A simple country girl of twenty, Raisa Danilovna had learned in a very short time that doctors could be as indifferent as shrapnel and that everything was nonsense—there was only life and death. She had become a patriot of survival.

Master of survival, Ilya Jaffee had thrown all his formidable energy into the task of dismantling the gigantic Kirov works in Leningrad, shipping all those tons of crates to Sverdlovsk in Siberia and reassembling everything there. Sverdlovsk was the new name for the city of Ekatarinburg, where on the night of July 16, 1918, the Tsar and the royal family were executed, the Tsar whom Ilya had seen three times, smoking nervously on the platform of the light blue imperial train.

By October 1941 Jaffee's factory had been unloaded, reassembled, and was back in production.

In Leningrad our factory had been making diesel aircraft engines for bombers that could strike deep behind enemy lines. This was the latest thing in technology and very important work.

After we'd set the plant back up in Sverdlovsk, we started producing those diesel engines again. Everything was going along just fine until one day in October '41, Malyshev, the deputy chairman of the Council of Ministers, arrives and there's another secret meeting.

Malyshev gives us a speech: "Comrade Stalin has instructed me to inform each of you of a secret that cannot be told even to our generals, not to mention other military or civilians. The whole war effort hinges on this. Comrades, the point is—we don't need diesel aircraft engines. We won't be bombing Berlin for quite a while.

"The enemy is at the gates of Moscow, and the only thing that can save us is tanks.

"And so, what we need is—diesel engines for tanks!

"All we have on hand right now is 412 tanks, and 412 tanks is a drop in the bucket. All other plants capable of producing such engines are still in the process of being relocated. If you don't switch to producing tank engines, we won't be able to hold the front. Is it clear why this is a secret?"

That came as a big shock to me. The enemy's at the gates of Moscow and we're here producing the wrong kind of engine? But there was no time for blaming Stalin, there was no time for thinking about anything but saving the country.

The Nazi drive for Moscow may have been slowed by mud and Soviet firepower, but the drive was relentless. The din of artillery was a few decibels more audible each day in Moscow. Then the first German soldiers appeared in the distant outskirts of the city. On October 16 panic broke out in Moscow. And it is one of the many uglinesses of war that those who fled were accused of cowardice by those who stayed—half a million going out to dig antitank trenches—and those who stayed were accused by those who fled of wanting to welcome the Germans.

One of those who stayed in Moscow was Joseph Stalin, and when that was announced it put some iron back in the city's heart. In the meantime, Stalin had depoliticized the war. The secret police were no longer arresting officers, and now the proof of a good officer was success in the field, not party standing. One of those good officers, Marshal Zhukov, was entrusted with the defense of Moscow, a grave responsibility.

But Zhukov had a Siberian ace up his sleeve. Troops from beyond the Urals, troops whose existence had not even been suspected by German intelligence, were shipped by fast train to the front and hurled into battle. Fresh and fierce, they gave the Germans some rude and bloody surprises. It was getting late in October, the ground was hardening, the first snowflakes had appeared—only for a minute or two, then they were gone again.

Moscow was in crisis, the Ukraine was a disaster. The capital, Kiev, had fallen, and now Kharkov, the second largest city, was about to fall. Colonel Starinov was assigned to mine Kharkov in preparation for its abandonment.

Starinov had heard Stalin's speech of July 3, stressing the importance of mines and partisan warfare. A training school had even been founded. But here it was October and he had neither the men nor the equipment to do even half the job. And he was being told to mine the city in such a way as to not only destroy as many structures as possible but to inflict maximum casualties on German personnel.

It was frustrating, insulting. He was going to have to do the same thing he had done in Spain, fight two wars at the same time—one against the enemy and one for the dignity and value of his art. But Starinov was up for both wars, especially because, in some obscure way, the restoring of partisan warfare would clear the names of the great generals and of his dear friends who had paid with years of life, or life itself, for crimes they had never committed.

After a few days in Kharkov we worked out a daring plan and submitted it to the top brass, *says Starinov.* Nikita Khrushchev was one of the people in charge of the front there. He reviewed our plan and made a few little additions, increasing the size of the corps planting dummy mines.

Khrushchev had his wits about him, and that made an impression. Unlike the other higher-ups, who were gloomy to a man, Khrushchev was full of vim and vigor.

More than a year before all this, I had gotten a letter from Kharkov. It was from the Spaniards I'd fought with in Spain against the Fascists. After the fall of the republic, they had sought refuge in the USSR.

I wrote them back saying Anna and I—I'd married her by then and we had children—would be passing through Kharkov on such and such a date.

It was a chilly, fall day. And there's Capitan Domingo on the platform and he starts yelling in Spanish as soon as he spots us. "Anna! Rudolfo! Olla, hombre!"

We threw our arms around each other and whacked each other on the back. All the passengers were watching.

But the train was only stopping in Kharkov for fifteen minutes. No face could ever look sadder than Domingo's. And he looked so sad when he said, "You're only staying for fifteen minutes?" that Anna and I stayed for a few days.

This time I arrived in Kharkov on October 1, 1941, and first thing I searched out Domingo. He made me strong, black coffee, Spanish style, and he told me there were twenty-two other Spaniards in Kharkov from the old partisan groups. They were working in a tractor factory and dying to get into the army.

Domingo says, "Help us out, we're not registered for the draft and no one will talk to us. But you know we know how to fight the Fascists!"

So I went to see General Nevsky and I told him about the Spaniards. I told him about Capitan Domingo, who had led the 14th Partisan Corps in Spain. I said how excitable Domingo could be, except in battle, where he was always cool and collected. I told him about Juan and Benito, what we'd done together in Spain, blowing up mountain bridges or trains full of Fascists.

"Those are some people!" says the general, and the next thing you know I've got permission to enlist them in our battalion.

We got orders directly from Khrushchev himself to mine the house where he was living. It was assumed that because of its size and location, the Germans would use that building for their commanders as well. I was against hurrying with the mines, they were a new type, detonated by a radio signal. The city was being bombed, a strong shock wave might set one off and cause a disaster.

Khrushchev was still living in the house. He said to me, "You believe in your technology?"

"I do."

"Mine the house!"

We took up a piece of the cement basement floor near the main wall, then dug a well-shaped hole more than six feet deep. We kept each layer of soil in separate, numbered bags so we could replace them in the same order.

Then we emplaced the explosives and the radio detonator. It was a tremendous charge, enough to blow up the building and the guards outside. We filled the hole back up and erased all traces of ourselves. But we knew that if the enemy didn't find any mines in a building that good he would become immediately suspicious. And so we set another mine to throw them off the track. Hid it in the coal pile near the real one.

The Spaniards were with us throughout the whole mining of Kharkov. They performed important and complicated tasks, and they were with us inside the city until October 24 when Kharkov fell. Demolition men are always the last to leave.

Just like the old days again, him with the Spaniards, and the Fascists winning.

*

Natalya Viktorovna hobbled through Moscow on crutches. She
had made a reasonable plan—take the train to Kiev and somehow
cover the eighty miles from Kiev to Zhitomir, where her husband
was visiting their children at her mother's. Nothing could be more
natural than to draw close to those you loved in time of danger.
But war, which created that necessity, obstructed it as well. The
train to Kiev, a straight line, a day, a day and a half at most in a
freight car, turned into a ten-day trek through waterless steppe that
ended in Moscow, five hundred miles northeast of Kiev. And it
wasn't only the result of "typical Russian muddleheadedness!" but
a sign of how deeply and disruptively Nazi armor had penetrated.
      Yet there was nothing for her in Moscow.

There were huge mobs in Moscow, wild mobs, people on
the run everywhere. Everyone was terrified of spies. More
than once I was surrounded by mobs suspicious that I had
broken my legs while parachuting in from a plane. So, I went
to Leningrad, to the communal apartment where we lived,
hoping that my husband might have brought my mother and
the children there. But our room was empty, the two children's
beds were empty.
      The Germans were advancing with terrible speed, and
Leningrad was already filled with refugees.
      I sent a telegram to Zhitomir but there was no answer.
The telegraph operators had a very strong sense of duty and
did not desert their posts until the very last minute.
      Everyone told me to evacuate Leningrad—how was I
going to manage there on crutches? Just as I was about to
leave, I received a telegram from my husband saying they were
all in a little place called Semikhatka. As soon as I arrived in
Irbit, a small town in the Urals, I sent a telegram to my
husband telling him where I was.
      That was late September. In early October I received a
letter from my mother saying that just as they were being
evacuated, a postman had come running up waving that
telegram from me. My mother said that she and the two

children had been evacuated on wagons because the trains were no longer running there. But there wasn't a word about my husband.

Finally, I received a letter from him in Leningrad. He had left my mother, who was fifty-six and in poor health, he had left our two children and gone off to Leningrad figuring I might be there.

He blamed me. He said I should have waited for him in Leningrad. But it never even occurred to me that a man could leave his children—a two-year-old and a three-year-old—in the care of a sick woman, to face an avalanche of Nazi tanks and go off to Leningrad looking for his wife. It was absolutely absurd!

We always did react differently to things, *says Natalya with a tragic sigh.*

The Nazis were winning everything but the Battle of Moscow, which now Hitler had decided absolutely must be won. But the Russians were fighting well now. It was no longer an invasion, it was war. The Red Army had cannon and cannon fodder. They also had the beginnings of a resolve edged in hatred.

Time and force had been lost in the Ukraine. Kiev had been taken and Leningrad encircled, but Moscow had not succumbed to the first great drive on it. And that could only mean one thing—the German army would now regroup and make a final attack on Moscow, one that would be even more desperate than its desperate predecessor.

It took them two weeks to get ready for the first offensive, it would take no less for the second. It was the very end of October.

Now, on the occasion of the anniversary of the revolution, Stalin addressed the nation twice, on November 6 and 7. He always flattered himself on knowing what Russians were really like; he had observed them with the clarity of a total outsider. They loved great rulers, great victories, icons, the language, Russia. The word "soviet" roused very little in their hearts. He still invoked Lenin, of course, but then quickly passed to Tolstoy, Chekhov, Tchaikovsky, and the great military leaders of Russia's past—from

Nevsky, who had defeated the Teutonic Knights, to Kutuzov, who had bested Napoleon. Stalin knew he had to appeal to Russian patriotism, because with the loss of the Baltics and the Ukraine, Russia was all that was really left. It was not a war to save the system but a war to save the country. Not the Soviet Union against Germany, but Russia against Germany.

But, as Stalin reminded his listeners, Russia had great allies now, the British were fighting in the West, the Americans were shipping supplies through Persia. Russia had almost unlimited resources and manpower. Then Stalin sent a signal to the collective psyche. "The German invaders want a war of extermination. . . . Very well then! . . . They shall have it . . . No mercy for the German invaders! Death to the German invaders!"

Stalin did not call for victory over the German invader but for "death to the German invader." Death, not victory; or rather victory through violence, Stalin's very specialty. It was a world-scale gang war, and the Russians could take some heart from knowing that their chief was a worse son of a bitch than Hitler. That was one reason, along with sincere patriotism and the lack of any other belief, why so many Russian soldiers went into battle with the cry of FOR STALIN AND COUNTRY! on their lips.

God gave Russia a cold November. The snow was heavy, temperatures fell to 30° below. German machine oil started gumming up, machine guns jammed. The Soviet tanks, the T-34s, now back in production, were superior to the German panzers. They could withstand stronger hits and put out a more powerful shot. But the Germans fought with an especially bitter ferocity, for this was the last chance to take Moscow.

Aside from fighting on and for their own soil, the Russians had another advantage—felt boots, the best protection against frozen feet, fur caps with fur earflaps, heavy quilt jackets. Not only were Nazi guns ceasing to fire, so were Nazi trigger fingers. Frostbite was rampant. The Germans had come to Russia dressed for victory, not winter.

Still, the German offensive rolled on until December 6, 1941, when it encountered the first Soviet counteroffensive that sent it back reeling through the ringing cold. The next day, the

Japanese bombed the U.S. fleet at Pearl Harbor, and four days later Hitler officially declared war on the United States. Now the entire world was at war.

As the Russians recaptured territory, they saw what the Germans had done to their land, transmuting simple hatred into a thirst for vengeance. In his travels, Colonel Starinov passed through the little railroad town where he had grown up watching his father halt the furious locomotives with a red lantern raised in the air, and where he had accompanied his father on his rounds inspecting track, staring down at those endless ties, that endless rail. The town had not been damaged too badly, but the Germans had managed to blow up seven buildings by sending in demolition men disguised as partisans. It was infuriating! The invader was using partisan methods that were still being slighted by the Soviet leadership, for all their fine talk.

But in late November the leadership took a sudden interest in the problem. Starinov was told to report to Comrade Stalin in the Kremlin at 2200 on the dot. Stalin rose late and worked late and made everybody else do the same.

Every button gleaming, all spit and polish, Colonel Starinov arrived ten minutes early. Stalin wasn't there yet, so he was told to take a seat in the waiting room. Sinking into a leather armchair, whose treacherous comforts had to be resisted, Starinov told himself not to worry.

But simply to be in Stalin's presence was dangerous. Some men were struck dumb, and in others the terror ran so deep it reached kidney and sphincter. A cleanup squad of secret police was always on hand with mops at the ready.

"All of a sudden, something changed in the waiting room. Nobody said a word, nobody made a sound, but everyone sort of came to attention. The man in the chair beside me took out his handkerchief and wiped the sweat off his forehead. Somehow or other everyone knew that Stalin had arrived. And sure enough, a few minutes later they started calling people in."

But that was the closest Starinov would come to making his case directly to the leader. At the last minute he was shunted off to one of Stalin's subordinates. Starinov argued with that subordinate about the wisest course until he realized that it was Stalin who decided what the wisest course was, and then fear silenced him. But now Stalin's main interest was in winning. Ten days later Starinov was summoned back to the Kremlin and given the go-ahead to set up a training school for partisan warfare. "At last! I was in seventh heaven!"

*

"No, I don't want to talk about it," says Natalya Viktorovna, seeming to brace herself. Russian speech has its peculiarities, and so does Russian silence. There are several such silences, distinct as grammatical forms. There is the silence of fear that overcame Starinov while making his case to Stalin's subordinate. There is the silence for the dead remembered of which there are two kinds—one for those who simply passed away, and one for those who were slaughtered by history. "No, I don't want to talk about it. There are details here I simply do not wish to recall. They come to me at night."

And if it is to be spoken, it must be said in the fewest possible words. "I received a letter from an evacuation center saying that my children were in Chelyabinsk, in the Urals and not that far away. My mother had died on the way there and her body had been thrown into a mass grave. I went to Chelyabinsk and found the children in the hospital, dying. I don't want to talk about it."

Still on crutches, Natalya Viktorovna brought her children back to Irbit, where she was living. The three-year-old son survived, the two-year-old daughter did not.

"Then I received a postcard from one of our neighbors in the communal apartment in Leningrad. The man was a real bastard but he had a traditional sense of duty. And even though he was only semiliterate he made it all sound quite official:

" 'Natalya Viktorovna, I consider it my duty to inform you that your husband died on December 22. Your room's been taken and your furniture's been burned.' "

The cold, which was a blessing for Moscow, was a curse for Leningrad. Under siege since September 8, the city was dying of cold and hunger, words that rhyme in Russian. Natalya Viktorovna's furniture would have been chopped up for firewood soon after her husband's death. Civilities were still observed, sentimentalities were not. Household pets were now eyed as sources of protein that had better be killed while they still had a little something on their bones.

The battle of Leningrad was not only for life but for civilization. And it was the perfect setting for that struggle. Leningrad is not an oak that grew from the acorn of a village. The city is an imperial fiat enacted in granite, a city built to order, a mélange of its founder Peter the Great's memories of his various trips to the West.

Pushkin saw Peter the Great as an artist of history, the city as the "creation of Peter." But other Russian writers, like Gogol and Dostoyevsky, found the city spectral for the same reason Pushkin praised it—it didn't have to be there. A city chosen without the least regard for those who had to build it—Petersburg built on bones—or for those who would live in its tubercular humidity, oppressive in summer, marrow-chilling in winter.

The city had its own patriotisms, as triune as its names. It was Petersburg until 1915, when it was changed to Petrograd, which means the same in Russian as in German, important since the country was at war against Germany. When Lenin died, Stalin not only had him embalmed and enshrined but renamed the old imperial capital for the man who had checkmated the Winter Palace.

Leningrad was not only the city of Peter and Pushkin, it was a great industrial city with a working class that was conscious of itself as a historical force. For it was there that Bloody Sunday had occurred in 1905, there that revolution had been won. And perhaps tragically lost in 1921 when the radical sailors had risen in Kronstadt, which guards the city by sea. And it was also there that Kirov, the boss of the Leningrad party, had won the popularity that cost him his life.

Both of Leningrad's great traditions—the shimmer of superior beauty, the iron of the proletariat—were united in Ludmilla Pavlovna. Her father worked at the Kirov Plant, where armaments were made. And her grandfather had been one of the Latvian

Rifles, Lenin's own fabled little army, thrown in at decisive moments to decide battles with their deadly fire. It might have been the Latvian side that gave a richer gold to her hair and some green to her Russian blue eyes. But the city's other dream—of rigorous beauty—was also reflected in her family.

My mother loved to dance. She would have given anything to be a ballerina. But her father was a worker at the Kirov armaments factory and that class had no respect for the stage. And that was the end of that.

But she didn't give up on the dream. When I was nine my mother enrolled me in dance classes. I may always have been a little too plump for ballet. Anyway, when I was thirteen I had a serious operation that put an end to any hopes of a professional career.

I was fifteen when the war started. I went to work in Factory Number 381 as a riveter. We assembled and repaired airplanes and were issued the highest bread ration, 250 grams a day. And they'd feed us a hot meal at the factory. It was hard work. Twelve hours a day.

A city is in desperate straits when a fifteen-year-old girl who lately dreamt of being a ballerina has to work twelve hours a day repairing airplanes. Leningrad had no electricity, heat, or transportation. People had to walk miles through the 30°-below cold to get to work, then work for twelve hours, and walk back. People were dying everywhere. On the sidewalk, on the assembly line, at their desks, in their chairs at home. People seemed to know when they would die, when there was only a day or two left at most. They would go around and say farewell, a word that in Russian also means "forgive me."

All the pets were long gone. People were eating carpenters' glue. Women stopped menstruating. Bodies were transported by children's sleds across the frozen city to the cemetery, where the frozen ground had to be dynamited to create mass graves large enough for a population that, at the peak, was dying at a rate of ten thousand a day.

But civilization was holding in Leningrad. The Red Army on the outskirts of the city continued to resist the Germans with stubborn valor. Part of Lake Ladoga to the north of the city was still in Russian hands, and that meant daredevil drivers could dodge German bombs on the ice while trucking food into the city. The Young Communists were out distributing food and fuel as best they could. Signs were posted advising pedestrians which side of the street was safer from German fire—the south side, for the Germans were firing from the south. Children went to school and recited Pushkin to dying teachers:

> I love you, creation of Peter,
> the elegant severity of your regard . . .

Everyone in the city was dying, just at different rates. But civilization had not died in Leningrad, and neither had the market for valuables. Ludmilla was lucky, she had a little furniture at a time when a nice, carved chair could buy a day's worth of life.

For a while we traded furniture for bread. Later, I started sleeping at the factory. I didn't even have the strength to move after twelve hours of riveting.

And then I came down with scurvy. My legs were in terrible pain. They were covered with open wounds, eight trophic ulcers. I was transferred to lighter work, repairing streetcars. That was considered lighter work.

My uncle's sister was executed for eating her own children. She had invited a friend over for dinner and when the friend looked in her soup she saw a child's fingernail.

Naturally, she hadn't killed her children, but when they died she had started eating them. She had gone out of her mind, needless to say.

When Lake Ladoga froze, trucks started coming across the ice with some food. We called that the "road of life."

In the spring everyone went out and cleaned up the city to prevent epidemics. All the bodies had to be cleared away.

In June I was evacuated with my factory from Leningrad to the Urals.

Ludmilla survived the worst her city would have to endure. She had not died or gone mad. She was injured but not crippled. The ulcers would heal and scar. She was not fusing with other liquefying corpses in a mass grave, she was among the living, walking in the light of day. Death would have taken her life and her future that held love, a husband, a son, and a daughter who would one day dance in the Kirov Ballet.

*

Natalya Viktorovna was getting around on only one crutch now. And it wasn't long after she enrolled in the journalism department of Sverdlovsk University that she threw that crutch away as well. She placed her son in a children's home that was half a live-in school, half an orphanage.

Some of the children's homes were hotbeds of juvenile crime, while others were models of care and instruction. But all were dismal, lice-ridden, hungry places. In many, the lights were kept on so that the hunger-crazed rats would not attack the children's cheeks.

Not that it was much better at the University, where the auditoriums were so cold that ink froze. And a student's rations were barely enough even to keep a little bird like Natalya alive.

Even though we were starving, we gave a half liter of blood every month because they gave you extra rations for it. Those rations included vodka, which you could swap for bread. Once I switched two hundred grams of bread for a matchbox full of rolling tobacco. I'd been smoking since I was thirteen. And I was always dying for a smoke.

Besides extra rations they also gave us a sumptuous three-course dinner. A soup that was nearly entirely just plain boiled water except for the few rotten cabbage leaves floating in it. The second course was a couple of spoonfuls of kasha and the third some inedible fat fried up in machine oil.

Russia was a nation again, bound by starvation and hatred. Moscow had been saved, Leningrad had survived, and the Red Army counterattack had driven the Germans back. But not far enough. The great battles that decide a war had yet to be fought.

Those battles began to be fought in the spring of 1942, and the Russians were losing them all. City after city fell. In the Crimean peninsula, which juts into the Black Sea, the Germans took Kerch and Sevastopol. Never a lucky city for the Russians, Sevastopol fell to the British in the Crimean War of 1854 as the Light Brigade charged and Florence Nightingale ministered to the wounded.

The Germans had regained the offensive and had decided to stabilize the fighting outside Leningrad and Moscow and press for both the city of Stalingrad, a major rail center whose name alone was a trophy, and for the oil fields of Baku in Azerbaijan. Hitler's generals warned—one or the other, not both. But that was why they were generals and he was the Führer.

Something happened that summer in Russia. A battle was won in the heart, where history is always decided and never recorded. A stream of panic coursed through the country like the one that had disgraced Moscow. But this one was repelled by hatred and courage.

The press called for "holy hatred" and "iron discipline." A policy had been determined and the right catchwords found. And the more holiness there was for the Germans to defile, the greater would Russian fury be. Stalin let the church breathe and pray for victory. Song was heard in the churches again, and the icons gleamed in candlelight. The mothers of the fighting men were now able to pray for their sons, and it would have been bad policy, insulting, to deny them that right. Stalin not only forgave the church, he returned his trust to the officers, issuing them gold braid, and switched to the policy of "single command," the officers unimpeded by political overseers.

Russia had its back to the wall of Siberia. "Not a step back" was the order of the day. Ilya Jaffee was at his post in Sverdlovsk producing diesel engines for Soviet tanks. Ivan Vrachov was fighting as a common private. But Raisa Danilovna, wounded in her first days as a Red Army nurse, was out of the war, keeping alive by doing road clearance for the Germans. Still, there were plenty of fresh volunteers, including Natalya Viktorovna, whose every attempt to join the Red Army met with gales of laughter—"Look at her, she's lame and skinny as a bird and she's asking to go to the front. Get out of here, you're useless." They, of course, had no idea of who they were dealing with.

Colonel Starinov was where he belonged, behind enemy lines. With a team that included some of the Spaniards, he was deep in the south of Russia, near Taganrog. It was an area of strategic importance, for it lay directly on the path of the German drive toward the oil fields of Baku. Starinov's men had begun their operations when the Gulf of Taganrog was still frozen solid. They were so busy that they had only taken forty-five minutes to celebrate the New Year before going back to work.

Their first attempt to strike behind enemy lines ended in failure. Halfway out on the ice they were caught in a fierce and sudden snowstorm. Some of the men did not return for a day, and, when they finally did, one of the Spaniards was barely able to part his frozen lips and say: "Muy frio."

A nd then there was the incident with the felt boot, *says Starinov*. One of the Spaniards, Angel, the leader of a patrol, fell in the snow and could feel his boot tangled in a wire. It could easily be a tension-action mine. The slightest attempt to remove his boot and the mine would explode, killing him and terminating the mission.

"Stop! It's a mine field!" Angel called out.

Holding the boot by the top, he carefully pulled out his foot. Then he got out a surprise mine from his bag, and just as carefully placed it in the boot. Then he wrapped his bare foot up with a scarf and, using a knapsack for a shoe, led the patrol on.

The group carried out its assignment of mining the road and returned safely to base.

A few days later a Russian who was working for the Germans deserted and came over to our side. He had a lot to tell, including the story of the felt boot. A German patrol noticed the strange object and the lieutenant ordered his men to retrieve it. Very painstakingly a German separated the boot from the trip wire and brought the spoils of war back to the shore. They took the small package, bound tightly with cord, from inside the boot. When they started cutting through the cord, the surprise bomb went off and they went to join their ancestors. After that we used to joke that Angel had figured out a way of kicking Nazis across the bay with just a felt boot!

Being with the Spaniards may have reminded Starinov of the lesson of the Trojan horse they had put to good use in Spain. But Russia had its legends, too; Russia had "Potemkin villages," named for Potemkin, the former lover of Catherine the Great, who had been ceded a vast province as his for services rendered. When Catherine decided to inspect the province under his governorship, Potemkin ordered all the fronts of the huts on her itinerary to be freshly whitewashed and all the peasants to be dressed in colorful folk costume, which would be torn from their backs as soon as the imperial coach had passed and be dispatched by special courier to the next village.

We pulled other tricks on the Germans too. One time, to sow some panic among them, we built a "Potemkin village." From scrap plywood, poles, wire, and bast matting our craftsmen built what looked like camouflaged tanks, trucks, howitzers, and so on. Even from a fairly short distance, half a kilometer, they looked like the real thing. On the night of February 26 we brought all those props onto the bay and positioned them about three kilometers from the enemy. About fifteen minutes after we'd pulled out, self-igniting matches began to go off. Of course, the Germans' searchlights converged on that "Potemkin village" and they opened fire furiously from field guns and mortars. To encourage the German gunners, we'd left matting soaked in kerosene, which the Germans' direct hits set on fire. They wasted a lot of artillery on that pile of junk!

But the bitter truth was also that Starinov's men still were not being supplied with sufficient men and matériel. The value of partisan warfare had yet to be fully acknowledged. The Red Army still had not seen what Starinov had made the Spanish command see—shells sometimes miss their mark, but mines always blow up just where they're supposed to.

Not to mention all the intelligence benefits that accrued from operating behind enemy lines:

One of our men found a notebook on a German officer who had been killed in a skirmish, and he brought that notebook to me. I couldn't make heads or tails of it. It looked like some kind of chemical formulas. I sent the notebook on to Moscow and it turned out that those were formulas for using uranium for atomic purposes. That officer had been in that recently captured territory looking for uranium deposits. This lucky find played its part in convincing the people up top to create a scientific center for studying the problems of atomic weapons.

Our men went behind enemy lines 110 times. Results were good. We killed more than a hundred soldiers and officers with our mines and rifles, put fifty Nazi trucks and two tanks out of commission, blew up seventy-four telephone and telegraph poles, two bridges, two barges, and four trucks with searchlights mounted on them. And all that forced them to bring up two additional infantry divisions to protect the shore.

As a reward for their service, the Spaniards were allowed to wear the uniform of the Red Army and were given ranks. Some of them requested to be sent to the front outside Leningrad, where Spanish Fascist troops, known as the "Blue Division," were fighting alongside the Germans. Their request was granted.

*

The battle for Stalingrad began in mid-July 1942 in all-too-familiar fashion, with the Russians doing their best to slow the German advance. On July 30, 1942, Stalin issued his orders: "Not a step back!" But the Red Army continued to yield until its back was to the Volga and the vast emptiness of the steppe. Because of its name, Stalingrad was a symbolic prize, because of its rail center a strategic objective, and because of its geography a last stand.

The battle for the city was joined on August 5, 1942. Once again the Germans possessed air and tank superiority, once again the Russian artillery was formidable and well situated on the islands and east bank of the Volga, which was over a mile wide near Stalingrad. The fury of the German onslaught reached its peak on August 23, when six hundred bombers attacked the city, killing forty thousand during one night. From a distance Stalingrad was a glow on a horizon made of steppe and sky. On September 3 the Germans had appeared on the outskirts of the city, which stretched for thirty miles along the Volga.

The Russian tanks from the factories that were evacuated to the Urals had performed very well, even though they were vastly outnumbered. But suddenly, by mid-September, the heavy weapons of war were no longer relevant. All fighting was within the burning city itself. In the rubble-choked streets of Stalingrad, tanks could no longer maneuver, wreckage became obstacle and barricade.

The battle of Stalingrad had become a bloody brawl fought with grenades, submachine guns, and bayonets. A Siberian regiment famed for its skill at throwing knives was even brought in. At first, the battles were for sections of the city, then for streets, then blocks, then buildings, then floors, and finally rooms.

Though the Russian soldiers now felt they were taking part in a legendary battle, they were still exhausted and only spottily supplied by the barges that made it across the Volga under heavy German air attack. And as the weather turned cold the river became less useful, the ice floes impeding the few barges that could slip across under cover of night. Not surprisingly, the Russians were ready for the oncoming cold, and, amazingly, the Germans were not. Arrogance had bifurcated the force of Hitler's intent, making him believe that he could take both the Caucasus and Stalingrad. Arrogance had kept the Germans from learning the lesson of Moscow—that a lightning war not won by winter will not be won at all. And the Germans had alienated the people in the towns outside Stalingrad, insulting the Russians by failing to even notice them, as if they were no more than horses in a meadow. And that turned civilians into partisans, glad to burn one building, shoot one German.

Still, the Germans seemed to be accomplishing their objective. They were moving swiftly through the Caucasus and had taken most of Stalingrad by mid-November. The Russians would be cut off from their supply of oil, the Germans having already severed rail traffic on the west bank of the Volga. But there was a system operating on the east bank. Reinforcements, tanks, and supplies flowed in for a counteroffensive, which began on November 19, 1942, the dimensions of which would catch the Germans by surprise.

In attempting to conquer Stalingrad and the Caucasus at once, Hitler had thinned out his best troops, his German troops, making up the numerical difference with Romanians and Italians, who did not fare well in the hostile vastness of the steppe. The frost ate at their discipline and fingertips. And when the Russian counteroffensive began with an immense barrage of artillery and Katyushas, it struck first at the weak Romanian–Italian flank.

Stalingrad was the turning point of the war, and the turning point of the battle itself took place between November 19 and December 11, when the Russian armies broke through those flanks and surrounded the city. The god of war perversely turned a victory into a death trap. Hermann Göring, the head of the German Air Force, assured Hitler that he could supply the German troops in Stalingrad with enough food and ammunition to hold out. Hitler ordered General Paulus, the commanding officer at Stalingrad, not to surrender; and, for whatever reasons, Paulus did not dare disobey.

December was fearfully cold, but the Russian tommy guns, stout little death-dispensers known as Pepeshas, could spray nine hundred bullets a minute in any weather. It was house-to-house, hand-to-hand again. Snipers dueled, the Germans even flying in Heinz Thorwald, the head of their sniper school at Zossen. After a four-day duel with a Russian sniper, the German, thinking he had made his kill, raised his head slightly and was instantly shot dead by the Russian.

Göring's airlift proved an empty boast, a drug addict's megolomania; by late December Paulus observed his men eating raw horse brains. To their honor as soldiers, the Germans fought bitterly to the end, which came on January 31, when Paulus surrendered. Hundreds of thousands of German, Romanian, and Italian prisoners were marched east across the steppe to atone for their sins with their labor and their lives. Precious few returned. In attacking the Caucasus and Stalingrad simultaneously, Hitler had gone double or nothing, but this time the wheel had stopped at double zero. The house had won.

*

The Russians had paid a fearful price in life for this great victory, but their armies were continually being replenished, among others by Natalya Viktorovna, who did not in the least appreciate being laughed at when she volunteered for the front and who was not in the least deterred by those rejections. "I had decided that I absolutely had to see war. And what kind of a mother can you be to a son when you're heart-stricken yourself? One way or the other, I had to put myself back together again."

She wangled her way into the army in classic Russian fashion, in which the forms are strictly observed while the rule is being circumvented. She now had a diploma in journalism, and after learning that the army was looking for people for its newspaper, she talked her way in. The officer had blank IDs and filled one out for her. Inducted or not, Natalya Viktorovna was now in the Red Army.

She was issued a uniform and was soon bounding along in the one-and-a-half-ton truck that carried a small newspaper staff and printing press, a "publisher on wheels."

There was a new man working on the paper, Novikov. He knew nothing about newspapers and could barely read himself. He was always being humiliated. I felt sorry for him. I was nice to him, showed him the ropes.

Then all of a sudden because Novikov was a party member they put him in charge of the division newspaper. And, oh, what a bastard he turned out to be!

He treated me like dirt and used the foulest language.

One night I brought him a copy of the first run of the newspaper to sign. This was very important, you could be shot for one little mistake.

"Any mistakes?" he says to me.

"I don't think so."

"Check the headlines again, you cunt."

Since I'm nearsighted, I bent forward.

"Stand at attention, you cunt!"

I'm a soldier, I obeyed orders, I stood at attention.

"Read the headlines!"

I bent forward.

"Attention, you stupid cunt!"

This went on for quite a while, him speaking to me like that, until finally I just could not bear it another instant. I ran out to our truck, grabbed my rifle, and was on my way back to blow his head off when a few of the other journalists caught up with me, grabbed me and locked me in the back of the truck, saying, "He's not worth it, not worth it."

Natalya Viktorovna was at war.

*

After Stalingrad, the German armies in the Caucasus melted away, but only to regroup for what would have to be their single greatest thrust of the war. Colonel Starinov was no longer needed on the Caucasus front, which had ceased to exist, but wherever it was the Germans would strike next.

No one doubted that the Germans would seek revenge for Stalingrad and attempt to seize the initiative again, *says Starinov.* And everyone agreed that the most likely place for this to occur was around Kursk in the Ukraine, where the German position was very strong. Still, those were only guesses.

I was recalled to Moscow and appointed deputy chief of the Ukrainian front's partisan movement in anticipation of a battle in the Kursk area. I was able to spend a few days at home in Moscow with Anna and my children. For a while, when the Spaniards had begun fighting with us, Anna had been pressed into service as an interpreter, but now she was back home.

At first I was so happy to be home I didn't notice anything. But at dinner I could tell there was something Anna wasn't saying. She waited until the children were in bed to tell me about our Spanish comrades who had died in the fighting, including Angel, who we used to joke had a felt boot that could kick Germans across a whole bay. And so our first reunion after so long a separation turned out to be joyless for us. Enemy dead can't bring your friends back to life.

But for those in the camps, war meant at least a chance to die with honor. Many of them volunteered. Revekka, now in a camp in northern Kazakhstan, almost as far as China, wished to fight for her country as did the others in her situation.

B ut they wouldn't take us. They took common criminals, they took professional criminals, but they didn't trust us.

We kicked up a row over it—if you're going to die, at least do it defending your country, not freezing to death in the steppes of Kazakhstan. But us they wouldn't take.

My reserves were gone. I had already tried suicide three times. I knew I had nothing left to draw on now and would be dead before the year was out.

Then one day the guard in charge of work assignments calls me and says to me, "Alright, dark eyes, I'm going to tell you a little secret, but one word about it to anyone and your life's not worth a kopeck. We've gotten orders to release women who are disabled or who have children. So here's your choice—either cut off a finger or move in with me. Soon as your child's born, you're free. And I'll give you a fur jacket and a skirt to wear in the meantime.''

I found him repellent, but I didn't give him an answer on the spot. I had to think about it. I knew the only thing that mattered was to survive. To live, to live at any cost.

*

Partisan warfare was at last being treated seriously, which meant Starinov now spent all his time in planning sessions in Moscow. In preparation for the battle of Kursk, he was given one final grace, one last sally behind enemy lines.

I t was a horrible feeling—we were flying over enemy lines and all of a sudden the Germans caught us in their searchlights. The pilot went into a dive that sent us all flying. Finally he got away from those searchlights. And then people started cracking jokes. But that didn't last long either. The nights were short in June and it was already starting to get light. Our unarmed plane would be easy pickings for any German fighter.

But then the landing lights were spotted and we set down in a large clearing by a birch woods. Partisans came running out of the birch woods, some of them in uniform and some in leather jackets they'd taken off dead Germans.

You could see they were the masters of that territory just by the way they brought us to their camp. They had a big table set up for breakfast in an open meadow. And we all had a wonderful breakfast.

I ran into an old friend there and we talked, but somehow we never got onto the subject of the generals we had both served under and who had been executed. And that cost me sleep that night, which I spent on hay in a tent made of parachute silk. I never got a chance to continue that conversation, my friend was gone the next day, *says Starinov with a grimace of regret.*

My assignment was to teach the partisans how to blow up trains and track. But how was I supposed to do that when the nearest railroad was miles away? The partisan leader suggested we have a look at their test range in the woods. I laughed to myself—what kind of test range could they have here? I figured the partisan leader was pulling my leg, so I went along with the gag. Sure, I said, let's have a look at the test range.

I couldn't believe my eyes—they'd built a perfect stretch of track along a perfect embankment, rails, ties, the whole works!

And the partisan leader says, "It's not the Moscow line but still it's something . . ."

Colonel Starinov went right to work imparting the secrets of demolition to able and avid pupils who in only a few days' time would be tested in the field of battle. But Starinov would not be there to hear the explosions or feel the shock waves through the grain. He was summoned back to Moscow, taking with him the assurance that the partisans would inflict serious damage that would help win the coming battle and win as well greater glory for their branch of arms. And the memories were nearly all good—breakfast in the meadow, the magical embankment, rails gleaming in the birch woods.

Everyone expected the attack to come at Kursk and everyone was right. There the Soviet front formed an overextended bulge into German-held territory, the contour of victory suggesting the next defeat. If the bulge was severed, surrounded, and destroyed, the loss in blood and morale could be sufficient once again to turn the tide in German favor.

The battle began on July 5, 1943. Though tanks, planes, and artillery had played their part at Stalingrad, in the end what counted were the soldiers. Stalingrad was a battle of armies, Kursk of armor. As usual, Russian artillery was liberal and lethal, and as usual the Germans had control of the air, their Stuka dive-bombers having sensed the soft spot of the Russian tanks—their rear ventilators. But as the tanks, three thousand on either side, closed in a series of battles, neither artillery nor air power was of any further use. It was just tank against tank, shell against armor. The air, thick with smoke, would suddenly clear, and then it was only a question of whose turret swiveled faster.

The battle lasted nearly seven weeks, until the Russian

victory was so clear that Stalin could order the great guns to boom earthshaking salvos on Red Square. What remained now for Russia was liberation, vengeance, and the spoils.

On August 23, the last day of the battle, the city of Kharkov was retaken from the Germans. It was important that this second largest Ukrainian city be back under Soviet control, both because of the area's industry and agriculture and for morale. And it was important to Colonel Starinov for another reason—he could check on the results of a certain experiment.

It was frustrating work, he so seldom got to see the results of his handiwork: a hollow roar in the distance, a flash like summer lightning seen through trees. Now he was going to be able to determine whether their ruse had outwitted the Germans as far as concealment was concerned and whether the detonator had been activated by the radio signal.

Their logic had been sound—the head of the force controlling a city lives in the best house. Khrushchev had lived at 17 Dzerzhinsky Street when the city was in Soviet hands, and someone of equal importance would replace him when the city fell to the Germans. The Red Army had fled in a hurry from Kharkov and may not have had sufficient time to plant many mines, but the Germans would of course operate on the assumption that important installations, like that fine house, would have been turned into time bombs. It was important to conceal the decoy weapon well enough so that his German counterpart would be satisfied that he had located the threat. The real bomb was planted deep in the foundations of the house, the decoy concealed in a pile of coal in the cellar directly above. Starinov had counted on the enemy thinking that not even a Russian would be dumb enough to place the two bombs right together. And he was still counting on it as he made his impatient way through the streets of Kharkov.

I could see that Dzerzhinsky Street hadn't suffered much. Except for one spot where there was a huge pit full of water surrounded by rubble and smashed chestnut trees. Number 17.

The people who lived in the house next door told me that a Nazi general had moved in there. A week later they were woken up in the middle of the night by a terrible shock and explosion. It was raining stones, they said.

Afterwards they went out and saw there was nothing left there, as if the earth had swallowed up the building. German motorcycles and soldiers and firemen had come racing over. They fought the fire, they put out the fire, but even after two days of looking they couldn't find any trace of the officers and men who had been living in there. Pieces of the piano ended up on the roof of the house next door.

As a professional soldier, Starinov made a mental note of all the eyewitness details, which did not prevent him in the least from savoring that description of his dream come true—a building full of German officers blown to atoms in the terrible suddenness that is explosion.

S everal days later I was asked to come to Front Headquarters where there'd be a surprise waiting for me. The surprise turned out to be Captain Karl Geiden, a German captain who had been directly involved in clearing mines from the house at 17 Dzerzhinsky Street. He told me that they found the mine in the coal pile but since they knew it could detonate in any number of different ways they worked very slowly on it. It took them almost two days to get it out.

Even though this Captain Geiden is keeping his eyes down all the time, and you can bet that was not something he did before, he still says he was surprised that the mine could be detonated by a radio signal—even the German army doesn't have mines like that.

So I said to him, "You still think the German army has better everything?"

"I'm sorry, Colonel," he says, "it's just a habit."

Russia had had its great victory, and now Starinov had had his.

*

After Kharkov, each week was a harvest of victories. From "Not a Step Back" at Stalingrad it was now "On to Berlin." But in a tragic land even victory brings tragedy to some. Raisa Danilovna, who had almost lost her arm and her life to shrapnel shortly after volunteering as an army nurse, had been clinging to life by doing road clearance for the Germans, who paid in meager rations. And now when they began to retreat they took her with them.

The Germans didn't beat us. Why should they beat us? We worked. We cleared roads. They didn't beat us. They fed us, of course just enough to keep you from starving to death.

They sent us to Germany and put us to work in a factory that made boots for the army. Then they switched us to a labor camp and I worked in the kitchen there because I could speak German. I had no great fear about going to Germany—I thought that if I hadn't died when I was hit by shrapnel, I wouldn't die in Germany either.

But being hit by shrapnel had really put the fear in me. I never felt fear like that again until the Americans started bombing Germany. That was terrible, that American bombing, day after day! To escape the bombing, a friend and I tried to escape to Switzerland and we made it nearly all the way. I had only one desire, to stay alive.

The Soviet secret police would soon find her allegiance to life treason to her country.

*

Natalya Viktorovna was now writing for the division's newspaper under the pen name of Nikolai Viktorov. All the journalists knew instinctively what to say and what not to, an instinct as essential to their survival as a sniper's knowing when and when not to raise his head. Everyone had heard the legend of the editor who had overlooked a misprint that turned "Stalin, Commander in Chief," into "Stalin, Commander of Crap," and who had paid for that oversight with his life.

Natalya had wanted to see the war with her own eyes, those nearsighted and oddly shaped eyes, whose pupils seemed to be standing on end.

Fortunately, our division commander insisted we always be right there where the fighting was. He was a Georgian, Koladzė, a man of absolutely insane courage. When it came time to attack and the men would be hanging back, he would calmly draw his pistol and walk forward into the attack. Him, all alone, with just a pistol. And the men would rise and go after him.

But then of course you must remember that there were secret police machine gun units behind the troops that would shoot anyone trying to flee the field of battle.

Ten or twelve miles from the front, death is still the exception, but near the front, and at the front itself, life becomes the exception.

I was interested in what people laughed at in war. A Polish army had been formed in the USSR and there was a good joke about it. That was supposed to be the real Polish army, Catholic, with priests as chaplains. So the priest gives a soldier the cross to kiss. He says, "Take your oath, son, and kiss the cross." But the soldier says, "I can't do it, holy father, I'm in the Young Communists." And the priest says, "Kiss the cross, you motherfucker, I'm in the party fifteen years myself."

But the laughing stopped for Natalya when her division arrived in Praga, a section of Warsaw on the other, eastern side of the Vistula River from the central city. Stalin, a man of several obsessions, was definitely obsessed with the fate of Poland. The war had begun with Russia and Germany dividing Poland and it would end with Poland totally under Russian control. To ensure that end, in 1940 the Soviet secret police had executed fifteen thousand Polish officers who had been held as prisoners of war, thereby destroying the most likely source of any resistance to Soviet postwar aims. A second decision in the Polish progression was to allow the Germans to suppress the Warsaw Uprising of August 1 through October 2, 1944, and to systematically detonate, block by chalk-marked block, whole portions of the city so that from the air Warsaw would seem a moon of ashes and scorched steel.

The Red Army encamped on the right bank of the Vistula did nothing to help.

That was the worst it ever got for me. The solitude of it was hideous. We were on the right bank of the Vistula and had total control of the territory. The Germans were pulling out and it wouldn't have cost anything to cross the river and help the people in the uprising. And every night they sent in little biplanes, which dropped medicine and weapons. That is, to prolong the agony.

I had to keep silent, which is what anyone would have done in my place. But I knew.

It was forbidden to speak of true evil, or true good for that matter.

This only happened one time, *says Natalya.* We were near a small town that had to be taken. I knew where the battle was to take place and I went there. And what do I see—the regiment that's supposed to take the town are all sitting in a field under trees and their commanding officer is sitting there with them. That surprised me and I went over to the CO and I said, "What's going on?" And he said, "Listen, you, keep your trap shut. I sent out scouts and they told me the Germans are pulling out. Why should I send men to their death?"

Of course that was something that should have been written up but I had to keep silent then too. As if he had committed a horrible crime, sparing human life.

*

Partisan demolition had played a pivotal role in the great battle of Kursk. But this was a Soviet victory, it had to be not only won but proven. Starinov's commanding officer understood that point quite clearly.

He ordered me to form a group to compile facts and figures on the effects of partisan actions on the liberated territories of the Ukraine, chiefly their effect on the railroads behind enemy lines.

"We have to compile figures on the damage the partisans inflicted while everything's still fresh. We need that information so we can know what ways and means to take in future partisan warfare," said my commanding officer.

"No one has any doubts on that score in our staff, Comrade General!" I said.

"In our staff, no, but some of the other comrades might have some doubts. We need facts in hand to prove our case."

He put me in charge. It was a huge job, but we got it done in a relatively short period of time thanks to the party and Soviet organizations that had been reformed on the liberated territories.

We inspected over nine thousand miles of track. We interviewed people who had been there—trackmen, switchmen, engineers, firemen, and the local population. But the best information came from the Germans themselves. They had kept scrupulous records of every partisan attack—time, date, losses suffered in track, rolling stock, number of regular army and officers wounded and killed. The Germans had obligingly done our work for us.

I was sent to Poland, after we had liberated it, to train partisan detachments there, and then I was transferred to Yugoslavia. Finally, I was sent to Germany. We weren't setting mines anymore then. Our job now was clearing the mines the Germans had laid. And that meant final victory wasn't far off.

Revekka was also about to win a victory of her own, and like everything she now did it was a curious mixture of virtue and guile. She had decided not to sleep with the guard who had told her of the new regulations concerning women and who had advised her either to cut off a finger or move in with him. He took his revenge by making her a milkmaid.

He liked the idea of a cultured woman milking cows. It was very hard work. I had seventeen cows to keep track of, take out to pasture, and milk. But this also meant that I could slip my friends a cup of milk each day and for some of them that was the difference between life and death.

Then one day disaster struck—one of the cows was missing. That would mean a punishment battalion, and that I couldn't take. There was an Asiatic people, the Chechens, who Stalin had exiled en masse to Kazakhstan and who lived on the other side of the river. If they spotted a stray cow they'd lasso it like an American cowboy and drag it over to their side of the river.

I figured that was what happened. I grabbed a horse and went out looking for the cow. I rode and I rode, galloping through the steppe, but I couldn't find the cow. Fortunately, it had come back by itself in the meantime.

There was a young guard who had served at the front before being sent to work at the camp. I'd known him for about two years. He was young, good-looking, well-mannered. He had been very worried about me galloping all alone through the steppe. When I came back, he said, "I'm never going to let you go riding off like that again!"

And so I said to myself, Having a child by him wouldn't be so bad. The child would give me a reason to live, force me to survive. And so I began sleeping with that kind young man.

Revekka could win her way back to life and freedom, but there were a lot of ifs—if the regulations didn't change, if the guard she rejected didn't seek further revenge, if she could conceive a child there in the camp and bring it to term and keep it alive until it was strong enough to travel. A whole year of ifs.

Under my pen name of Nikolai Viktorov, *says Natalya Viktorovna*, I wrote some pieces about wartime humor for that worthless rag of ours. War distorts your sense of humor and you laugh at things you shouldn't laugh at. By then we were crossing the Oder River into Germany. The crossing was of strategic significance and so there was an entire antiaircraft regiment there to protect us. We now had complete supremacy in the air.

Then out of nowhere a single German plane comes flying up. Of course, the antiaircraft guns set up such a terrific barrage that the plane couldn't get anywhere near us. It wheeled around and started flying away. Just as the order for the cease-fire was given, one of the gunners got off a last shot. A direct hit! The plane fell, bombs and all, onto the command post of the 38th Division. Blew it to smithereens. That kept the army laughing for days.

The Russian soldiers were raping every German female from eight to eighty. It was an army of rapists. Not only because they were crazed with lust, this was also a form of vengeance. Those soldiers had now seen what the Germans had done to their land—the burned-out villages, the partisans hung in the squares, people herded off to Germany as slave labor.

The Russian soldiers robbed every German man and killed most of them too, and they raped all the females. They only knew two expressions in German—*"Frau, komm"* and *"Uhr,"* meaning wristwatch. In those days, it was still rare for a Russian to own a wristwatch.

Stalin knew the value of the medieval custom of giving a captured city over to the soldiers for three days of rape and looting. It's very good for the soldiers' spirit.

But after those few days it would all be brought to a stop with an iron hand. And then the officers would begin having mad, passionate affairs with the German women. So much Slavic blood was mixed with German . . .

There were jokes about all that too. A soldier is demobilized and sent home from Germany. His wife welcomes her conquering hero home. They have a great meal and they drink and then they go to bed. But he can't get it up. So, he says to her, "Get out of bed." She gets out of bed. "Get dressed," he says, and she gets dressed. "Now," he says, "put up a fight."

One time we went into a house in Germany and saw that it had beautiful furniture and a radio and lace napkins. To

a Russian it looked incredibly fancy. Then we found out that
the house belonged to a shepherd! Now Russians had seen the
world a little and had a new standard to measure by. And just
because they knew too much, many of those Russian soldiers
were sent immediately to the Gulag.

It's like the joke about the American gangster. The big
boss asks one of his men, "Bob, how much is two times two?"
"Four," says Bob. The boss shoots him dead and says, "He
knew too much."

We'd linked up with the Americans by then. The officers
were drinking together. The Americans would go into a
German farmer's house and ask for sausage. If they didn't get
it, they'd fire off a burst into the ceiling, to show they meant
business.

As a private, Natalya Viktorovna could only look on as the officers
fraternized. Perhaps that fraternization had been a gift from Stalin
to his officers, like the raping and looting was to the soldiers. In
any case, it didn't last long either, ending with an abruptness that
signaled the highest authority.

Stalin, who carved out Eastern Europe for himself at Yalta,
was now busily deceiving his allies. He did not want to share the
glory of taking Berlin, nor the power that would accrue from it.
Besides, it was only just—the Russians had done the real fighting,
the real bleeding, the real killing. The Allies hadn't even opened
up a second front until June 1944, and by then Russia had been
cleared of Nazis. Stalin wanted to go down in history with Berlin
pinned to his chest.

Pretending to agree with Eisenhower's strategy of cutting
Germany in half at Dresden, Stalin sent two armies headed by rival
generals toward Berlin, still ruled by Adolph Hitler. By then Hitler was living in an underground bunker, where he moved flags of
nonexistent armies and seemed happiest when petting his new dog,
Wolf. Much of the fighting was now being done by the young and
the old, a grandfather holding an antitank weapon in a city-street
trench, his grandson beside him with a rifle.

The Russians were fighting differently now, both more cautiously and with more ardor, to get it over with. Russians were still dying, and there is always a special sadness in being killed late in a war. There were still strong German troops defending Berlin and they had good reason for fighting hard—better to surrender to the Americans and British than to the Russians. Learning of the Russian army's intention to blind them with searchlights turned horizontal and then subject them to furious artillery, the Germans simply withdrew and allowed the Soviet shells to churn the ground. But that barrage of fifteen thousand guns, which had thundered so mightily and then came to such a sheer and vertiginous halt, could be repeated as many times as necessary. Russian soldiers were already avenging their grandmothers on the outskirts of the city. The Berlin Zoo came under shelling. The cages were hit. Zebras raced the streets of Berlin, flamingos rose above burning cathedrals.

Hitler committed suicide on the very last day of April, an act containing an implicit vow—through April but not a single day of May. For of course May would bring the fall of Berlin, of Germany, of everything. By May 3 it was over and the guns began falling back into their ponderous silence.

Natalya Viktorovna was to the north of Berlin, where she could feel the peace gradually settling in.

"At the time we were staying in an absolutely beautiful house. It even had a bidet, which I knew about only from reading. It was an architect's house. The architect had fled but the maid had stayed on. And every day at seven o'clock when I got up she was already dusting and cleaning. There wasn't a speck of dust anywhere but she was forever dusting the figurines. The war was as good as over, I'd seen everything I'd wanted to. Even the bushes didn't grow right in Germany. I was getting terribly homesick. It was all too much for a Russian person. Those figurines!"

The war was over for Natalya Viktorovna and for Colonel Starinov, the war was over for Russia and Germany, and the war was over for the world. But the fighting was never over for Starinov. There was always plenty to fight for—to demonstrate in lectures, articles, and books the significance of partisan warfare and demolition, thereby, in some war, atoning for his own sin of doubt against the innocent.

"Four wars, not bad," says Starinov, who even near ninety is still bluff and hearty, rubbing his wounds like old dogs. But now he has the sense that death is closing in on him, maneuvering in ways that are eerily familiar. He counterattacks with a light, healthy diet and joie de vivre and by marching twice a year in the big parades through Red Square—May Day and Revolution Day, November 7.

"I have lots of medals. I was awarded the Order of the October Revolution and the Order of the Great Patriotic War, Second Class, many, many medals. But I only put them on for May Day. In November you need a topcoat. Who's going to see all your medals?" he says, and only after a taut second of silence does Starinov detonate with laughter.

Bad Blood
(1945–1953)

Having wangled her way into the army, Natalya Viktorovna now wangled her way out.

I ran to the infirmary but I was limping when I came through the door. I told them my bone tuberculosis was giving me trouble again and they were glad to discharge me right on the spot.

By then I was staying in another fancy house, one crammed with Japanese porcelain. The owner must have dealt in it. I had a very small handbag, and I decided to take a miniature coffee service, a tiny pot, and six cups as small as flower petals. And the guys in our press unit had given me a present—a ring with a large sapphire, probably from some looted store. And so, apart from a few clothes in my knapsack, that's all I had with me when I started home.

There was only one way back to Russia, by hopping a ride in a freight car. Waiting in the yard for a train bound east Natalya was approached by a man of about thirty-five, who was there for the same reason she was.

W here are you going?" he says.
"Home," I say, "I've been discharged."
"Me too," he says. "Let's travel together, it'll be easier that way."
"Why not," I say.
Then out of the blue he says, "Give me that ring as a present."
I took off the ring and gave it to him. It was nothing I needed. He was no officer, a soldier, maybe a sergeant, who the hell knows. Anyway, we climbed up onto an open platform car that was carrying rails, girders, something made of steel. Rough traveling. We had a special way of sleeping. You take off your overcoat and use it as a blanket, one sleeve rolled up for a pillow and the other over your head to keep it warm, your knees tucked up.
Anyway, I gave him a ring. And then he starts proposing.
"Are you alone? Do you have anyone?" he says.
"No, no one."
"Where are you going?"
"Leningrad."
"You have a room there?"
"No, my room was taken."
"Listen, come live with me, marry me. We'll have a good life."
He was such a likable guy. And it was a long trip too. Sometimes we had to sit on the couplings between train cars. We'd sit there on the couplings with our legs dangling down over the tracks. One slip and it's all over. We'd hold on to each other. It made for quite an interesting trip.
But he was simple, much too simple, from some small town in the middle of Russia, and that's even worse than a village. But he seemed serious about saying that he loved me

and wanted to marry me. He was even starting to make plans for us.

"What do you mean?" I said. "I've got plans of my own."

"What kind of plans can you have, a woman alone with a kid? Get your kid from the Children's Home and we'll have a good life together. I'm in love with you."

But I shrugged it off with a laugh.

"What's that in your suitcase?" he said.

"A beautiful porcelain coffee service that I like very much."

By the time we got to Russia our train was unloaded and we could ride on a flatcar again. He was going to start heading for somewhere in the Ukraine. And he was very tender in saying good-bye to me.

"It's still not too late, won't you come with me?"

"No," I said, "I won't."

He climbed down from the flatcar, which was just starting to move, and he walked alongside it. He was almost crying and he was looking at me with such love in his eyes, saying, "Come on, let's go, change your mind, you'll be happy with me."

"No," I said. "Good-bye, and good luck."

He stopped, letting the train take me away. Then all of a sudden he breaks into a run until he catches back up with the flatcar. Then what does he do—he steals my suitcase.

I couldn't stop laughing.

Raisa, who had been taught by the suddenness of her wound that only living mattered, was also returning home. But there was no laughing for her. She was about to taste a bitterness that would infuriate her for the rest of her life.

The Americans and the French came around asking people, Do you want to go home or not? And I say, I want to go home. They put us on a train to Hungary. And then the interrogations started. I never felt anything more humiliating than that suspicion.

"How come you survived?" said the secret police. "How is it you survived? You're a Soviet woman, you should have been killed, not survive and work for the Germans. Why did you work for the Germans? How did you end up in Germany? You should never have gone to Germany. You should have been killed."

It was so humiliating. It was so deeply insulting, *she says, as her tears flow down a face stony with unforgiving anger.*

*

Revekka's son survived birth in the Gulag.

B ut when he was four months, he was near death, they weren't even letting me feed him. He had to live, he was my reason to live, without him I'd never get out of there. I begged the doctors for help. They helped, my son survived.

When he was five months old, I received my release. But it said that I had to live by the camp and work in it as a civilian employee.

"No," I said, "I have the right to leave. I have a child. And you have no right to keep me here."

Three weeks later I was issued a new release stating my place of exile.

By then it was November and freezing cold. I was going to have to travel twenty-five miles by horse to the railroad station. All the other women were yelling at me, "You barbarian, you madwoman, where are you going with a child, you'll both freeze to death on the way."

But when I said I was leaving they tore up their blouses and skirts for diapers and swaddling.

The station was packed with soldiers who'd been discharged. Even the officers were sleeping on the floor.

The train starts to pull in. I can see that the steps are very high and covered with ice. There's a rush for the train. I know I don't stand a chance of ever getting on. Some officers were lining up to one side. I ran over to them and I said,

"If you men don't get me on this train, I'm throwing myself and my baby under the wheels."

And I said it with such sincere determination that they picked me and the baby right up and carried us onto the train.

Stalin had done enough trusting for a lifetime. Now he betrayed both alliances that he forged during the war—the one with the Allies and the one with the Russian people. The Americans had the atomic bomb and that made them a superior power. To be allied with them meant to be in an inferior position. There would be a secret project to build an A-bomb, overseen by Lavrenty Beria, the head of the secret police, and sparked by the brilliant, patriotic young physicist Andrei Sakharov.

And the country had been twice destroyed, once by retreating Russians, then again by retreating Germans. The track Colonel Starinov had blown was Soviet track, and the dams the partisans destroyed even included the great hydroelectric Dnieper Dam that Ilya Jaffee had gone off to build in the flower of his youth.

But now, Ilya Jaffee was no longer what he had always thought himself to be, a "typical representative of the rank and file Stalinist intelligentsia." Having thrust all doubt aside when throwing himself into the production of the tanks that won the Battle of Kursk, Ilya now experienced his first crisis of faith since the reading of Darwin and the sight of his father being crippled by the Whites had converted him from Judaism to communism.

He could no longer hide the truth from himself. "Stalin was a psychopathic criminal. But what could I do? One wrong word and I'd disappear, just disappear.

"When the people around Tsar Pavel realized that he was insane they simply strangled him. Out of all of us, there wasn't even one capable of strangling Stalin.

"It was clear as day. There was nothing I could do till Stalin croaked."

I love you, I love you, I love you, and then he steals my suitcase, *says Natalya Viktorovna, her fragile shoulders bobbing with laughter.* In Russia the men think women were born to be lied to and tricked. It's an honor for a man to deceive a woman. There was even a little joke they used to tell at the front about a girl bragging that she'd tricked a soldier. She'd let him sleep with her but she wasn't going to marry him.

Russians are great liars. First of all, because it was always necessary to lie to the authorities and the bureaucrats. That's not just a Soviet trait, but an age-old Russian one. Russians have no respect for the law because they think it's only a tool in the hands of the masters. Every Russian knows the saying—The law's a wagon, it goes where you turn it. Russians take an almost aesthetic pleasure in beating the system. Even Stalin couldn't break them of the habit.

It took ten days to travel from Germany to Leningrad. There I found out that after my husband's death our room had been taken over by a KGB man.

I had always liked that communal apartment, which had eight families living in eight rooms. The people there had realized that you had to live in peace, to give in every so often. There were arguments of course, but not too many . . .

I went to the building's administration office. The woman there remembered me from before the war.

"Listen," she says, "the KGB man who took over your room has another apartment, he's keeping this one as a spare."

"Do you know the address?" I say.

"No, just the street."

I went to the office which had a list of all addresses. I gave them his name and the name of his street. But they couldn't give me the address or his telephone—they were classified since he was in the KGB.

And so I went to that street. It was a big street with one seven-story building after the other. I started going house by house. For about fifteen days, like a detective, I kept going into courtyards and telling people that I was this man's relative until I finally found out where he lived. I also found out that he had two wives, two families—one in the country, and another in this part of town.

It was a time when people became complete animals or

else displayed extraordinary humanity. I went back to the housing bureau where I was given papers indicating that the man who was registered to live in my room had a two- or three-room apartment in another part of town.

Then I took those papers to the district housing administration. The section was run by a plump blonde covered with makeup. Everyone in Leningrad was lean and hungry after the siege and there she was like a fatted calf. There was another man there too, a middle-aged soldier who'd been discharged for illness and was now also trying to get his room back.

"No," she says, very official, "you have no grounds to claim that living space."

And that was even after I'd explained that the KGB man had an apartment as well as my room. She wouldn't hear of it. And the soldier was such a meek sort that he was already getting up to leave. I realized cursing the bitch out wouldn't do any good, and so I said to the soldier, "Say, listen, which front were you at?"

"The second Belorussian."

"Me too," I say. "And did you ever think when you were in the trenches with the bullets flying past your head that this would be the sort of welcome you'd get in your own home town?"

He picked up on it right away and, paying no attention to her, we started telling each other where we had been and what we had been through.

Then tears started coming to her eyes. Maybe she'd lost someone, a brother, a father. She wrote us both out residence certificates, him for his room, me for mine. She was a real bureaucratic bitch, but even her heart wasn't entirely dead.

In the beginning of August, after three months, I got my room back. There was nothing in it except for two chairs and a metal trunk. The windows were boarded up with plywood. It was dark except for a small, bare bulb dangling on a cord.

The electricity was back on in Leningrad by then. The

buildings that had been damaged by shelling were being torn down quickly. Pictures of windows were painted on the plywood covering the broken glass so that the city would look a little nicer. There was an invasion of rats. All the cats had disappeared during the siege of Leningrad, when people would pay two hundred rubles for a cat. Now the rats were fat from feeding on corpses. People had been dying in their homes and sometimes it was days before the corpses were taken away.

I don't know about other cities but the amnesty had caused Leningrad to flood with criminals who were cutting people's throats in broad daylight. They had daggers made of sharpened steel files and they'd say to a woman, Hand over your fur coat. People were afraid to get involved. The criminals also had razor blades between their fingers and would slash the eyes of anyone who tried to interfere. Still, people who had fought at the front in hand-to-hand combat would sometimes band together and deal with these crooks, either killing them right there on the spot or dragging them off to the police.

The streets of the city were mostly empty. Having survived the war, Leningrad was empty and beautiful.

At the beginning, people's spirits were good. There was enthusiasm for rebuilding the country, which was in ruins from the western border to the Volga River. But the squeeze was put on the peasants, and city people were on rations. The country was both becoming richer and poorer at the same time. People thought life was going to be better after the war. There was a certain unity among the people, hope that the pressure was going to be lifted. But quite soon it was clear that nothing would be any better.

Ivan Vrachov, who had supported Trotsky because he believed that to be Lenin's behest and who had defied Stalin to his face, had not been killed during the Terror, and his luck held during the war as well. His tainted background forced him to enlist as a private, pretending he had lost his draft card, some of the niceties being overlooked in those first chaotic days of war. By the time of the victory Vrachov had worked his way up to sergeant major. But the staunch Leninist did not like what he saw in Stalin's army.

M y years in the army were a time of great moral suffering for me. I saw so many monstrous shortcomings. I saw the inexperience of the new commanding officers replacing those who had been wiped out before the war. People held posts that were not in keeping with their training and experience. I could not accept the disappearance of the Red Army's spirit. Gold braid and aides-de-camp were introduced. And vodka for the fighting men—why did they need to waste grain and labor on making vodka for the fighting men, who never got much of it anyway? Most of it either rotted in warehouses or was drunk up by officers cavorting in cushy jobs at the rear. The nation was going hungry and grain was being used for vodka. We never had anything like that during the Civil War.

Stalin had corrupted everything, even that beautiful instrument, the Red Army. This only stiffened Vrachov's resolve to outlast the bastard. He was going to need all that resolve because arrest, which had somehow overlooked him in the thirties, caught up with him after the war.

Ivan Vrachov disappeared into the camps without ever learning that Revekka, who had so loved him as a girl, was alive, living with her two children, the one she had had with her husband, who was executed in the Terror, and the one she had had to win her freedom from death and the Gulag.

Revekka had returned to life and was herself again, her father's daughter. "Papa always said the working class is the healthiest element of society. Yes, sometimes they're crude, but they always know what's what, what really counts. Put your faith in the working class, he used to say."

Now she did more than put her faith in it, she joined it, disappeared in it, found security in that mass of kerchiefed women and workers with grey caps tugged over one eye. Now she had good reason to live—to stay alive for her children and to keep her children alive.

Everything else could wait. Clearing her father's name could wait. Had to wait. For that could never be done as long as Stalin was alive, Stalin who had slipped into their box at the Bolshoi, his tiger-yellow eyes mesmerizing Revekka.

*

During the celebrations of the victory the sky over the Kremlin had exploded with fireworks and the sidewalks had overflowed with the piss of ten thousand drunks. Between prison and exile, Ruth Bonner had illegally visited her daughter Elena in Moscow. "All Moscow was celebrating the victory. My daughter's room was packed with young people, some of them in uniform, some not. Oh, what young lions they all were. But I was absolutely alienated from all of it and all of them. Absolutely alienated."

The only people with whom she felt even the slightest affinity were those soldiers who had seen the horrors of war, of which they never spoke. But war was at least war, the camps were a horror of a higher order and she had seen it all. All faith was burned out of her. Ruth slipped away into her exile before anyone could report her.

I t was the era of the stool pigeon, *says Natalya Viktorovna, her arthritic hands shaking slightly as she lights another cigarette, the oversize oval black stone in her ring bobbing.* They were trying to recruit everyone. Apparently, their pool of stoolies had dried up. Especially in Leningrad, where the siege and the war had taken a colossal number of lives. And so they started trying to recruit everyone. Everyone in our group, all my close friends, and me too.

A person could refuse. You just had to flat out refuse. What happened to me was that I took a job with State Publishing. The editor in chief, as he called himself, was an old secret police man. And of course he was still working for the secret police. But he wasn't on staff now as he had been before. He reminded me of a hyena. He even looked like one. But he had his good side too and could even be quite human.

I hadn't been working there long when he said to me, "We need informers. If you're a good Soviet . . ."

"I'm not going to inform," I said. "I was at the front, I volunteered, I've proved I love my country. Of course, if I hear of a plot against Stalin's life or something of that sort, I'll come right in and tell you."

He even came to my room to try to recruit me. One time my lover was there and threw the man out, kicked him down the stairs. I didn't know what to think. The man was my boss, after all.

The next day he said to me he could see that the two of us can't work together. He was transferring me to copyediting and proofreading. He didn't fire me. And I consider that very human on his part. Especially since the pay was better in proofreading.

I had a neighbor who worked in the tool storeroom at a factory. She signed out the tools and signed them back in. But because she was only semiliterate she made all sorts of mistakes. One day there was a surprise inspection and they found everything in total disorder. She was put on trial and given ten years. For nothing, a messy stock room.

Then she was summoned in by the KGB. They said to her, "Do you want your sentence revoked? Work for us." Without even a second's thought she signed the agreement saying she would collaborate with them. Her husband had been killed in the war and she had two children. She couldn't leave them for ten years. They gave her instructions—the workers who got their tools from her knew her and weren't afraid of speaking in front of her. She was to make a note of what they said and report it to them.

Everything was fine. Her case was closed, she went back to her job. As soon as she returned to work, she said to the workers, "You guys say whatever you want, but not in front of me. Keep your mouth shut around me. If you need a chisel, just say you need a chisel, that's all."

A few days later she was summoned in by the KGB. There were other informers where she worked who had informed on her.

The KGB punched her, they slapped her face, they drew their pistols. But, in the end, all they did was fire her as a stoolie. And the woman went back to work.

But then there was a man I knew who after the war had begged me to bear him a child. His story was terrible. During the Civil War when he was sixteen, he made friends with a White officer and had also fallen in love with the man's wife. It was purely platonic, just endless declarations of love. But the White officer and his wife fled abroad after the Civil War was over. My friend was arrested for his links to the Whites and told he would be executed if he didn't agree to cooperate with the secret police. He signed an agreement saying he would collaborate. He was just a terrified kid. And this poisoned the whole rest of his life.

He always did everything he could to avoid denouncing anyone and would always speak of a suspect in the most exalted terms. They'd draw their pistols, punch his face, scream at him. He was a refined intellectual, a talented writer, a sick man. He couldn't stand the strain. He started having fits. One day he was visiting me. He had a fit and started raving incessantly—I want to see Stalin hung! He was thrashing and hollering—I want to see Stalin hung! Needless to say, we couldn't call an ambulance.

The secret police had penetrated absolutely all of private life. There was nowhere to escape from them. They were like the very air.

But even in Stalin's Russia, where history and life were almost one and the same, life was still the greater. Wild with youth, Vitya hated his stepfather even more than his stepfather hated him.

"He didn't treat my mother well. I hated him, he hated me. It was impossible for me there. And so when I was twelve I ran away and joined the Gypsies," says Vitya, slapping his thigh both to emphasize the point and to prove to himself that those three years with the Gypsies hadn't all been a dream.

It is a warm June day in 1989. Vitya is sitting with Alyosha on a ten-foot-long log embedded in the ground that serves as a bench. Alyosha has made the hour-long train trip out to the country to see Vitya, from whom he rents a room for the summer so he, Lusya, and their children can have a few weeks away from the shouting and the dripping laundry of the communal apartment on Sretensky Boulevard to breathe the fresh air of meadows and birch groves.

The sky is vast, domed, turbulent. June thunder reverberates across the plains like artillery a city away. The land behind the bench is a garden, one of those little plots that can keep a family going on Russia's staples of tomatoes, cucumbers, and potatoes, bounded by tall sunflower stalks, their heads leaning forward, heavy with grey seed. The yard is busy with hens, roosters, goats, dogs, and cats. The animals run to Vitya's hand, accept his touch, return his touch, then run off.

Alyosha has now folded himself into the posture of the perfect listener. But Vitya has let himself be interrupted by a baby goat, to whom he coos diminutives. He calls each animal by name. And each one stays for only as long as it wishes, then bounds back to the yard, where the hens are always indignant about something and the young goats cannot contain themselves.

Vitya is fifty, with jet-black hair and the startlingly blue eyes of a man who is pure of heart and drinks too much clear vodka. He is a blacksmith and has the arms to prove it. They are covered with the homemade green tattoos favored by soldiers and prisoners. The largest reads—I'll never forget you, mother mine. His white T-shirt seems to glow with vitality after he has rubbed an animal or has been rubbed by one.

"Let's go down to Hitler's bunker," said Vitya with a laugh, leading Alyosha to his small, low-ceilinged cinder-block cellar, nearly all of its space taken up by chicken-wire cages full of parrots, doves, and chickadees. A flurry of excitement runs through the cages—Vitya's here, Vitya's here! Birds come flying to him, they squabble in the air for his attention. Vitya reaches and chooses one to bestow his affection upon, rubbing it against his cheek, a bird he once fed from his own mouth.

"Look, how they fly in pairs," says Vitya. "He takes a stick in his beak and brings it back to their nest and puts it in. And the female starts fitting it into the nest. And soon as the male flies away, another male comes and swipes the stick. Just like people, no honor among thieves. And sometimes it happens that a male dove will see the female cheating on him. That means you got to sell one or the other of them, because he'll kill her. And the parrots have communism. If one of them starts doing better, two, three, four, five others gang up on him. Birds' lives are like people's, just simpler."

By the time Vitya and Alyosha are back out on the log the sky's grey has darkened almost to black. The thunder is closer. June is still the month of sudden storms, as it had been for the pagan Slavs who worshipped the god of thunder, Perun, and who, during lightning storms, would roll naked with their animals in dew vivified by heaven. Now Vitya is ready to speak of his youth and the Gypsies.

T he Gypsies would let you live with them if you could go out and beg and bring back money. By and large, Gypsies like Russians but if you didn't have a talent for begging, out you went. We had all sorts of tricks. Sometimes we'd do a dance and then go around saying—twenty kopecks, please. Sometimes you'd get a kick in the ass but then you'd do a somersault in the air, land on your feet, laugh, and hold out your hand again—twenty kopecks, please.

There was one Russian kid who'd pretend to be crippled. He'd get on a train and limp along with his accordion, singing a little song. And everyone would say—Oh the poor boy, so young and a cripple . . . By the time he was done with the train, he'd have made more money than a miner. You had to turn in all the money to the leader of the Gypsies. He could take the whip to anyone he wanted but you couldn't lift a hand to him.

They sent out their women to beg too, to trick people

out of their money, or steal it. And we'd go along to see what
we could swipe. If a Gypsy woman came home empty-handed
she'd be whipped. They'd put on special dirty clothes to make
people sorry for them, and take their children with them. The
women would carry the children on their backs, and they'd be
all filthy and in rags. And if they didn't have children of their
own, they'd borrow somebody else's.

Some of them had a talent for looking a person dead in
the eye and saying, Come here, my friend, and I'll read your
palm. They had a way of looking that person in the eye so that
they'd become hypnotized and lose their shirt before they knew
what hit them.

The ones who didn't have that talent would just steal.
The men were known as tinkers and smiths and when they
would come to a Cossack settlement—these Gypsies lived in the
south, in the Kuban region—all the people would come
running to get their things soldered and patched. Meanwhile
the women would roam around looking for anything that was
loose—a loaf of bread, eggs, a chicken. They never went
around alone, always in twos or threes, some of them telling
fortunes while the others went inside the house and cleaned it
out, stealing kerchiefs, rugs, whatever they could fit under their
skirts. They were special wide skirts, their working clothes.

The Gypsies don't have harems. A Gypsy has one wife,
and no lovers either. And God forbid a Gypsy woman betrays
her husband. That nearly never happens. But when they fight,
they don't fight with their fists like Russians, the Gypsies use
knives and chains, especially if they're drunk.

There were about twelve wagons in our band. The
Gypsies would sleep in the wagons and us kids underneath, on
big feather beds, big enough for four and we'd sleep with our
arms around each other to keep warm.

They spoke their own Gypsy language but they swore in
Russian. If they were brought to court for stealing a horse,
they'd say, "I'm walking down the motherfucking road and I
see there's a horse laying across the road. So, I say to him—get
off the road, you motherfucker. But the horse doesn't budge.

And wouldn't you know it as soon as I try to step over the fucker, up he gets to his feet, and goes galloping away with me. Good thing there was a policeman around, I could have been hurt, and me with a wife and nine kids."

They had a whole science for stealing horses. Say we'd been out five of us and stole five horses. We'd come racing back with the owners right behind us. But everything'd be ready at the camp. Special chemicals. In two shakes, they'd have changed the horses' brand and given them white marks on their foreheads. There was no way their owners could ever prove they were theirs. And if they did call a policeman, all the Gypsies would start yelling and cursing, they'd even pinch their babies to make them cry, there was no way the policeman could ever get it all straightened out.

And they had good tricks for selling horses too. They'd take one that was on its last legs and just as they were bringing it into market, they'd stick a hot potato under its tail, and the horse would come in, rearing up, looking very spirited. They'd sell it for five times the going rate and it'd croak in a week.

It is that delicate moment when you can't quite be sure if it has started raining yet. In the east the grey-black sky is cracked by revelations of lightning, and thunder stirs the birch leaves.

B ut there was nothing better than when the Gypsies celebrated. The women would put on their gold. And oh did they have gold. Pure gold too, with a reddish tint to it, more gold than a Russian could ever dream of.

They'd build huge bonfires and sing and dance around them all night. They played guitars and violins and they sang in their own language. And could they dance! One after the other, from the youngest to the chief, they'd all dance around the bonfire. And when the chief danced they'd all dance in a circle around him. And if they were near a settlement the people there would stay up and listen to the music for the sheer pleasure of it. And the Gypsies would all sing and dance until dawn, especially if they'd stolen something good that day!

Vitya stands up and claps his hands and dances. The memory of those days, gold and bonfires, Gypsy silk and Gypsy music, won't allow him to sit still another second. Vitya claps his hands and dances to show Alyosha what it was to be thirteen years old and living with Gypsies—but, fortunately or unfortunately, no words or dances are equal to that magic.

Even though it has started raining, Vitya sits back down on the bench in a distracted silence, his smile fading to wryness. Suddenly sprinkle is downpour and they race for the house.

The dining room is filled with bird cages. "Grisha, my Grisha, so little, so smart," coos Vitya.

Vitya's wife, Marina, has set them a table of light bread and dark bread, cucumbers, tomatoes, smoked fish, boiled eggs, and a bottle of vodka, white with ice.

Well, to tell you the end of the story. It was after I'd been in the army and married Marina. The Gypsies from my old band started coming by to see me. They drove me crazy, they'd come ten or fifteen at a time. The older ones had died off, these were the younger ones, they were more settled, they had cars. And they had all their teeth capped with gold whether they needed it or not.

Finally, I said to them, "I'm sorry but this is no hotel." But they wouldn't go away. And then they started stealing. Even from me.

And so I broke off diplomatic relations with them. I said, "I'm sorry but you've insulted me. I can't be friends with you any more."

How else could it all end with the Gypsies?

*

Stalin gave up smoking. Perhaps no great struggle was involved, even tobacco may have lost its savor for him. Reasons of health might have been involved—not so much that he thirsted for life as that he very much did not wish to die. That would only benefit those closest to him—Malenkov, the heir apparent; Beria, head of the secret police and a potential usurper; and Molotov, aspiring only to second place.

Of late his successes had been mixed. In 1948 Andrei Sakharov, as part of a team of Soviet scientists whose lives were considered too precious to risk in plane travel, watched as an atomic bomb consumed the dawn in the desert. But that same year Tito had broken with Moscow, a lesson that would not be lost on the three-quarters of a billion Chinese. As the Russian saying goes, a bad example is infectious.

Why shouldn't others turn against him too? Especially those closest to him who would stand to gain the most by his death. He knew they were always registering his vital signs, the spring of his step, the gleam of his eye, his memory for detail.

He must act against them before they act against him. He must act against them even before they realize they are going to act against him.

At his age he was most vulnerable to doctors. And as he knew well, nothing could be easier than murder by pharmacology.

Most of the Kremlin's doctors were Jews. Stalin's daughter Svetlana had just married a Jew. And a Jew from Israel, Golda Meir, had caused spontaneous demonstrations of joy when she visited Moscow, proving that the Jews of Russia had at best a dual allegiance. And the Jews of America were turning their country more and more against Russia.

But Stalin had already struck back a few times. Everyone knew that the campaign against the "rootless cosmopolitans" was a campaign against Jews. And when a half a dozen Jewish writers faced the firing squad for treason, Russians could be counted on to draw the larger lesson.

On January 13, 1953, *Pravda* revealed that several important party officials had been murdered by doctors, most of whom were Jews. Terror and hysteria rippled through the land. The "Doctors' Plot" was clearly the prelude to Stalin's grand finale.

A t the time of the Doctors' Plot, *says Natalya Viktorovna, edging crumbs off the table,* I was working for State Medical Publishing, Medpub. Those were years of true happiness for me, I had found the work I wanted to do. What interested me most in the world was biology and medicine. I was also editing dissertations because you couldn't live on what Medpub paid. And every dissertation is a monograph. I was learning all the time.

Anyway, just when the Doctors' Plot broke, we were getting ready to publish a multivolume set entitled *The History of Soviet Medicine During World War II.* There were fifteen volumes, I think. Not an especially important publication, though there were some interesting entries. But an awful lot of hack stuff too.

Still, it was an elegantly done job, all fifteen volumes in hard cover and hand bound. It was going to be quite a sizable edition because all party members were obliged to subscribe, and so were prominent physicians, professors, deans.

But there was something I couldn't quite fathom. It was clear that the campaign against the rootless cosmopolitans had been anti-Semitic but this time Russian doctors as well as Jews were arrested. I thought they may have known too much and may even have taken part in some of Stalin's crimes. Stalin had decided to get rid of them because he always got rid of any witnesses to his crimes.

Suddenly we discovered that the volume we were publishing in the hand-bound edition consisted nearly entirely of articles by the very doctors who had been arrested in the Doctors' Plot. So, they put in a rush order for articles by some medical hacks, unbound all the bound books, took out the old articles, inserted the new ones, and rebound all the books, but by now the huge volume had shrunk and become very slender indeed, *says Natalya with a laugh, recalling the power of terror to wither a fat volume to thin.*

In those days no one ever turned the radio off. We even slept with the radio on. And all of a sudden there was a medical bulletin about Stalin. He was ill. There was a full report on his condition, including his urinalysis. I realized then and there the situation had to be hopeless. Otherwise, Stalin would have had the heads of everyone who could even imagine that a god urinates and that his urine was subject to analysis.

And what I felt was fear for the country. Fear mixed with relief and joy.

On March 5, 1953, Stalin made his last and greatest contribution. He had either died of a cerebral hemorrhage or the men closest to him had in fact used the very weapon he suspected they would.

Stalin's body lay in state at the Hall of Columns in central Moscow. Hundreds of thousands streamed toward the body, hundreds being trampled in the oddly silent city. As funeral music played, each of those hundreds of thousands passed by the flower-heaped coffin where Joseph Stalin lay in state, all five feet, four inches of him.

I was at Medpub the day of the funeral, *continues Natalya.* Thirty-two of us met to listen to the funeral on the radio. Everyone was crying except me. I couldn't cry and I couldn't pretend to. They all kept looking over at me in amazement.

On the other hand, I did find the speeches very interesting. Molotov just dissolved in tears, he wept and wailed and even started hiccuping. Beria, the head of the secret police, made a repulsive speech, you could feel what a repulsive person he was. Then came Malenkov, who everyone thought would take over next. He delivered the funeral oration. He spoke of their grief but his voice rang with joy. It soared. That was very striking.

Anyway, to make a long story short, a few days later it turned out the doctors weren't guilty of anything at all. And that meant we had to unbind the slender volumes, reinsert the articles by those doctors and hand bind the books all over again!

Natalya laughs at the thought of all those pages rustling in Stalin's dying breath. "Still, by and large, people loved him. One man even said to me, 'Without Stalin who're we going to die for?' "

After the Death

To the astonishment of her coworkers at Medpub, Natalya Viktorovna not only refused to feel or feign grief as they listened to the radio broadcast of Stalin's funeral, but had followed the orations with unseemly curiosity. She had been repelled by the voice of Lavrenty Beria, the Georgian chief of the secret police, a murderer who affected intellectual ways, including wearing a pince-nez, and who liked to rape teenage girls chosen at random on the street. When Molotov spoke Natalya heard him choke and sputter with grief. He had the stooge's love of the boss. No boss had been greater than Stalin, and no stooge greater than Molotov, who not only signed the deal Hitler and Stalin made but did not so much as peep when Stalin arrested his Jewish wife in the prelude to a pogrom that never happened.

And the third speaker, in whose voice Natalya Viktorovna found indecent elation, was Malenkov, the heir apparent, a tubby bully whose girlish face the Politburo mocked behind his back.

The three speakers soon formed a triumvirate, with Malenkov dominating. His obvious rival for power was not Molotov but Beria, who knew too much, was too closely tied to Stalin, and whose removal would allow the Russians to take vengeance on at least one Georgian. Beria had to go, and Beria went.

And, as Beria himself well knew, if there is the political will, then to arrest a man and shoot him in the head is the merest nothing. The new head of the secret police is said to have done the honors himself.

Beria was replaced in the triumvirate by Nikita Khrushchev, a tough and energetic man who knew how to lead. He had run the construction of the Moscow Metro, he had been the boss of the entire Ukraine, and he had commanded a front during the second World War. Miraculously, his humanity had survived, almost alone among the others. Malenkov had neither personality nor ability, and Molotov was inert. Khrushchev could not help but predominate. Sheer vitality would win the day, as it so often does.

The spell of exile was broken as it was cast, with a magic word. But no word got to Ruth Bonner, who, after nine years in the camps, was in her eighth year of exile, isolated in a village of moonshiners deep in the Russian sticks.

Rumors didn't even reach there.

In September 1954 I was summoned to the Military Board of the Supreme Soviet. I was shown into a very nice office and the man at the desk was in full military regalia, a colonel, a lieutenant colonel, I could never keep them straight.

It didn't look like the usual interrogation. He offered me a seat, in an armchair, not the usual stool where you're perched with a bright light in your face. But as soon as he pulled out one of those questionnaires that investigators use I was on my guard. And when he started asking questions about my family, my friends, and people I'd known in the past, he sounded just like any other investigator. I clammed up. I was scared.

But he tried to convince me that all that information was very important and could help clear up any injustices that might have occurred. But I wouldn't have any of it, and said as little as I could.

Though the camps taught the true value of kindness and beauty, their most persistent lesson was that mistrust is essential to survival. And Ruth had been in the class of '37.

I went back to that remote village very alarmed. It was such an out-of-it place that my daughter Elena had to come there to inform me that I had been re-ha-bil-i-ta-ted, a strange, new word at the time.

I was summoned to the Military Board of the Supreme Soviet in Moscow this time, and this time I had no fear about going. I was met by a colonel at the foot of the stairs. He took me to his office, offered me a plush armchair, asked if I wouldn't prefer to rest up from traveling first, or would I like something to eat, perhaps some coffee or tea. I refused all of it.

The colonel began by saying, "The man you saw in Leningrad isn't sufficiently experienced. He didn't understand what was required of him, he did not succeed in winning your trust that what's at issue here is complete rehabilitation for you and your husband. And there are other people who must be rehabilitated too, and we need your help in that."

I still wasn't saying a word.

"How can I convince you to trust us?" he said. "I know it must be terribly hard after all these years, but everything's changed here, the old people are out, we're all new here. We're trying to find the people who are still alive, we're trying to help them. You were one of the first we found and, look, you won't even cooperate."

I said something without really saying anything.

"You know what," he says, "I'm going to bend the rules and show you something you're not supposed to see."

He showed me a document that stated after a review of our cases my husband and I had been fully rehabilitated. The first signature on the document was Khrushchev's.

I didn't say anything.

And then he pulled a document signed by my daughter Elena stating that she had seen the official report on the review of our case.

"Is that proof enough for you?" he said.

I still didn't say anything. It was only after a long pause that I finally said, "It's proof enough."

Now that the spell had been broken, everything moved rapidly in the opposite direction. From living in a hovel in exile Ruth could return to Moscow, where she would be given an apartment in a building originally intended for Central Committee big shots, just recently completed in the early fifties by German prisoners of war. Deprived of all rights as a Family Member of an Enemy of the People, she was now to have an internal passport, just like any other Soviet citizen.

"When I went to get the passport, the head of the passport office took a look at me as he handed me the passport and he said, 'You've won this time!'

" 'I hope it's not just this time but once and for all.'

" 'We'll see about that,' he said. 'We'll see.' "

Ilya Jaffee, that "typical representative of the rank and file of the Stalinist intelligentsia," had turned against Stalin. Communism could still be saved but not as long as Stalin lived.

"When that criminal maniac Stalin started to croak all alone in his room and then died surrounded by his cronies, I realized that as a member of the ruling party, it was my duty to speak out. By 1954 I no longer felt in danger of being arrested or of disappearing. By then I was nearly fifty and had been in the party for twenty-five years. I realized that there'd be smart guys by the thousands ready to criticize, but there was no point in that. I felt it was my duty to present a rational solution to the problem, one that should not be violently imposed but should retain the basics of the system."

The "member of the ruling party" began his grand review. Ilya, who had sat hunched over Talmud and Darwin, now read through all the fifty-five volumes of Lenin. He could not live with-

out faith and faith was not yet dead in him, the Restorer of the
Faith. This was a serious business—but it did not, however, pre-
clude all mischief.

"One time I made a copy of various remarks by Lenin from
his article 'On National Pride' including one that said the Russians
were chauvinist tyrants. I left it on my desk and somebody walks
by and sees it. 'What's all this anti-Soviet stuff?' he says. 'Just
something I'm using in a report,' I say. 'But where did you get this
garbage?' 'I'll show you,' I say, and open the volume of Lenin to
that page. What a commotion that caused!"

1956 was a rich and fateful year. Khrushchev made his "secret
speech" denouncing the crimes of Stalin, and Revekka returned to
Moscow to petition her government.

I insisted that I be rehabilitated since I had been unjustly
imprisoned. And I was given my rehabilitation. Meaning an
apology, an acknowledgment that you had not been guilty of
anything. And the fact that you had spent eight years in the
camps and two in exile, well, that was another story . . .

I was now given the legal right to live in Moscow and I
found a room in a home for old Bolsheviks. They helped me
with the paperwork connected with getting a residence permit.
And then I had to find a job, I had a young son to support. By
then my other son was grown up and in the army.

I decided not to go see anyone, not to make use of any
past connections. Instead I went to the employment office of
the District Executive Committee. The man I talked to was a
decent human being. I told him my whole story and I could see
the compassion in his eyes. And I was as touched by that as he
was by my story.

And I said to him, "I only want to be with the working
class."

"There's a factory by the Belorussian station, the
director's a good man, they'll take you on there."

Everyone was very nice to me at the factory and even
though I didn't know how to use a sewing machine I learned it

quickly. And it wasn't long before I was active again in various factory organizations. I was happy there, people were warm. But I did feel that I stood out a little, those twenty years had left their mark on me.

Still, after a short time I was asked to work in the factory's party office. But I had never been a registered party member, and no one in the factory knew my story. People in certain government agencies knew, but you couldn't keep telling it to one person after another. And so when the party office proposed that I join the party, I was frightened, startled. I had been raised a communist. But how was I supposed to enter the party carrying all that baggage, all those years in prison! For me the party was the noblest and the purest of organizations that carried on the highest and best ideas of Lenin.

And I said, "I think you're making a mistake. The party doesn't need me. What the party needs are fresh young forces. And it has nothing to do with what I want or don't want. I was a Pioneer, and I was in the Young Communist League, and then I was a communist, though I never applied for formal membership."

But they said, "You're being nominated by the working class and that's a great honor."

And, yes, it was just as her Papa had always said—the working class knows what's what.

Secure, rehabilitated, and now able to fight for something more than surviving the hour, Revekka assumed her mission: "to clear my father's name and have him reinstated in the communist party."

*

In the fall of 1956, the Hungarians revolted against Soviet authority and were crushed by Soviet tanks. "I was born that year," says Lusya, interrupted by Pasha, her eleven-year-old son from her first and disastrous marriage. He wants a few rubles to escape the bickering women and dripping laundry of the communal apartment on Sretensky Boulevard and go to the neighborhood video parlor and watch action films on a VCR. He has the same brown eyes and hair as his mother, but he also has a woodland creature's quick, slinky alertness, which his mother does not. He leans against her and whines like a child half his age, as if to remind her of when he was young and they spent all those years alone together. "I have no will power," sighs Lusya, digging a three-ruble note from her purse, "not even with children."

I was born just before the Hungarian uprising, in October '56. And that was quite a story too, *continues Lusya.*

My grandmother was always saying she hoped her daughter would marry a Jew because they were family men, didn't drink, and made good providers. It wasn't that she felt any special joy when my mother married a Jew, it's just that she thought it was more practical. Needless to say, my father turned out to be a lush and a ladies' man who never earned a ruble in his life!

My mother was pregnant. My father was still living with his parents and didn't care about my mother. She was afraid to go home to her own mother, pregnant like that. She had nowhere to live and so she slept in the park. And she was on a park bench when she went into labor. They rushed her to the hospital, where she gave birth prematurely to a daughter who lived two days.

I had a mystical bond with that girl. And with the fact that she was only in this world for two days. Sometimes I felt that she was my predecessor and there was a deep connection between our births. And at other times the feeling was that I was her; that she was my failed attempt at being born. Later in life when I was baptized and accepted Christianity, I realized that none of that could be so, but still it all felt so fateful. And my mother's fate was even repeated in my own experience. When I was pregnant with Pasha, I too had no place to live and I slept on a park bench too.

The atmosphere quickly turned choppy under the erratic Khrushchev. He freed tens of thousands from the camps but crushed the

Hungarian uprising. He hounded Boris Pasternak to death and helped Solzhenitsyn into print. In one year alone, 1961, the Soviet Union sent the first man into space, built the Berlin Wall, and, under cover of night, slipped Stalin's body out of the mausoleum.

It was in those years of swift change and reversal that Viktor Krivorotov discovered that he was what he had no desire to be.

Looking back at himself at twenty-one, he smiles at fate, which is as obvious in retrospect as it is invisible at the time. Now, at fifty, in the prime of life, he is an icon painter in Tbilisi, the capital of Georgia, a city loved by many Russians for its mountain air and Italianate architecture, the red wine and lamb of its legendary hospitality, the handsomeness and sexual frankness of both sexes. He has just completed an icon for the ancient and holy monastery of Zagorsk and is anxiously awaiting the arrival of the monk who is charged with taking possession of the icon and of its safe delivery. But Zagorsk is near Moscow, a thousand miles away, and, as Russians know well and often say, anything can happen.

Rasputin in a blue and white jogger's suit, Viktor has long hair and a longer beard, and the light in his eyes can be gently radiant or flash with the memory of evil in everyone, himself included. The evil that is vanity, the arrogance of self-importance, which is the source of the anxiety he is now feeling, an unworthy expenditure of spirit. He returns to the workshop to check the icon one last time and to confront the image he has given to the great, thousand-year-old church of Russia.

The passages connecting the rooms in his house are narrow and low, hutlike. His assistants, five women, including his wife, look up with anticipation when he enters the workshop, whose walls are covered with icons, saints and saviors in gold and brown: the room would seem the interior of some ancient chapel were it not for the large technicolor photograph of an American astronaut in a shining silver suit whose sleeve has been autographed: "Rusty Schweickart."

In a hush the women unwrap the icon for one final look. A final check of the spirit's craftsmanship, no sins of inattention in the application of the colors, every line the line of a prayer.

With a quick, definite nod, Viktor indicates that the ties are to be redone.

He goes back to the kitchen and sits down at the table, where he is served lunch by one of his assistants, a Georgian architect who gave up her profession to follow him. Her features are like those on Byzantine icons—high forehead, thin, arched brows. The electricity has been off for the last two hours. Outside, even the light seems to be fasting.

I didn't want to be a healer like my father, *says Viktor.* He was a well-known healer, my father, a very kind and gentle man. It used to baffle me—how could a man like him even exist in our society, which is a constant battle for survival with people tearing things out of each other's hands. I even condemned him for being too good. I'd say, That man deceived you. Why forgive him? Why help him? And he'd say, What do you mean, the person needs help. Even though I rebelled against all that, it left its mark on me.

My mother's sense of organization and my father's kindliness were significant in forming me. I'm grateful to them for that, since I am very well aware how hard it is to acquire any positive traits. How very hard.

For a moment he looks like a man for whom every moment of life is a struggle between the good and the evil in him, a man who is not yet entirely convinced that the good will prevail.

My father made a career of the military and was the head of the research and development department for the Trans-Caucasus Military District. He was able to combine a military career and healing because he accepted no money for treating people. That's what saved him. At that time, if he had taken money, he'd have been thrown in prison.

But he did not heal people to make money but because he loved people and wanted to help them. He was always helping people the doctors had given up on. There was always a steady stream of people coming to see him. With my own eyes I'd seen him heal people many times but I hadn't the slightest desire to be any part of it. I had decided to become an engineer and enrolled in the Polytechnical Institute of Tbilisi.

Politics didn't interest me at all. I'd heard all sorts of stories about '37 but it all went in one ear and out the other. All I cared about was sports—volleyball, rowing. I was a top athlete and took part in national competitions. Sports played a big role in my life and taught me self-discipline.

But meanwhile by the time I graduated from Tbilisi Polytech I knew that engineering bored me to death. I was twenty-one, I had to do something. So, I started helping my father in his work. And then all of a sudden I threw myself into healing.

*

Sasha Gorodetsky became a clown to avoid arrest. He was the only one who couldn't see what was apparent to everyone else—that the roly-poly, mischievous, good-natured boy was born to clown. Comedy was even inscribed in the large curves of his shoulders and head. And now, in his mid-thirties, with his hair thinning and his head seemingly all the more massive, his eyes slanted, he is a Buddha laughing at all creation. Or nearly all creation, for he can no longer find any humor in the apartment he shares with his wife—a tiny kitchen, a tiny bathroom, and a very small bedroom that is the living room when guests come.

He was not one of those boys who cannot wait for childhood to be over; Sasha was very alive in his school days, and his school days are always alive for him.

I had an absolutely typical Soviet childhood. I hated kindergarten, you were always being forced to do something. I don't want to rest. You must rest! I don't want kasha. Eat the kasha! I'd throw tantrums in the morning—why leave a warm house to walk through snow to a prison?

And those absolutely imbecilic songs we had to sing!

After that year in kindergarten my parents sent me to

summer camp, where things were a little freer. But there was
one counselor we all hated. She was always on your back. We
could read by four or five and so some of us had already read
Jules Verne and other adventure novels. So we decided to put
what we learned into practice. My friend and I came up with
the idea of setting a trap for her, digging a large pit for her to
fall into.

But we weren't strong enough yet to dig a pit that deep
so we had to find a hole that was already there. Unfortunately,
the one we found was at the edge of the camp's land, where
nobody ever went. And so that meant we'd have to lure her
over there. But just as we were trying to figure out how to do
that, my friend, who was six at the time, had a sudden insight
into the meaninglessness of individual acts of terrorism. He
said, "She'll fall in the pit and they'll just send another one."

He became a historian when he grew up.

I missed the first couple of months of first grade due to
illness. And when I was well enough to start going, it turned
out I was too fat for any of the school uniforms. So they
bought me a sailor's suit. A fat boy in a sailor's suit, I stood out
like a sore thumb. And I had to get into a lot of fights to prove
I was no mama's boy.

First grade. Purple ink, inkwells in the desks, wooden
pens with metal nibs, the ink was forever spilling, your hands
were always ink-stained, your notebooks all smudgy. It was all
so boring you could scream! I was always turning around in my
chair, tugging at someone. And when I started popping
ink-filled balloons over people's heads they called my mother
into school.

By third grade I was smoking.

I was inducted into the Octobrists, the first stage in
communist youth groups. They spent a long time telling us how
happy we were going to be and there were those stories about
Lenin as a little boy, his conscience bothering him because he
broke a pitcher. You could scream! But mostly we played
outside, we played war, the war of 1812, if we'd been reading

about that. And after we saw a movie about the Teutonic
Knights we put pots on our heads and fought with wooden
swords.

My father died when I was still young. My mother was
working as a director at the Crooked Mirror, which was half
cabaret, half theater. I grew up backstage. All the actors treated
me like family and felt entitled to ask me what kind of marks I
was getting at school.

In fifth, or maybe it was fourth, I was around ten,
eleven, twelve, they inducted us into the youth group known as
the Pioneers with great pomp and ceremony. With drums and
banners, beside a tractor in the Museum of the Revolution. It
was there we took the oath—I, as a Young Pioneer, do here
solemnly swear before my comrades . . . and so forth. We did
everything but sign our names in blood.

We wore triangular, red neckerchiefs and we had to
know what each of the three corners stood for—one was the
Pioneers, one the Young Communists, and one the
Communists.

For the first two weeks after the induction we all kept
our neckerchiefs as nice and clean as we could, but after a
while that got boring so we tried to see who could get his the
dirtiest.

In sixth grade I developed a real taste for drinking beer.
I knew that it wasn't right to go into a beer shop wearing my
Pioneer scarf and so I'd always take it off before going in. The
beer was sold from machines. And I'd sneak onto buses without
paying. I already knew there were two different worlds. At
home, I was always being told, Sasha, don't you ever say that at
school.

Our teacher was a real Stalinist. Cruel, tough as nails,
she ruled with an iron hand. But still she was always
emphasizing that we were all brothers, all equal. All problems
could be solved through her. We were supposed to go to her
and squeal on our classmates—Petrov copied his homework
from so and so. She encouraged us to inform on each other. In
the classroom there was a large portrait of Pavlik Morozov. We

were told that during collectivization some of the peasants hid
their grain. Pavlik's father hid his grain too and Pavlik
informed on him. He was a hero, a real Pioneer, who had
helped his country. He did not spare his own father for the
good of the country. A Pioneer is supposed to tell the truth
and that's what Pavlik did. And it was for telling the truth that
he was killed by some of the other peasants. The country and
the party are more important than your father, that was the
conclusion we were supposed to reach. But I didn't take any of
that seriously. My mother used to say, Sasha, informing is bad,
squealing is bad. That I knew anyway.

I did join the Young Communists because I knew I
couldn't get into an institute otherwise. I never did anything,
just paid my dues. I had gotten very interested in chemistry and
when I finished school I enrolled in the chemistry department
of the Petroleum Institute. It only took three months for me to
realize that petrochemistry and I were two very different things,
but I stayed on in that institute for three years, gritting my
teeth with boredom.

Finally, I graduated and spent the next year and a half
not doing much of anything, picking up a little money here and
there. That brought me to the attention of the police. By Soviet
law, if a person hasn't worked for two months, he gets a
warning, then a second warning, and then, if he still hasn't
found a job, he can be given a year in jail or be sent out of
Moscow. The charge is "parasitism," vagrancy. A policeman
started coming around to see me and insisted I find work. He
was a great big Ukrainian, a very good-natured guy. I'd run
into him on the street and he'd say, Get a job or I'll throw you
in jail.

It was nothing personal, he liked me fine, that big
Ukrainian cop. We used to laugh and kid around. But that
wouldn't keep him from tossing me in the clink. Now I was
really on the spot.

One day Polyakov, the head of the theater where my
mother worked, came to the house and slammed his ivory cane
on the table.

"You're going to work," he said. "You choose. Either a stagehand at the Writers' Club or an electrician at the old Moscow Circus."

I thought—the Writers' Club had a restaurant and two buffets, and I realized that if I took a job as a stagehand there, I'd become a total alky. Plus, the circus sounded like more fun.

They took one look at all 220 pounds of me and said, This kid could be a clown.

*

W hen some part of your body aches, you naturally touch it with your hand, *says Viktor, rubbing his shoulder as if he had a sore ligament there.* It's perfectly natural. And very ancient. There are classical references to healing, and the laying on of hands is spoken of in the New Testament.

But before you begin healing someone, you have to talk with that person, find out what the ailment is, what caused it, what brought him to it. You have to have long conversations with the patient, and they have a certain psychotherapeutic quality.

Healing is a spiritual process. A person opens up completely and tells everything about himself. All his troubles, what's bothering him now. Souls touch in healing. It's a very deep form of communication.

Then the healing process begins. I activate my hands. I know how to do that, to concentrate my energy in my hands, *says Viktor, glowing with the certainty that his hands have restored health, eased pain.*

Essentially, it's love that heals. If I do not feel love for a person, he can't be healed. If someone irritates me, and there are people like that . . . , *says Viktor, and as soon as he remembers them and what they make him feel, his eyes lose all their elation.*

First Viktor was convinced that he did not want to be a healer, and then with equal certainty he was convinced that he wanted only to be a healer. And with time, he saw that he did not wish to be only a healer. Needing another source of income, one that would allow him independence, Viktor chose art.

I started drawing a lot. I studied painting. First, I was an abstractionist. My gods were Kandinsky, Malevich, Larionov. Then came the Impressionists. Then American painters, I was very taken with Rauschenberg.

It took me thirteen years to make the transition. Then I had my first one-man show in Tbilisi and my painting started appearing in group shows that traveled the country.

Then I started doing nothing but portraits. What I wanted was to study human psychology through the portrait. I set myself the task of painting one portrait a day.

When I saw icons in the museum, I had absolutely no idea what they were all about. I knew that in the past the icon had been held in very high regard. I began analyzing them in an attempt to understand what they were about.

First, I just studied their colors. Then I noticed the use of deformation in them. Modern art is based on deformation, Picasso's work for example. But that was a point of connection for me—the icons also used deformations. I'd go and stand for hours in front of one icon, trying to understand what the master had wanted to imbue it with.

Little by little I entered the world of the icon.

And then came the desire to paint icons myself. I asked my artist friends to help find me someone who knew that art form. In Moscow there was a Spaniard by the name of Dioniso Garcia, he was one of the Spanish children who'd been brought to the Soviet Union after the Spanish Civil War. He had learned how to paint icons and though he was a Soviet citizen, being Spanish, he could work still more freely. And so it was a Spaniard who taught me the ancient methods of making Russian icons.

First of all, they're done in egg tempera, colors which the painter grinds himself. If you don't grind your own paint, don't feel your own paint, you're not considered capable of painting an icon. Paint in a tube, that's civilization. Paint's not artificial, it's from stones. Paints don't spoil either. They can keep for millennia.

The stones are ground and mixed into the egg, which

acts as a binder. This is also a symbolic process. The egg is a symbol of birth, of life. And the stone is a symbol of the world.

But before you even start priming the canvas for an icon, there's a whole ritual you must perform. First, we bring the canvas to a priest and have it blessed.

Before starting to paint, we fast and pray. There are special ancient prayers that have to be said. Then we attune ourselves to the saint we're painting. To us he is a real person, he exists, and contact can be had with him. And the better we are attuned to him, the better the painting.

But if you don't attune yourself well enough and don't feel infinite respect for the image you want to create, then nothing will come of it. It'll only be a painting, an ordinary painting. But what you have to do is make an image that a person could walk up to and pray to. A picture someone could repent to.

The image has to create that desire in a person, to repent, to purify himself. And the artist has to know what it means to repent and to purify himself. Painting icons is a great responsibility. A priest helps us. And when the icon is done he comes and blesses it again.

At the same time as I was learning to paint icons, my work as a healer took a different direction. I realized that I was only healing people's bodies, not their souls. And it is the psyche, the soul, that determines what happens with the body. I'd cure a person of an illness and a year later he'd be down with it again. I became more interested in mental illness, in helping people to overcome their fears and go back and lead a free and normal life.

Egotism is a grave illness and the source of all other illness. Our entire civilization is built on role-playing. We all want to appear at our best to one another. And, in the end, we're even afraid to find out what our real essence is. That's the most horrible thing of all—to hide from oneself. And that's where the real problems come from—from having to play a role but also having a real essence which isn't being fulfilled. And that produces inner conflict and can lead to degradation.

But in the Russian Orthodox tradition you don't forbid yourself to act a certain way, you develop some new quality in yourself that squeezes out that other negative quality.

I run groups. People come to me and I try to help them change themselves. They have to look into their subconscious, and stop being robots of automatic behavior. People need to be conscious of what they do, not just react like automatons. In the group, two people might interact and the rest of the group will observe and then analyze their behavior. This helps a person recognize his own strengths and his shortcomings.

We have several groups and some of them are in other cities. Some of the groups have been in existence for ten years. There's really no end to the process. The deeper you go, the more you find what's wrong with yourself.

Viktor starts as someone drives up in back of his building. It is not the monk from Zagorsk, only a neighbor. It is almost raining, in the distance some houses have the electricity back on.

*

First time out Sasha flopped as a clown, and nothing could be more lugubriously clownish than that. Ordered into a clown suit, kicked in the pants to get him into the ring—"all that light, two thousand eyes"—he left unaccompanied by the clown's only true applause, unstoppable laughter.

"But that didn't bother the director. He knew I just needed more training. And I became a perfectly good clown. The only problem was that I wanted to be a talking clown, not just one who did sight gags. But this was the Soviet Union and any word spoken by any clown in the country first had to go through the censorship."

After two years of working as a clown, Sasha discovered that it was not at all his true calling, especially if it meant being a silent clown. But he could not confine his ample spirit to that narrow form. His was not the rotundity of the clown but the girth of the impresario.

I went to theater school and I became a Director of Clowns, Magicians, and Eccentric Music Groups, which is now my official title. I work out the routines with the performers. It takes a very long time to polish a routine.

Circus life is horrible, always on the road performing those same routines day after day. And there's no real money in it. Tours abroad are the only chance of making any money, preferably tours of capitalist countries, and Japan is the sweetest of them all.

Here's how it works. A performer makes a contract with some Western impresario, but he doesn't receive any money. He's paid back home in rubles. If the contract designates thirty performances a month and he does more, then he's paid by the impresario.

But the real money's in the per diem. And so when Soviet performers go on tour abroad they pack their suitcases with the most pathetic stuff—macaroni, dry soup, canned food. It's called "soup in an envelope" in circus slang. And a foreign hotel manager knows the first thing to do when a Soviet troupe arrives is to get out the spare fuses because they'll all be using hot plates. Every cent of their per diem goes to buying goods, which they sell at a great profit when they get back home.

All circus performers are glad when they bring the lions and tigers along since they are fed meat and you can always try to wangle yourself a little slice.

There's even a joke about it. There's a big elephant and on the wall beside it there's a sign—Daily ration: Apples, one hundred pounds. Bananas, fifty pounds. Beets, twenty pounds. Oranges, thirty pounds. Someone walks by, reads the sign, and asks the guy cleaning up the elephant's stall—Can he really eat all that much? And the guy says—Maybe he could, but who's going to give it to him?

One time the American impresario Sol Hurok brought over the Bolshoi Ballet to New York. And since they were in New York they walked everywhere to save money and lived entirely on soup from envelopes. By the first rehearsal they were so weak they couldn't lift the ballerina into the air. Hurok understood in a flash and paid for their food out of his own pocket for the duration of the tour.

Begging for lion's meat, hot plates blowing fuses, ballerinas fainting from hunger, what could be more pathetically demeaning, the very stuff of comedy. Sasha laughs but then grows serious as he ponders what has happened to people in his country.

"The Russians have forgotten how to laugh. Some of them have been through too much, some of them are just worn out. They all sit there guarded, tense, in pain. It takes titanic efforts to get a laugh out of them. But it is my belief that it is a great service to help people laugh. It may not be a cure for all their ills but at least it kills the pain."

*

The lights come on at Viktor's—startling, intrusive, though still faint, the yellow has a slightly old-fashioned yellow-orange to it, electricity from the twenties. Outside, the daylight is waning. No sign of the people from the monastery. There is no telephone. In certain places it can take ten years to get a telephone, and some places seem to never get one.

Struggling to subdue his impatience, Viktor says:

A s soon as I heard that the American astronaut Rusty Schweickart was coming to Moscow, I knew I had to meet him. He was of great interest to me from the psychological point of view. He was the first man to have walked in space and that made him unique. I wanted to feel what he was like. I threw everything aside and went to Moscow.

We met at the house of the famous healer Dzhuna, who was supposed to have treated Brezhnev and other Soviet leaders. Schweickart struck me as a man who had accomplished a great feat. He had been ready to die. You don't see that much. We all cling to life, *says Viktor with a sudden grimace of distaste.* He struck me as a strong person and a deep one. His consciousness was quite global. He was interested in the problems of mankind. And how could his consciousness be anything global when he had stepped outside his own life, so to speak. People who cling to themselves, to their little problems, their little possessions, they are capable of nothing and of no interest.

When everyone was getting ready to go to a restaurant, Schweickart said that unfortunately his wife wouldn't be coming, she was at the hotel, not feeling well. People asked me to try to help her and they gave me the address.

I went to the hotel to help her. And I wanted to bring her to the restaurant as a surprise. I arrived just at the critical moment, she was just losing consciousness and had to be lifted from the bed.

I worked on her for about an hour, maybe less. I cured her, I took her to the restaurant. And that made quite an impression on everyone. And brought Schweickart and me even closer.

Suddenly a small car drives up. The driver hops out and opens the back door, from which a monk emerges. His hood and robe are Bible-black, a gold cross flashing under his stiff, black beard as he strides toward the house.

The knots on the icon's covering are quickly undone for the epiphany. For a second Viktor and his apprentices fear that their repentance was insufficient to create an image worthy to be a mirror of the spirit and a window onto heaven. But then the priest smiles and nods, his black beard touching the gold cross.

After abbreviated bows and blessings, the icon is rushed from the house to the waiting car, as if Russia needed all the holiness it could get.

The House on
Pushkin Street

When she returned from the front, Natalya Viktorovna had to battle for months to win back her room, which had been taken over by a KGB man with a complicated erotic life. She had lived quietly in those years, happily, doing work she liked with people she liked. Most important, she did not lose anyone she loved, as she had in the terrible December of 1941 which took her daughter, her husband, and her mother. Natalya had gone to war for many reasons, to see what it was like, to fight, but not for "Stalin and Country," just for country. Mostly she went to war because, after the terrible December of 1941, war was the only force on earth with the power to shake her out of her grief. War would either kill her or bring her back to life.

Natalya was happy under Khrushchev—"Why do people remember him so badly, he did so much good." In the early sixties, as Natalya approached fifty, she could see clearly that, after a life of wandering and communal apartments, she wanted a place she could call home. The pretty, chestnut-haired girl whose near-sightedness always drew her close to things and people and whose frame had the attractive diminutiveness of a miniature was, when she was resolved, no more afraid of the Soviet system than she had been when grabbing a rifle and marching off to shoot an officer who had spoken unforgivably to her. It would take hustling, deals, scams, payoffs, wheedling, pleading, conniving, it would take papers and signatures, stamps and seals, hours and hours in dim corridors lined with sullen petitioners, but she would do it.

In 1962, the year after Khrushchev, the Fernando of space, had sent a Soviet Columbus into orbit, Natalya Viktorovna had been granted by the country's one landlord a two-room apartment, a seventh-floor walk-up until the elevator began working a few years later.

Natalya did not have this entire apartment to herself, nor would she have wanted that. The whole point of the enterprise, in fact, had been to find a place where she could live with her closest friends, Zoya and Regina. All three had much in common—they had all worked as editors and were all interested in collecting folklore. But that was not what bound those three, rather it was only one sign of it. What they shared was a sense of what life was about and how people should treat each other. Other than that they couldn't have been more different.

R egina was almost an invalid, *says Natalya*. She had a congenital heart defect. She was intelligent, sensitive, and possessed what I'd call telepathic abilities. Somebody once called her an emotional amplifier. She was pretty much bedridden. The place by her bed became known as the "confessional" because people would come to her and make confession to her. She knew everybody's secrets.

Regina wasn't well adapted to life because of her illness. Zoya's reasons were different. I don't think she had ever once in her life gone into a store and bought herself a coat, say, or a dress, or shoes. There was always somebody who'd take her by the hand, and bring her to the store, get someone to let her try something on and then pay for her after she said, I'll take it. She was as tiny as an elf, she couldn't have weighed more than seventy pounds. And very timid. Unless, that is, she felt insulted. I once saw a man call her a kike in the post office and Zoya turned pale and went right for him, a great big guy, and she no more than seventy pounds. He ran away. It was the look on her face that did it.

In any case, neither of the two were suited for running the household and I wore the pants in the family, so to speak.

I'd always thought that people had lost the art of socializing. Both Zoya and Regina were completely with me on that point—that people no longer knew how to be together without drinking vodka. They had forgotten how to talk over a cup of tea. And so we decided to have an open house where people could relearn this art. And in time our place became known as The House on Pushkin Street.

The accommodations were not luxurious but the address was brilliant—Pushkin Street in Pushkin's city, Leningrad still the capital of the culture, if not the government. Near Natalya's building there was even the first statue erected to Pushkin in the city, a statue whose lightness and elegance—Petersburg values—Natalya particularly admired.

In the Khrushchev years, such dreams—a home, a place where people could congregate in human fashion—were not only permissible reveries but practical possibilities. But it was in the same year that Natalya and her two friends opened The House on Pushkin Street that Khrushchev almost brought the world to an end in the near-nuclear confrontation over Soviet missiles in Cuba. Khrushchev was too rash and erratic for the rest of the Politburo, who felt more directly threatened by Khrushchev's attempt to limit the party's power in 1963 than by his apocalyptic bluff of 1962.

Nikita Khrushchev went on vacation in October 1964 as the leader of the Soviet Union and was called back to find himself somewhere between a pensioner and a prisoner. He did what people in that position do—enjoyed the sunshine on his face and the grandchildren scrambling on his lap, and wrote his memoirs.

But what he had done proved not easily undone by the undoers led by Leonid Brezhnev, a dapper bureaucrat with a taste for fast cars. Stalin could not be returned to the mausoleum, the best they could do was to begin reenhancing his legend—as a man who took Russia from a land of poor peasants and made it a mighty industrial power that defeated Germany and went on to become an atomic superpower—and finally, sensing that the time was ripe, to erect a ten-foot bust on his grave, which was located directly beside Lenin's mausoleum, to its left from the point of view of people on Red Square.

Khrushchev had overstimulated expectations—people wanted justice, food, apartments. Limits needed to be reset. The new leadership made use of a device that Khrushchev himself, to his disgrace, had brought into practice—psychiatric punishment for dissenters.

All the blame cannot be laid at Khrushchev's door, however, for this was an old and honorable tradition, dissenters having been declared insane as early as the eighteenth century. And in the early nineteenth, the great philosopher Chaadaev was forced to admit he must have been mad in saying that Russia might not be an organic part of the history of the world but might just teach the world one overwhelming lesson before vanishing forever from the stage.

*

Lusya and Alyosha's friend Mark would rather listen to his uncle Ilya tell of seeing Tsar Nicholas three times than tell his own stories. He would even rather witness his mother Raisa Danilovna's tearful fury as she remembers the KGB begrudging her her life after she returned from German captivity. He does not want to tell his story, for stories always take you to their source.

His usual darting edginess leaves him, but his stillness is too sudden, of the sort that precedes a fit. The circles under his eyes seem smudges left by darkness.

He looks from the water in the reservoir, doubly stagnant on that breezeless, overcast day, to the large building beside it—a windowless, concrete monolith that any Soviet would know not to approach unless he had specific business there—then back to the water. He glowers recalling the rumor that in the event of nuclear war, those who work in the monolith will be evacuated through an underground tunnel to a survival bunker located beneath the reservoir. What you can't see always matters most.

I was attending an elite mathematics school and the course load was murderous, *begins Mark.* We worked something like twelve to fourteen hours a day. I was seventeen when I finished the course work. Instead of taking the exams I went away for a rest and that probably was the beginning of my breakdown.

I was sent to a psychoneurological outpatient clinic. That goes on your record and sticks with you forever. They stamped my draft card saying I had been exempted from military service due to point 4. Everyone knows that the first 10 points are for psychiatric disorders. And the lower the number, the graver the illness. Point 2 is epilepsy.

Then for reasons I can't understand, my condition became worse. I became exceedingly nervous. Since the doctors are responsible for the health and the life of a patient, they must have decided there was some danger of suicide in my case. And a suicide could cause them a good deal of trouble. And so as soon as the first signs appear, they try to have you dragged off to a hospital where you're under such supervision that suicide is impossible.

They told me I'd be comfortable in the hospital, I'd have peace and quiet there, I could study. It would only be for a few weeks, a month. I had no objections to that. They asked me how I'd get to the hospital and I said I'd take public transportation. But then the doctors suggested they send someone around for me.

I was home, it was already dark, around nine, ten o'clock. The doorbell rang and in came two strapping men. You could see their white uniforms under their topcoats. They spoke with my mother for a moment then took me by the arms, as if to help me down the stairs but really so that I couldn't escape. I was escorted to a minibus with barred windows and a red cross on its sides, known as a "nut wagon."

We spent another two hours driving around Moscow, I wasn't the only patient they had to pick up that night. When the minibus was packed they drove till they came to some kind of gate. The gate opened, we drove in, and the gate closed automatically.

I went through all the procedures, an examination of some kind, the showers. They took my clothes and gave me a patient's gown. Then I was taken through endless brightly lit corridors. I felt as if I were underground and in fact the hospital's complex of buildings are joined by underground tunnels. I was taken to my bed.

And it was only in the morning that I began to have some idea where I'd ended up. I was in the violent ward. Among people who needed constant supervision or else they might get into fights or try to kill themselves. I saw two suicide attempts. One man went racing head first at a radiator and the other bit a thermometer and swallowed the mercury. The orderlies grabbed him by the legs, turned him upside down and kicked him in the stomach until he had vomited all the mercury and glass.

There was a certain system to it. I was on the second floor where there were bars on the windows and no mirrors, and you weren't allowed pencils. The third floor was for people who were recuperating, and things were more liberal up there. They had walks, movies, television, but we didn't have any of that down on the second floor.

People knew that any violations of the rules could land you in a hospital where people stayed for years. Those hospitals are prisons and don't come under the health ministry but the ministry of internal affairs.

What frightened me most and put me on my guard at once was the use of chemical torture. As punishment for breaking the rules, or for fighting, patients were given injections which have no medicinal effect whatsoever. Sulfazine was used to inflict hideous suffering. For a few days after the injection you run a very high fever, 104° or even higher.

We had people from every walk of life in the ward, there were even some political prisoners. I met one, an artist by the name of Andrei Reznitsky. He told me that he had given an interview to one of those companies like the BBC. That was in November 1967, right at the time the fiftieth anniversary of the revolution was being celebrated with great pomp. They decided to clean out all the troublemakers from the city. And Andrei was a drug addict too. He was about to leave town when they came and arrested him.

He told me what he had said in the interview. "The Soviet government had seized power by military force and maintains its power by cruelly suppressing the people. Those men are gangsters and they do what gangsters do—exploit everyone and take everything for themselves." I'd never heard anything like it before!

There was a worker there too. After his pay had been illegally reduced and he was transferred to harder work, he was so furious that he tore up his passport and said he did not want to be a citizen of the USSR. He was immediately committed. He'd have severe restraints on his civil rights for the rest of his life and could be confined again for the slightest infraction. For years. And it's all completely legal!

There were twelve to fifteen people in the room, very crowded, pairs of cots, someone right beside you breathing, sleeping, snoring. The windows are barred and the doors are double-locked. Each of the staff had two keys. A person might get one key away but two would be much harder. The food was revolting. One day Reznitsky the artist said, "They feed us garbage, it's inedible." Another patient said, "Yes, but on the other hand a Soviet spacecraft has just landed on Venus." Reznitsky said he didn't care about Venus, he wanted some soup he could swallow.

In our ward there were also violent criminals awaiting psychiatric evaluation. And there were the chronically ill who had been there about twenty years. They made for about a third of the ward. They could no longer speak coherently, and could not differentiate between the edible and inedible. They had lost the sense of disgust. They would eat excrement.

But the most horrifying thing I saw was this. Every so often people wanting to work would be put to work, say, shoveling snow. They'd form a group of ten or fifteen, give us shovels, and two orderlies would keep an eye on us while we worked. One time we were going down some kind of corridors, down staircases, it was very poorly lit and very filthy. Then we came to what I thought was the boiler room. It was almost pitch black and there was a highly unpleasant smell, the smell of urine. Suddenly I could see figures separating from the walls, an old woman in a shapeless patient's gown. I looked in and I could see a great many beds, and people stirring on them. It was some kind of a horrible underground pit where people lived in darkness and filth . . .

I witnessed one escape. The orderlies didn't even notice him missing until dinner, when there was one egg left over.

The man who escaped went home and drank tea. Going home is the worst thing you can do and 90 percent of them do it. They went right to his house and arrested him. They brought him back to the hospital and he was punished very severely, with heavy doses of sulfazine.

I talked with people who'd been in the camps and they all said it was much better there. You could walk around after a day's work. But here there were walls everywhere.

After a breakfast of mush came shock therapy. You're given a large dose of insulin, the sugar disappears from your blood and you go into shock. This is considered a good way to treat schizophrenia. You're tied to your bed with strips of torn sheets, not ropes.

When they're in shock, people go into convulsions. They scream and howl. Their eyes look like they are going to pop out of their head. Then, after the correct amount of time nurses come around giving people shots of glucose. A strong shot of glucose will bring a person around in ten or fifteen minutes. One orderly holds your arm in an iron grip and another winds a piece of rubber tubing around your upper arm, and when the vein is fat and swollen the nurse jabs it with a hypo. The nurse never missed a vein. She was rough but accurate.

The psychiatrists there seemed mentally ill to me. Once a day one would come over to my bed and, holding his finger horizontally, he'd say, "So, how are you?"

If you're doing better, you hold up one finger and point it up and if you're depressed you point it down. Then after about two or three weeks you're called in for a two- or three-hour examination that's more like an interrogation; then once or twice more, the last time just before you're released. Other than that, there's no treatment.

The staff used stoolies, everyone knew that. The doctors based their opinion of a person's health on indirect reports from stoolies who told them whether somebody was excited or apathetic or looking for trouble.

Everyone knew that any protest would cost you demerits. If a person even asks when he's getting out, they give him a huge amount of demerits. And if a person says he's well and wants to be released, he runs the risk of being transferred to one of those hospitals where people stay for years. I started to feel that I would never get out of there. I was totally in the power of people I considered insane.

I realized that the only possible approach was to say that I was doing well and just wait. And that's what I did. I waited until they transferred me from the violent ward to a regular ward. And I waited there until they transferred me up one more floor where things were even better. Only one stage to go. But they kept me there a very long time. And then I started to feel as if I were on death row without knowing when I was going to be executed. Maybe in a year, maybe in a week, maybe never.

Then all of a sudden they tell me I'm free and the joy hit me like an electric shock. When they released me and I got on the bus, it felt like I was on a spaceship!

Mark's face lights up with a brittle incandescence. He has survived the telling of the story just as he survived the experience itself, riding the spaceship of a bus back to life and freedom, to marry a woman whose grey-eyed, fair-haired beauty has a modesty that almost keeps it from being noticed and with whom he has had three children.

The madhouse haunts his art. In black-and-white ink drawing after black-and-white ink drawing, he portrays the shrieks he could not shriek in there, a darkness stirring with shapes.

His memories are fed by new fears, for he knows that in Russia the powers of darkness are always just under the surface, like that underground corridor, like the shelter beneath the reservoir, able to burst forth at any minute as they did in August 1968, when Soviet tanks roared into Prague, dispensing the ultimate demerits to a nation mad enough to declare itself healthy and free.

*

The Russian thaw and the Prague Spring both ended that August. Faceless Soviet Stalinism without Stalin triumphed over socialism with a human face. Still, great countervailing forces were at work. Natalya Viktorovna's apartment was a full-blown institution by then and was referred to as The House on Pushkin Street. Tea and free speech flowed. The rarity of the atmosphere and its human comfort so attracted some people that, once having experienced it, they could no longer go on living as they had before. In The House on Pushkin Street they found the truth they had been looking for without quite being able to name it. For one woman, Galya Dozmarova, The House on Pushkin Street was so irresistible that she moved into a communal apartment in the building to raise her young daughter, Masha, near that benign oasis.

But Galya was doing it for herself too. She had never had a home or family. Her mother, a pilot who flew in the war and was always rushing from one place to another, had given birth to her on the steps of the Kursk train station in Moscow. And all she knew of the family history was what her mother's brother—an engineer who had been recruited for lifetime service in the KGB against his will—has said in his dying delirium.

Born in 1935, a former geologist who made field excursions to the Soviet Far East, Galya has a face whose fine tectonic lines are echoed by her aboriginal hair. Her laugh is roughened by tobacco. She looks as well used by life as her daughter of twenty-five, Masha, a tall and slender beauty, looks fresh, though she already has a marriage behind her. But Masha still has a virginal purity in the grey-green luminescence of her eyes and the spontaneity of her gestures, a beauty marred only by her teeth, discolored by Leningrad's disastrous water.

Galya was twenty-seven when she first visited The House on Pushkin Street and was still under the influence of her society, which had once, when she was in the Communist Youth League, caused her to rip the red scarves off two Pioneers who had, in her judgment, misbehaved. But she was a person of innate goodness, which can never be satisfied with "correct" behavior. "I became a different person after I met Natalya and the other women of Pushkin Street. It's because of them I am a self-respecting person. They helped me develop what was in me, my God-given abilities, they helped me become a human being. I fell in love with that house immediately. I said, I can't live without this house. And I had only been there once."

Pushkin Street was long ago. Galya has her own apartment in Leningrad now, where she is frying potatoes for dinner. Masha, grown up now, is making call after call on a phone whose receiver is bound with a tourniquet of black electrician's tape. She is on a piece of furniture that is a couch if you are sitting on it, a settee if you are lounging on it, and a bed if you are sleeping on it.

"Soviet television calling," says Masha in a crisp voice that demands attention. Galya smiles, her face cracking like parched earth.

"The door was never closed on Pushkin Street," says Galya. "It was always open house. There was always food, very unpretentious food—black bread grilled with salt, tea, sugar, jam. Tea was served every evening at nine o'clock. On the dot."

Hanging up, Masha is no longer a Soviet television producer but an alumnus of Pushkin Street, still mystified and exhilarated by life. "You had to have a very solid excuse to be late for tea. Tardiness was viewed as a violation of tradition," she interjects, glad to be remembering those years. After a pause, Masha adds:

Those were the Brezhnev years. Boring times, nothing was moving, it was like a swamp. The only place you could relax was in the kitchen on Pushkin Street, where you could say whatever you wanted and know you'd be taken right.

I didn't want anything to do with the outside world, I didn't want to communicate with my classmates at school. Everything was so good and so interesting in that little world on Pushkin Street. I grew up there and I even considered myself a part of their generation. And it was only much later that I could see that I belong to my own generation too.

I lived in the closed world of Pushkin Street. I did not suffer from any split in consciousness because I had practically nothing to do with the outside world, with people my own age. But when I started working for Soviet television, all of a sudden I could see that something was wrong. These people had a different way of looking at the world. First I kept my distance from them but then I had to speak with those people who had a different mind-set. Unconsciously, I went on my guard, that must have been the instinct for self-preservation. Once I was talking with a director and an old woman came by. Everyone was waiting for her to retire so they could replace her. The director says, "Oh, and how are you today?" to her but when she was past he said, "Good Lord, when is she finally going to die?" That shocked me.

I changed a lot working there. I lost my naïveté and spontaneity. I became very guarded. I used to say things without a second's thought but I don't anymore. I have to keep myself under control all the time, I have to think about nearly every word I say. It's become automatic with me, and it's spreading even into things that have nothing to do with work.

Sincerity does not prepare you for hypocrisy, sanity is not a good school for the world. When founding The House on Pushkin Street, Natalya Viktorovna had very limited and specific aims.

Masha grew up in our house, *says Natalya.* And we helped inoculate her, figuratively speaking. But we never paid any special attention to the children's upbringing, I thought educating the grown-ups was more important.

When Galya became pregnant with Masha, the father was against having the child and used that as the reason for leaving her. But Galya had made up her mind to have the child. She stayed on at Pushkin Street, she lived one floor down, and gave birth to Masha, who grew up in our kitchen.

There were always new people showing up at Pushkin Street. Dissidents who had been released from the camps would come to our door and say, I'm so and so. You always had to feed them. But there was always fried potatoes, salted mushrooms, bread, butter, jam, and tea. That wasn't a problem.

Every day was open house and sometimes it just got to be too much. One time we decided to post a list for our regular guests, telling them which days of the week to come. One of the dissidents just back from exile tore the list down in a fury—Why are you drawing up lists for the KGB!?

Needless to say, there was a whole surveillance network around the house. And it looks like they had some informers among us too. I could tell by the way they searched the apartment the one time the police came and made a search. They never touched the shelves where the illegal literature was kept. They didn't want to initiate a case against us, just put some fear in our hearts.

Also to put fear in people's hearts the writers Andrei Sinyavsky and Yuli Daniel were tried in 1966 and sentenced to the camps and exile for statements made by their fictional characters. The entrance of Warsaw Pact tanks into Czechoslovakia in 1968 had been more than an invasion, it was a message as to the limits and the rules. And, as one Czech writer remarked with Central European rue, The pen is mightier than the sword, but not than the tank.

That wasn't entirely clear. For in that same year Andrei Sakharov made a fateful decision. He allowed underground distribution of his essay "Progress, Co-existence, and Intellectual Freedom." For twenty years he had served the state, helping in the creation of the first Soviet atomic bomb and fathering the hydrogen bomb and had done so out of a patriotism honed by war and a sense that a nuclear balance was stabilizing. Now, with the publication of this essay, he shifted allegiance from the state to the society. He had had his fundamental insight about the world—a society without human rights for its citizens was a threat to all societies in which human rights were observed. The invasion of Czechoslovakia and the publication of *Progress* were the opening salvos in a war both sides declared in 1968.

The next year Revekka Mikhailovna retired from her job at the factory. She had raised the son she had given birth to in a labor camp, the son she bore to win her freedom and a second chance at life. She had taken her beloved Papa's advice and returned to the working class, to simple humanity, rough but good, and healed her hideous wounds among them, the wounds of losing father, husband, and brother all in that year, '37. And, on the insistence of that working class, she had joined the communist party, which for her always meant the party of Lenin, the party of her father, and the party of her father's great friend, Ivan Vrachov, whom she had so loved as a girl, running across the floor and up into his arms. But there wasn't a sign of Vrachov. He had been a perfect candidate for execution—he had challenged Stalin to his face, he had called on his comrades to rise up against Stalin in what he called "Russia's last hours of freedom." And, if by a miracle, he had, unlike Revekka's father, escaped execution, he would have either dropped of emaciation in a camp or been killed in the war. That was a given for Revekka.

Naturally, I was sure that Ivan was dead. I didn't doubt it at all. And life had been such a struggle for me all those years I didn't even think of him much. I knew a person who worked in the diplomatic service and when he found out who my father was he kept on asking me over and over how he could be of help to me. One day, he said to me, "Today I'm in a hurry. I going to the Military Society to meet with Ivan Vrachov."

And I said, "Please do me a favor. When you see him, mention my name to him. If he reacts in any way, tell him my address. But if he doesn't react, drop the subject."

The next day I called up my friend in the diplomatic service. He said, "If you could have seen how happy Ivan Vrachov was to hear your name, he jumped for joy. He said, 'I can't believe she's alive.'"

The diplomat gave me Ivan's address and said that Ivan and his wife would stay home for the next two days expecting me. I couldn't bring myself to go on the first day but the next day I went. When he opened the door, I thought to myself, He looks so old.

But a great friendship sprang up between us. He wrote me letters every day, he came to see me, he shared all his feelings with me. But when the friendship started becoming dangerous I insisted that he stop coming to see me. He was a married man. And then he confessed that he was in love with me. And I told him, All I can promise you is this—if, God forbid, something bad ever happens, you can count on me.

We didn't see each other for a long time. And then his wife died and he came to me and said, "Something bad happened."

That was in 1969, the year I retired, and the year I married Ivan Vrachov.

*

For a brief period in 1942 the Warsaw Ghetto was reachable by phone, Hell could be dialed direct. There was something similar about the fate of the Soviet Jews who applied to leave the country in the 1970s and were denied a visa. They could be phoned, they could be visited, but they too were sealed off, in a NO EXIT designed by some Sartre of the KGB. They were in a bubble that seemed made of space-age material, transparent but indestructible, that punishes a person by cutting him off from everything while leaving him in the very midst of life.

Yuri Chernyak comes out of his building, a slab the color of dirty snow, and heads for his car. Sandy-blond, compact as a gnome, with broad lips shaped to smile, he moves quickly, for he has many errands to do even though everything he does is only a form of waiting. Walking to his car is one way of waiting and taking the windshield wipers from the glove compartment is another. Left on the windshield, the wipers would have disappeared within ten seconds and would have been on the black market within the hour, and so, the gesture of replacing them is as automatic and distracted as unlocking the door.

For him, as a physicist, driving a car is like sitting inside an equation and taking it for a spin in various vectors and at various velocities. At least until he remembers that he is not really driving but only waiting. It is March 1988, and that means he has been waiting twelve or seventeen years, depending on whether he dates it from the moment he applied to emigrate in 1976 and was refused, or from 1971, when it became absolutely clear to him that he could no longer live in that country.

I didn't even know I was a Jew, *says Yuri.* I didn't even know my father was a Jew. He was from an assimilated Russian-speaking family, they came from Vitebsk, which Chagall made famous. They knew Chagall, my father's older brother was his friend. I grew up with art and literature, Snow's "Two Cultures" was never a problem for me.

I was born and grew up in Moscow and my upbringing was typical of the time. When I was asked who I loved most, I'd automatically answer—Stalin. Everyone said you had to love Stalin more than your mother and father. Stalin first, then your parents.

My father cried when Stalin died. And he was shattered when three years later he was assigned to work with the Supreme Court on cases of rehabilitation. They had been told that they had their work cut out for them—in a year and a half they would have to review thirty million cases.

In the middle fifties, there was a change in the air. The camps were being opened. Suddenly people had grandparents.

Samizdat, underground literature, became a real part of my life, a major part of my life, at least half of what formed me as a person. For me that literature was both information and morality. I read the writers from the beginning of the century, the Symbolists, the philosophers, as well as accounts of the

camps, memoirs. I was around fourteen then, and it was also
the time I fell in love with physics, a love that may or may not
be requited but one that has lasted to this day.

Identifying as a Jew and becoming alienated from the
Soviet system were parallel processes with three definite turning
points. The first came when I was reading all that samizdat
literature and I remarked to a friend that as an idea socialism
was good—brotherhood, the redistribution of wealth. And my
friend said, Just what makes you think it's a good idea? I
suddenly understood: The idea itself was meaningless. As an
idea, it's on the order of thinking that it would be nice to flap
your wings and fly around for half an hour before breakfast.
The air's so fresh by the forest and exercise is good for you.
The only problem is that it's impossible. The idea of socialism
was unrealistic, impossible. And putting that idea into practice
results in tragedy.

The Six-Day War was the second turning point for me.
My awareness of myself as a Jew shot up. Mostly it was a sense
of pride—the Jews had been transformed from victims to
victors. Until then I had always thought of Jews as people of
the mind—Christ, Marx, Einstein, Freud. I never thought of
Jews as fighting men, capable of carrying out brilliant
operations. I had no image of the brave and daring Jew. Of
course Jews had fought in the Civil War and many commissars
were Jews, but there was still a certain stereotype.

The third and final impetus came in 1968 with the
invasion of Czechoslovakia. I felt ashamed and disgusted. At the
time I was in a Moscow State University summer camp on the
Black Sea. The Czech students studying in the USSR had been
detained and sent to our summer camp. They had not been
allowed to go home though they wanted to. We'd go over to
them and whisper words of solidarity. And thus my disaffiliation
from the Soviet system allows of precise dating—August 1968.

Now came the tricky part, reaffiliation. But the anti-Semites
helped out. They forced Yuri to remember something he had not
even known as a child, that he was a Jew and basically unwel-

come. At the time Yuri was supervising a top-rank group whose task was to make mathematical models of how various metals would react to the stresses of space, a project one might think the state would set great store on. But, no, it was clearly demonstrated to Yuri Chernyak that the metals could wait, the Jew had to go. It was the pettiness and the stupidity of it that were the most infuriating.

Seventeen years later he pulls up in front of a grey-brown apartment building. He has papers to bring to his friend, Yuli Kosharovsky, who has been a refusenik even longer than Yuri and who is now in the eleventh day of a hunger strike.

In the front hall, Yuri removes his boots and chooses one of the many pairs of slippers available to guests, an old custom that induces coziness and saves wear on floors. A hunger strike also requires the quietness of slippers; after eleven days, every sound is intrusive, tiring, and words can only be whispered.

With his shock of grey-brown hair, his sharp goatee, his pince-nez-like glasses, Kosharovsky looks every inch the Russian intellectual, a strict violin teacher, a professor of chemistry.

His young son enters the room, taking special care to restrain his innate high spirits, and looks at his father. His father nods, the boy turns and runs. A few seconds later he is back with a bottle of Borzhomi, a cloudy, Georgian mineral water. Kosharovsky sips and listens as Yuri reports on world reaction to the hunger strike and confines himself to only the most concise questions. He saves his words for his two main worries—that the West's attention was becoming harder to keep and that the lunatic anti-Semites, especially those in Pamyat, a group whose name means "memory," were becoming more vocal, more powerful. Sensible enough when they talk about the need to protect the Russian environment and Russian culture, the Pamyat people only reveal themselves as madmen when they seek the "enemy"—all of Russia's sufferings could not have been mere accident—and find him in a secret cabal of Jews and Masons.

"Here," says Kosharovsky, rising slowly and walking to his bookcase in the kinetic equivalent of a whisper, "here is their latest manifesto." As he extends the smudged xerox, he smiles with wan irony, but winks as if to say, It's spicy reading.

*

If two women like Natalya Viktorovna and Elena Bonner were in the same city, it would not be very long before they would meet. They were both in Leningrad in the early fifties. Elena Bonner graduated as a pediatric physician from the institute of which Med-pub, where Natalaya Viktorovna worked, was a part. Elena's mother, Ruth Bonner, had spent seventeen years in the camps and in exile, and Elena's father, the fiery Armenian revolutionary Ge-vork Alikhanov, had been important enough to have been executed at once in 1937. She did not need any lessons on the meaning and the pain of injustice, and she had the temperament to fight it at every turn.

"Elena," says Natalya, "was asked to write an in-house review on a book by one of my editor's cronies. The editorial board there were outright bandits. They handed out book contracts as favors. The editor in chief was an ignorant drunk. They gave Elena one of those books to read. She read it and said that it was totally useless, illiterate, raving lunacy, and must not be published. And the editor said, 'He's my friend, go rewrite your review.' She refused and they fired her."

People who were daring in the early fifties, when it could still have been very costly, became even more daring in the late sixties and seventies. Dissidents, or people who simply wished to demonstrate they were free, would gather outside the courtrooms where the state was using the law to commit injustice just as it used psychiatry to derange.

In October 1970 the trial of two dissidents, Pimenov and Veil, was switched from Moscow to the provincial city of Kaluga, away from the glare of publicity and world attention. Elena Bonner and Natalya Viktorovna made the trip together. And it wasn't all anxiety either—Natalya enjoyed the sight of the faded, aristocratic, eighteenth-century buildings, and there were funny moments, as when the local bumpkin KGB were walking from one little group of intellectuals to another in the courthouse lobby and, overhearing the mathematicians talk, were clearly wondering if they were speaking in some kind of code.

W e were all there in the lobby, *says Natalya,* and all of a sudden a person appears, someone I had never seen before. His face was so striking that I just stood there stunned and could not tear my eyes away from that face. I had never seen a person whose face radiated such spirituality and intellect. And he started walking very confidently through the crowd. And when he was passing by me, I just naturally reached out and stroked his shoulder and arm.

When he reached the courtroom door, he pulled out an ID and said, "I am Academician Sakharov. I have the attorney general's permission to attend the trial."

That same day Elena Bonner sent out for rolls and kefir. And when she offered Sakharov some, he refused, saying he didn't like cold food. That was the first time they met and spoke.

The three of them became friends at once. Now if Sakharov was in Leningrad he was on Pushkin Street and if the Pushkin Streeters were in Moscow they were at Andrei Sakharov's and Elena Bonner's, for the two soon recognized and declared their love.

"The KGB stepped up their surveillance on us after Andrei became a frequent visitor," says Natalya, edging crumbs off the table with the side of her arthritic hand. "But I wasn't worried because I never engaged in any of those dissident activities like signing letters, which I considered absolute nonsense. I always thought that the system had to be resisted on the personal level. You have to defend yourself against the system and resist it on the moral level. People had to rally and realize they were human beings and not cogs. The main thing was to instill people with a sense of their own dignity. Dignity is the source of all resistance."

Masha laughs. "For me, as a little girl on Pushkin Street, Andrei Sakharov was the nice, kind man who used to take me on his lap.

And sometimes he and I would listen to children's records together." Her smile turns a touch wry as she recalls that Sakharov had figured in her divorce as well.

"My husband was an actor by training but worked directing TV. He joined the party for the sake of his career. I was against that, but not enough to keep me from marrying him. Then he started saying I had a bad reputation, I knew too many of those Sakharovs and foreigners, and that was holding him back in his career. And so he said I should join the party. And I said, I'll never join, the party's philosophy doesn't coincide with mine. And so we broke up. On ideological grounds."

The dissident movement in the Soviet Union naturally formed into two camps, those who, like Sakharov, favored Westernization and those who, like Solzhenitsyn, insisted that Russia's destiny was always uniquely her own. Neither man suited the powers that be. The KGB's Solzhenitsyn problem was solved in 1974, when he was simply picked up and deposited in the West, which he so abhorred; KGB solutions are often punishments with a moral. The next year, Andrei Sakharov won the Nobel Peace Prize for his championing of human rights in the USSR. He was neither allowed to go to accept in person nor would he have gone, fearing that the way home would be barred. Neither of those examples deterred Yuri Chernyak from applying to emigrate the next year, 1976.

It took six months to have his application processed and rejected.

Needless to say, I was fired from my job. Actually, it was by mutual consent. They told me, If you stay on here, your life will be hell.

And they blackmailed me, The other Jews in the institute will suffer because of you.

I gave up modeling the stresses metal would be subject to in space and ended up painting cars. A Russian, a good guy, took me on, and insisted that we split everything fifty–fifty even though I was just learning how to paint cars.

Over time, Yuri phased out of that line of work and into doing translations and giving English lessons. But that made for a precarious income, a precarious situation. Like a heart attack, the police could come at any moment.

"I had a tough time of it with the police. My various incomes were in fact illegal, and not only because I didn't pay taxes on them. Many refuseniks tried to pay their taxes but their money was simply not accepted," says Yuri, laughing at the very notion of normal countries where people cheat on their taxes.

"The police came to my house fairly often. They'd demand I tell them where I was working. I'd say, That's what you get paid for, go find out yourselves. But when the police have so much power and you have none it isn't easy to keep up your resistance and hang on."

The KGB actuaries must have worked out the probable number of fatal heart attacks that would be suffered under a regime of isolation and harassment, the stress of being a prisoner in your own life. Yuri thought so.

And the KGB was definitely around.

I took part in the seminars on Judaism, the Jews of Russia, the questions of emigration, to Israel or to America. Those seminars were then banned. When they threw Abramovsky in jail, we tried to get into his apartment to demonstrate that the seminar was going to take place anyway. We were stopped by some KGB gorillas. While we were arguing with them, a minibus drove up with one of its doors open. That was a warning to us—they could shove us in the bus whenever they felt like it.

I went over to the subway station and told a policeman that we were being harassed by hoodlums. He went back with me and walked over to one of those KGB men. The KGB man bent over and whispered something in the policeman's ear. You should have seen that policeman's face! He was totally paralyzed, incapable of speech! *says Yuri laughing merrily.*

But the heart attack did finally come, like the police pounding at the door. The intellectual's pleasure in espresso and cigarettes, producing the caffeine–nicotine buzz of inspired conversation, was now to be rationed, sips of dangers. And there is of course such a thing as the second heart attack, which, too, can come at any minute. But life must not become a matter of waiting for that heart attack, for that will only increase the tension and thus the probability. And of course they must have figured that out too.

The years passed and nothing changed. And that was dangerous in itself, to become "old wine," as Yuri calls it, smiling, his lips smarting with the irony. "Young wine is cheap, they sell it by the truckload, but old wine they sell by the bottle."

Bad as the waiting is, it is not the worst of it. What's worst is feeling the truth of his condition. "The feeling is so horrible, so monstrous, that you practically never allow yourself to feel it. Once a year, maybe twice. You have your ideas and your plans, then suddenly you realize that they're all meaningless. You are a slave. You can't do anything without their permission."

Yuri pulls up in front of his building, the color of dirty snow now fading into a twilight of that same color. He removes his wipers, locks them in the car, and sets off across the bluish, hazardous ice.

A cuckoo clock is ticking above the small formica table. Sweet, red wine ages in a stout jar on top of the refrigerator. Yuri's wife, Natasha, lyric as he is dynamic, is just about to start serving the dinner. Their son Dmitri comes in. Tall, his face handsomely impassive, he would make a good honor guard, and in fact will be eligible for the draft in a matter of months. He could be assigned to a missile unit that would make him a security risk and keep the family prisoners in Moscow forever. His younger sister Julia, just twelve, comes giggling into the kitchen direct from girlhood.

Dinner at the end of day is important to them in the way it is to any other family, but they must also reaffirm their solidarity in the face of a force whose pressure can collapse the heart's walls.

Suddenly the food loses all taste, aroma becomes pure steam. This is not food, not life, not home, but a prison of perfect abstraction. Stricken, they bear through the hideous instant until they are on the other side of it, again a family speaking of the day as butter melts into potatoes.

*

Natalya Viktorovna tried to avoid all politics and all underground activity. But sometimes it could not be avoided and a choice had to be made, as when a mysterious couple showed up on Pushkin Street saying they'd been sent by the well-known dissident Bukovsky, who had been exiled in a novel way, in exchange for a Chilean spy.

The man said he was an Englishman. He couldn't speak a word of Russian. The woman spoke some Russian but with a very thick accent. She said she was from the Baltics. The man, she said, had been sent from England by Bukovsky.

I immediately warned them my apartment was bugged. And that meant we had to communicate by writing. I got out paper and pencils. She wrote that Bukovsky had shipped some kind of espionage device along with that Englishman and I was supposed to pass it on to someone in Moscow!

I had only a split second to decide whether to trust them or whether this was a KGB provocation. All I had to go on was my intuition.

I took the risk, I took the device. It was a miniature tape recorder concealed in a belt buckle. Of course, it wasn't for espionage purposes but to record trials, interrogations.

The woman I was supposed to pass it on to lived in Moscow. I wasn't from Moscow, I didn't know the city. So I brought the belt buckle to Elena Bonner, who lived in Moscow. Did she ever give me an earful for that! But somehow she found someone who got the job done.

Though many dissidents had been forced to leave the country or had been stripped of their citizenship while abroad, the struggle was still on. In 1976 the Helsinki Watch Groups were formed to monitor Soviet compliance with the human rights declaration it had signed the previous year. Though this was perfectly in keeping with the dissident strategy always to obey the law and to fight the regime by trying to make it obey its own laws, people continued to be punished in prisons, camps, and psychiatric wards. In 1977 the World Psychiatric Congress condemned Soviet abuses, exactly ten years after Mark found himself recovering from an ordinary nervous breakdown that had been diagnosed as schizophrenic and treated accordingly, with insulin shock therapy.

Suddenly, everyone was leaving. Either for America or prison, Israel or exile. Sometimes it seemed that the only people left were the Pushkin Streeters and those around Andrei Sakharov and Elena Bonner in Moscow. Then in 1978, Natalya Viktorovna's only son, Igor, certain he had no future in Russia, decided to leave the country with his wife and three children.

"He pleaded with me to go, but I told him I didn't want to leave Russia," says Natalya. "At the passport office I had to sign a paper indicating why I wasn't going and I wrote the same thing there as I'd told him—I don't want to, and that's it.

"At the airport he said, 'Mother, think it over, and come live with us.'

"And I said, 'Igor, if it turns out I'm the last one left at Pushkin Street, then I'll come. Death'll decide.'"

Decisions

On December 24, 1979, the Soviet Union invaded Afghanistan. Andrei Sakharov protested, and a month later he was abducted and exiled to the city of Gorky, three hundred miles east of Moscow. Solzhenitsyn, the lover of Russia, had been expelled from the country, and Sakharov, the great Westerner, was to be deprived of all contact with the outside world. His apartment in Gorky had a policeman at the door round-the-clock, his balcony was watched, his radio jammed, his movements tailed. Gorky was a city closed to all foreigners but Russians were, in principle, as Russians often say, free to travel there. Natalya Viktorovna was one of the first.

The House on Pushkin Street had been under surveillance since Sakharov had begun visiting it, and the chances of Natalya moving undetected by that surveillance and by the one around Sakharov in Gorky were very low.

One day after that first trip the three of us—Regina, Zoya, and I—were having breakfast on Pushkin Street when the doorbell rings. In comes the handsomest man you ever saw. Where do they get all those handsome young men in those impeccable suits? You might even think they were intelligentsia but in fact they're agents or investigators. And the handsome young man said, "Natalya Viktorovna, the KGB would like you to come by." He handed me a warrant for two o'clock that day, and it was already ten. Of course Zoya and Regina were in a panic, but I said, "Don't worry. I'll be back."

So I went. I was shown to a regular office where I was met by a man in uniform who held up his ID and said he was Captain something or other, I didn't catch the name. And since I'm nearsighted, when he started taking his ID back, I grabbed his hand and pulled it close enough for me to read, and I read it out loud—"Captain Kulakov."

There was a small table perpendicular to his large desk forming a sort of "T" and that's how you could tell it was an interrogation.

"Don't worry," he said, "I've just been assigned to tell you something."

"I'm not worried. Why should I be."

"What I have to say is that we don't recommend you traveling to Gorky."

"Your recommendations don't influence me."

That surprised him. "I'll be blunter then. You are forbidden to travel to Gorky."

"I'll go anyway."

He laughed. "You won't be let in," he said.

"We'll see about that," I said, and then I laughed.

"You know that Sakharov has deeply insulted our organization."

"It's hard to insult an organization as glorious as yours. And Andrei Sakharov is incapable of insulting you. And the way you treat him is disgraceful. And I could say more."

"Go ahead."

"It's disgraceful that the KGB spends so much money on one person, a person whose only power is his voice, which you're trying to silence."

"Sakharov insulted both us and the government very deeply."

"When was that, when he gave you the H-bomb?"

But he tired of it all soon enough and said, "I've told you what I was supposed to. Take it into account."

"I won't do anything of the sort," I said.

And less than a month later I went to Gorky again.

The first casualty of Sakharov's exile was Regina, one of the three founders of Pushkin Street, the invalid whose bedside was known as the "confessional."

"Regina died in 1980," says Natalya, "and I think it was because she couldn't take Andrei being exiled. She had a stenocardia, which lasted three weeks until her death, with up to twenty-five attacks a day. The doctors said it was hopeless, but each time we dragged her back with our own hands."

Still, there were two of them left, Zoya and Natalya. They could carry on the traditions of Pushkin Street. That was the bargain that Natalya had made with her son and with death.

*

In an apartment on the far outskirts of Moscow, beyond the last stops of all the subways and buses, reachable only by taxi or train, a young mother is telling stories about her children, as young mothers will.

"My six-year-old son was arguing with his communist grandfather, that's what he calls him, 'my communist grandfather.' His grandfather says, 'You say you don't like the communists but you eat bread and it's the communists who make the bread. You wear clothes but it's the communists who make the clothes.' So then my son plucked up his courage and said, 'The communists didn't make my clothes. This is Italian, this is American, this is Finnish. That's one thing. And another thing is that everything in the world was made by people. There wasn't always communism and still things got made. You make it sound like the sun wouldn't rise if it wasn't for the communists.'"

She laughs with maternal pride and hearty scorn, then washes down some Swiss chocolate with Armenian cognac, smooth and with a lazy bite. It is past two, late in a city where the Metro closes at one, the drunks, suddenly sobered by the thought of freezing to death, racing for the last train, police everywhere.

Sometimes Alyosha needs a late night, a break from the communal apartment on Sretensky, where lately the women have been coming to blows in the kitchen beneath the canopy of dripping laundry hung from the high ceiling. Sometimes lateness itself can be a narcotic if taken with oranges, chocolate, Armenian cognac alternated with espresso and cigarettes. And what better people to sip lateness with than Suzanna and Vasya.

Blonde, with an earthy sensuality, Suzanna flies into furies or laughter with equal ease. "I won't let that idiotic murderous system ruin my children's minds! I hate this country. I hate it so much.

"I want to live in France, where children are taught to think, not obey. I want to live in France but not for so very long, say, forty years." Suzanna chases a bawdy laugh with brandy.

Even Vasya smiles. He has the long, fine hair and porcelain eyelids of a Flemish John the Baptist, but one whose eyes flash with sarcastic amusement.

I 'm what we call a businessman, *says Vasya, delectating the larcenous insinuations of the word.* I got involved in 1980, and I wouldn't have done it if I had known what I was getting in for. You can't beat the system forever here. Sooner or later they get you. In a year, two, seven.

I knew my friend was involved in some kind of business but I didn't know what kind. I needed money. And so I went to him and asked for work. He said, "I'll give you a month's tryout at three hundred rubles."

The business was the production and distribution of religious literature, prayer books, New Testament Bibles, books by the church Fathers of Russian Orthodoxy. Religious samizdat. We used government presses at night, on the sly, paying off people. For some of us it was pure mission, but for most it was just business. For me, it was a mixture of the two.

A standard edition was one thousand copies and the

usual profit ran to six or seven thousand rubles, which had to be divvied up among the fifteen people involved in the actual production of the books. The distributors took the books at a certain price and then made whatever profit they could on them if they weren't doing it as a mission.

Vasya found that he felt comfortable both in the underground and in the underworld. As a seeker of truth, he read the Church Fathers, the religious philosophers like Berdaev, and the mystics like Gurdjieff. But business was money, danger, freedom, life.

I n business you make your own decisions. And it's all up to you whether you go broke or make a fortune, *says Vasya.*

There's many different kinds of businesses, and each one has its own name of course. An "iron" is someone who changes money. And the "money men" are the ones who buy from the "irons."

Weapons can be bought. There's a special mafia for that. For 300 to 400 rubles you can buy a German Luger with one clip. And there's a pistol from West Germany that fires nerve gas, that goes for around 350. Refill cylinders with gas cost 100. These weapons are primarily for bank robbers. A police uniform costs 400.

I had no problems with being picked up for being a vagrant, a parasite. I always had all the working papers I needed. If you're going to do business, you've got to have working papers. They can be bought. The price varies. Right now they usually go for one hundred rubles. For that amount of money they'll do all the paper work and you get your ID marked. If someone calls your place of work to check if you really do work there, they'll cover for you. Aside from the one hundred they get for giving you working papers, they also take the salary you're receiving for the job you hold and split it among themselves.

Most of my own business was connected with books. There's a big market for mysteries and adventure stories. They're an escape from this life where nothing ever changes and nobody can do anything about it. Mysteries are an escape, a narcotic. And for the intellectuals reading all that philosophy late into the night gives them the illusion that they're still spiritually alive.

Video is big now. Blank tapes, cassettes, VCRs. Rambo III when he's in Afghanistan was very hot for a time. Of course, there's narcotics and pornography too but that's very risky business.

I learned the theater business too. There's a big mafia of scalpers, especially for the Bolshoi. Some sell tickets for rubles and some only for hard currency. Each mafia has one theater it controls. It does swaps with other mafias. No money is ever involved. Each show is graded and gets a certain number of points. The highest is sixty–seventy. *Boris Godunov* at the Taganka gets sixty points, *Hamlet* gets sixty too. Then, all goods that are in short supply are also assigned a certain number of points. Sausage, tea, candy, chocolates with cream or fruit fillings, coffee, deodorants—thirty points, perfume, detergent.

"Two deodorants equal one *Hamlet*," says Alyosha, who has been mostly quiet until then and they all laugh.

I was just imagining myself in a cafe by the sea in France, *says Suzanna, looking down at the gold hair on her forearms as if expecting to see it stirred by a breeze.* Who knows, maybe they'll give us a visa just to be rid of us. They've been on our backs since '82 when they started cracking down on the distribution of religious books. Friends of ours were arrested. The building manager started sending all sorts of people to work on our apartment, this was leaking, that was leaking. One day at six o'clock in the morning someone rings our doorbell hard and a young woman's voice says, "Telegram for you." I say I don't want it. And she says, "Take it, it's for you." "Slip it under the door," I said. And as soon as I opened the door a crack to pick up the telegram four big lugs come bursting in and press me against the wall. That was the first time in my life I ever saw the muzzle of a gun pointed right at me and it's something you don't forget. I thought they were robbers but then one of them pulls out his red ID and says, "KGB. Here's our search warrant."

They confiscated a lot of literature but they didn't take the Berdaev, they took the cash but not the bankbooks, they took the silver candlesticks though they missed all the gold, one gold chain I had was worth all the silver they took. And it was no secret that the arrest usually comes fairly soon after the search.

Vasya the businessman who has been methodically listing the cost of everything in Russia suddenly comes to life: "As soon as I heard their boots on the stairs, I jumped from our balcony to our neighbor's. I thought I'd sit it out there. Then a boy about twelve walked very calmly up to the balcony doors and opened them for me. I was wearing slippers and asked him if he had any sandals. He went and he got me a pair. Then I just walked out the front door and past their car. The driver was in the car but he paid no attention to me. We left Moscow a week later, we went to Riga, Vilnius, Tbilisi, the seaside resorts in Georgia. We stayed on the move for eight months. After about a year the whole thing blew over. I went in, made a deal that cost me nothing, nobody cared by then. Now it's just waiting to go to France."

"I have a sister in France," says Suzanna. "I'll just lie down on her doorstep with my children and say, If you don't let us in and help us, we'll lie here till we starve to death."

Alyosha smiles at her vehemence and asks, "How are you going to stay alive in France?"

Suzanna flares again like brandy touched by a match. "I will never believe for a single second that I am the product of the Soviet system and cannot exist outside it! I speak French and English. I'm self-reliant, I have strength, desire, ambition. Nothing can stop me. But they don't need anything like that here, here they don't need languages or abilities or education or beauty or elegance, all you need here is a good pair of elbows. I hate this fucking country!"

*

Either to prove a point or through mind-boggling naïveté, some Russians wishing to see Andrei Sakharov went right to his front door, where they were promptly detained by the police and sent out of Gorky on the next plane, after being issued a serious warning. Natalya Viktorovna never made that mistake. An appointment to meet somewhere in Gorky would be made well in advance when Sakharov or Bonner called onto an interurban line from the Gorky Central Telegraph and Telephone.

I was supposed to meet Andrei and Elena in a cafe at two o'clock. And I arrived in Gorky at twelve. There were long lines for the buses but what did I know about Gorky's bus routes. And the line for cabs was three hours long. Then I see a car, a taxi, but he seems to be waiting for somebody because he didn't pull up to the taxi stop. Then the driver comes up to me, another guy in a good suit, and he says, "Where're you going?"

"To the Russian souvenir store."

"And then?"

"To a cafe."

"Get in."

I got in wondering if it's off to the airport where they'll put me on a plane out of there. He took all kinds of back ways but that may have been because the town square was closed to traffic. In the end he brought me to the store.

I got to the cafe first. I found a table for four and took a chair against the window. When Andrei and Elena came in a few minutes later, I said, "For the love of God don't be upset, Andrei, but if they try to drag me out of here, I'm not going of my own free will. I won't resist but they'll have to carry me out."

*

Natalya Viktorovna said it loud enough to be heard by any of the handsome young men in the well-cut suits taking seats at nearby tables. She correctly calculated that though the KGB hated any defeat, their code of male honor would prevent them from bodily removing a petite, nearsighted woman in her fifties from a cafe table, especially since she had taken the precaution of sitting by the window and was thus barricaded by the table.

Sometimes, in spite of herself, Natalya Viktorovna would wince with compassion for Brezhnev when watching him deliver an incoherent speech on television, a walking, puffy corpse on whom medals were continually being pinned. There were rumors that the famous healer Dzhuna was being summoned to the Kremlin, only she able to keep a spark of life in him.

Ilya Jaffee was old now. It had been sixty-five years since he had seen the Tsar. Now Ilya was waiting for Brezhnev to die as he had waited for Stalin "to croak." Having thought through the whole tangled history of communism in Russia, Ilya Jaffee had hit upon a way to save the system, but no one wanted to hear about it, as his contacts with the Central Committee clearly demonstrated to him. There was not much Ilya could do but live the life of a hale man in his early seventies, vehement and confident as ever, except for those rare nights when he woke in a cold sweat, remembering the five peasant families he had consigned to their doom in the fever of collectivization.

But for Boris Yampolsky, the Zek raconteur and great reader, those couldn't have been better years. It was at that time that Boris made the acquaintance of Natalya Viktorovna, but he avoided all the entanglements of The House on Pushkin Street, visiting it only rarely. He withdraws a Russian cigarette, pinches the hollow cardboard mouthpiece in the same place but at opposite angles to give it the properly raffish shape. His sarcasm very gentle, Boris says, "Those were good years. There was absolutely nothing to do. Speaking with foreigners, underground literature, that was all too dangerous and I'd already spent ten years in a camp. So, what could you do? Reread the classics, Dostoyevsky, Turgenev, and with all the time in the world for it too!"

"Alive. Alive. Dead. Wounded. Alive," says Lieutenant Andrei, touching the chest of each of the five soldiers in the photograph taken on a blindingly bright day in Afghanistan, the soldiers' green and khaki camouflage blending with the bare hills.

His own uniform now folded over the back of a chair with discipline's pride in care, Lieutenant Andrei is wearing a short-sleeve shirt, jeans, and sandals on a warm June evening and, except for the precision of his haircut, looks like any Russian in his late twenties who grew up on rock 'n' roll but has since come to terms with life. He has the peace of a man who has been in combat and who has answered certain questions about himself. But he also has the tension of a man who has been in combat and has never quite relaxed since.

One black-and-white glossy jolts him slightly. In it, a Soviet soldier is feverishly reloading as an Afghan guerrilla raises his rifle with both hands, about to club him. "It's only by accident you ever get this close. Two to three hundred yards is the usual distance for combat. A Kalashnikov is accurate to five hundred yards."

He touches both soldiers in the picture as he says, "Neither was hurt. We disarmed the Afghani before he could do anything."

But the photograph's tension is not dissipated by the memory of the incident's safe resolution. Andrei continues staring at it until finally he sighs and turns to the next one in the pile, of himself on the day he arrived in Afghanistan, the black-and-white photo catching the darkness of his eyes and hair but missing entirely the ruddiness of his pale skin, the complexion Russians call "blood and milk."

Pausing to reconsider in a moment all the forces and factors that brought him there on that day, Andrei says:

My parents were both in the party. My father was an anti-Stalinist, and had great respect for Khrushchev. My father was a peasant by origin and Khrushchev did a lot for the peasants. My mother was more of a Stalinist. No one in her family was arrested. Actually, her father was arrested but after four months he was released, it was a mistake. And that only elevated Stalin in her eyes. The KGB even spread the legend that Stalin looked into every case personally. And even when my mother found out the whole truth about Stalin, she'd still always say, "Doesn't matter, it was still better then, I don't care what they write, things were better then."

And I am a member of the communist party too.

I was raised the traditional way, to think everything was pure and good here. I was one of the first in my class to join the party. I believed every word Brezhnev said, Yes, of course, there's some problems but we'll overcome them.

When I decided to go to military school, everyone said, Andrei, the army's not you. But somehow it felt right. Civilian life was too dirty for me, I wanted something that had some purity.

And I wanted to test myself, my strength, my character, I wanted to find out whether I was a man in the true sense of the word. Or just a piece of shit.

I went to a military school, graduated an officer, and was stationed in Tashkent, which isn't far from the border with Afghanistan.

Finally, I was transferred there. We believed we were going there to help, to fight for freedom.

Afghanistan was going to be our Spain.

I was attached to a paratrooper brigade as deputy political officer. I was responsible for discipline, political instruction, and morale. In Afghanistan every officer's first responsibility was to be able to lead men in battle. That means able to read maps, direct artillery, command soldiers, select positions from which to engage in military operations.

After a day of hard training, we'd sit around and sing songs, songs about the war in Afghanistan, and sometimes World War II songs. Otherwise we'd listen to cassettes. The Moscow group Time Machine were my idols, but I also loved Deep Purple and The Beatles.

Then it was time to go into combat and find out what it was like and what he was like. But it was not quite what he expected.

Y ou always engaged the enemy at a distance of two
hundred–three hundred yards. If you were any closer then
it was probably a mistake, either yours or theirs.

One time we were caught by surprise. The Afghan
rebels came at us out of nowhere, they had some caves nearby.
Fire opened at around thirty yards. The whole thing took about
fifteen minutes, twenty at the most. Modern weapons make for
quick decisions. Whoever fires first wins. We were a little
thrown at first but we were first to open fire.

War is war. You can't let your guard down for a
second, you always have to be on the alert. If you relax for a
minute, if you lose control, if you let your men relax, you're
dead. You're in a state of constant tension, your nerves are
tight as a fist. You cannot allow any fear to slip in.

Our main tasks were protecting cargo shipments and
ambushing guerrilla bands based on previous intelligence.
Sometimes we were sent to areas where a rebel base was
located. Our task was to seize or destroy that base, and
establish the Kabul government there. Then we also did
propaganda work with the civilian population, explaining what
we were doing there, and supplying them with food and
medicine.

There were three problems in that war. One was that
there was no real front and you never knew who was your
enemy and who was your friend. Some of the locals were
farmers by day but would take up arms against you at night.
The second problem was the absolutely unfamiliar terrain. And
the third was the weather, the heat would hit 110°.

In the cities some of the children and merchants spoke
Russian but not in the countryside. We had interpreters with
us, Uzbeks and Tadzhiks, and some of them even had relatives
in Afghanistan. I don't know if they believed in Allah or not
but they were faithful to Muslim traditions and at first they
didn't want to fire on their brothers. But after one of them was
killed, no one went into battle more furious for vengeance than
them.

And there were plenty of cases when somebody had to

stay behind so that the lives of the others could be saved. You couldn't order anyone to do that. He had to volunteer. There were always volunteers.

Connections don't matter at the front like they do everywhere in civilian life and everywhere else in the army for that matter. At the front we were pure. And after that we could never be like other people who say, Do me this favor and I'll do something for you. I can go see any one of my friends from Afghanistan at any hour of the day or night and he will give me the shirt off his back and ask nothing in return. Or I can write one of them a letter and say, I have to see you. And he'll drop everything and travel hundreds of miles. That's what counts.

The best soldiers we came up against were the mercenaries, foreigners who had fought before and knew tactics. The guerrillas would never engage in close battle. One time a detachment of ours was surrounded. They were heavily outgunned and were wiped out. When we retook the position we saw what they had done to our dead and wounded. They'd cut off everything you could cut off. Eyes gouged out, bellies slashed open. And naturally that made us hate them all the more.

Andrei learned what he had come to learn, that he was a man, not a "piece of shit." He also learned what most soldiers learn—that it isn't long before the only reason you're fighting is to kill the people who killed your friends and who are trying to kill you.

"You get terribly homesick for Russia, the real Russia. You start to understand what your country means to you, you discover it again. And you start dying to see birch trees again, especially with everyone singing those Russian and Ukrainian folk songs. And if you get leave in Tashkent even though it isn't really Russian but just Soviet, still, there are birches there. When you see them you feel like crying and falling to the ground and kissing the earth."

He picks up the next picture. Two young men seeking the delicious shade of the east, their faces spattered by light.

He's alive. *He touches the one on the left then the one on the right, saying:* He was wounded but he survived. I was wounded too. In Gazni. We were surrounded. A helicopter was trying to evacuate the wounded. The copter was hit. We dragged out the wounded and started crawling with them to some rocks. We were just a few yards away when we were caught by a burst. The guy dragging a wounded man beside me was killed and I was hit in the upper body, right side. The men who were already wounded were saved.

The wound is still very fresh. You never forget about it. The skin there is very thin, very sensitive, sort of a naked feeling, *he says, touching the wound.*

War is war. Some people on our side used drugs, looted, deserted or even went over to the enemy. But it was a strange war, a war in which we won every battle but did not emerge as victors. If we had to take control of some area, we took control of it. If there was a guerrilla band we had to wipe out, we'd wipe it out. There was no assignment we didn't carry out. And when we left, the civilians threw flowers at us, and I would have given my whole two years there just for that.

But the war was a mistake. We had no right to be there. We should have known what war meant from losing twenty-seven million people during World War II. I realized that war only means killing and never makes anything better, whether it's in Vietnam or Korea, Afghanistan or Grenada. And the army general staff had been against the war and warned that it would end badly. But the Politburo wanted it. Brezhnev wanted it. If he had to go to war or send his son to war, he might not have wanted it so much.

After a while we saw that it was a civil war, their business, let them decide it themselves. For centuries the army was always considered the elite of Russia, examples of dignity and honor. And now that prestige had been damaged. We came back from that war and people spat at us. We were perfectly well aware by then that the war had been a mistake, but knowing it was one thing and saying it was another when you had friends who had been killed there. It takes time, years, to make that kind of mental adjustment and some of the guys just never could make it.

Our Spain.

*

On November 7, 1982, the sixty-fifth anniversary of the revolution, Leonid Brezhnev waved from atop Lenin's tomb to parading soldiers whose cheers resounded like retorts in the brick acoustics of Red Square. Three days later he was dead.

Yuri Andropov now went from head of the KGB to head of the country, though he probably had a good hand in running things during Brezhnev's long demise. He began tightening the machine at once. People frequenting movies and bath houses in the afternoon would have to prove to the police that they were not unlawfully absent from work. All the various spigots on the state's immense vat of vodka were closed with a few turns. But Andropov went after corruption in high places too, so rank and rampant that very little ferreting was required.

The second of the three original Pushkin Streeters, Regina, who didn't even know how to go shopping for clothes by herself, died at the beginning of Andropov's reign. Only Natalya Viktorovna was left. Death had decided.

But there would be one last trip to Gorky before Natalya Viktorovna kept her bargain and went to join her son and her grandchildren in America. Her most recent experience had demonstrated to her that there were no safe phone lines for arranging meetings with Andrei and Elena. The arrangements would have to be made in writing, hand-delivered and confirmed by the same person, everything scheduled at least a month in advance. The only problem was eluding surveillance in Leningrad, but, with a little help from friends, that was hardly insurmountable.

In writing I asked a friend to buy me a ticket to Gorky thirty days in advance. He went to the train station and stood in line and no one knew who the ticket was for. Then very, very quietly, I started getting ready. And not a word to a soul about it either. I also made arrangements with another friend. He came by on the day I was leaving to pick up my ticket and my bag, which he then took to the station and boarded the train with. I left the house and was immediately tailed, they were always dogging my heels. I started off in the wrong direction but then gradually started making a large circle until I was finally near the train station's freight yard. You can get to the platforms from there. I meandered around for a while then went straight to the platform. There were literally thirty seconds till the train left. My friend jumped off, handed me the ticket, and on I got.

The agents tailing Natalya Viktorovna arrived a few seconds too late. Now, to its own dishonor, the Leningrad KGB would have to call the Gorky KGB to inform them that the old dame had given them the slip again. They couldn't stop the whole Leningrad–Gorky train just to drag off a woman who had to use the handrail to mount up the high steps before vanishing in steam and train dust, just as the man who had slipped her the ticket was vanishing in a crowd of grey and brown coats, pausing only to take out an old-fashioned cigarette, squeeze the cardboard mouthpiece twice in the same place but at opposite angles, and to light the inch of tobacco with a match that flared like the glee in his eyes.

Yesterday

The Eighties

Part One

Lusya's children have knelt on their beds and watched the green and red fireworks over the Kremlin on the seventy-eighth anniversary of the revolution. All three had been so excited by the explosions of beauty that it took an extra hour to calm them down for bed. And even then they kept running from their bedroom through the common hallway to their parents' room for comfort, water, company.

Pasha is allowed to stay up a little later. He is at the age when it is an unconscionable humiliation to be treated the same as the little ones. If he can be allowed to go out and play by himself in the capital of a crumbling nuclear empire, he can hear a few of the stories grown-ups tell each other, especially today, when the story is a very good one. Vera, the fireball from Siberia, and her husband, Dima, smuggled a priest into the apartment while the KGB family was out and had their newborn son baptized in the bathroom on the anniversary of the revolution. Alyosha and Lusya laugh with the humor given only to believers, but Pasha laughs too;

351

he knows the bizarre patterns of Russian life and can already appreciate some of the tastier combinations.

Lusya takes a mother's pride in the intelligent gleam of real understanding in Pasha's eyes, deep brown but with a quicksilver alertness, but it also makes her sad and angry, sad that her son's childhood and innocence are ending, angry that they are ending there in that communal apartment on Sretensky Boulevard, where time drips as slowly as the laundry hanging overhead in the kitchen. She sends Pasha off to bed with a brusqueness that startles him. He knows at once that none of his tricks will work. His mother is not a woman angry by nature and she usually struggles with the anger she does feel, but the anger that does finally break free is hot and sharp, and to be avoided.

But he can kiss them good-night. The hug he gives his mother is so warm and gentle that it makes her ashamed. Alyosha gives Pasha a good squeeze and a wet, long-bearded kiss.

Pasha is my first child, *says Lusya,* and I went into the maternity hospital early with him, because I was worried about giving birth prematurely. I had slept on a park bench pregnant with him like my mother had done with me. So I checked myself in early.

But Soviet maternity hospitals are like prisons. Once you're in you can't get out. You can be there for nine months and not ever even go out for a breath of fresh air. And they don't let anyone in to see you either. My mother, who lived in Latvia, was coming into Moscow on her way home from Bulgaria and so I asked for just ten minutes with her. It was refused.

I went into the maternity hospital early on a Saturday evening and was put in a labor ward with sixteen other women. All of them were in one stage or another of giving birth.

There was a nurse midwife there but she spent the first forty-five minutes or hour I was there on the phone talking to her boyfriend. "What do you want to do tonight? The movies again? I'm sick of the movies. Let's go see Tanya? No? The movies?"

And she kept shouting to the women, "Keep it down, I can't hear!"

The women are crying out in pain, and she can't hear!

"Help, help," the women are crying, and the nurse says, "Right away, one second."

But when she was done with her phone call, she just walked off, that's all, just walked off.

The ward was unbelievably filthy. The sheets were filthy, the gowns were stained. Rats ran by.

At first I was able to endure it. But it became a nightmare. One night I said to the woman beside me, who had already gone into labor, "Are you having labor pains right now?"

"No," she said.

"Then please go find someone to help me, I think I'm about to give birth."

She ran out and looked in every room on the floor but there was no one around, no doctors, no nurses.

It was two or three o'clock in the morning and they'd all gone off to sleep. I had to lie there weeping and moaning, unable to speak, unable to even move my lips. At ten o'clock the next morning the new shift came on. By then I had gone into convulsions and could not even cry out to them. And so I lay there a few more hours until a woman doctor began going up to check on each woman individually. I'm lying there thinking, hurry up, for God's sake, hurry up.

She came over to my bed and saw that I was turning blue. She listened to my stomach, then flew out of the room like a bullet. Suddenly, I was surrounded by ten or fifteen doctors, all in white gowns running back and forth through the ward.

Then I was on the table. The child had already dropped so low they decided to bring it out with forceps. And when they put those forceps in me without any anesthetic and began pulling Pasha out, I screamed so loud all Moscow could hear it.

I passed out from the pain. When I came to, they were holding up a little boy.

Later, when they showed Pasha to me again, I was horrified to see that he had a deformed face, his jaw all off to one side. I didn't know it was just the effects of the forceps and would wear off. I decided he was deformed and said to myself, It doesn't matter, I'll love him all the more.

Giving birth to a boy was somehow a creative triumph for me. My next child was Nesya, a daughter, me to a T. I had a different feeling when giving birth to her, a disappointment, no, not disappointment but a feeling that giving birth to a daughter was just natural.

After my first experience with Soviet maternity hospitals, I decided to hire a private physician for a hundred rubles. That was especially important since, after the difficulties of the first birth, the doctor determined that I should have a cesarean for the second. But of course my doctor had just gone into the hospital herself for a kidney stone operation, when I went into labor.

Alyosha put me in a taxi and we went to the maternity hospital where we were signed up. Alyosha walked in very proudly and said, "Lusya Polshakova is here to give birth." Needless to say, no one had ever heard of me there. Finally, the receiving nurse had me fill out a form and then told me to take a shower. "But," she said, "there's one thing you should know—there's no hot water."

"You can get pneumonia like that," I said. "And I took a shower this morning."

"Doesn't matter," she said. "You have to take a shower."

I don't like breaking rules and so I went and took a cold shower. When I came back, she sat me down in a chair and said, "Wait here, a doctor's coming from another hospital for you."

She went off to eat her dinner and I was left all alone, in labor, sitting on a chair! An hour and a half passed. Finally, Alyosha, who could see me in the chair howling with pain through the waiting-room window, stormed in and said in a decisive voice, "Get your things. We're going to another hospital."

Just as he was abducting me, another nurse appeared and said, "What are you doing?"

"I'm in labor," I said, "and I've been sitting here for an hour and a half and no doctor's been to see me."

"Oh my God!" she said, and grabbed me by the arm, taking me to the birthing room. There she asked me, "Are you Lusya Polshakova, the one that's supposed to have the cesarean?"

"That's right," I said.

"Oh my God!" she said. "We can't operate on you. We have no OR nurses or anesthesiologists on duty, and there's no sterile anything! Oh my God, why did you have to come here, they'll put us in prison if anything happens to you!"

Just then the midwife comes in and says, "What do you need a cesarean for? Look how peacefully she's lying there, bearing up to it all so nicely. Let her be, she'll give birth fine and easy."

"No, no," I said, "I almost lost my first child."

By then they were all running around like madmen trying to get three doctors to sign a paper stating they had decided not to perform the cesarean, but no one would sign.

Meanwhile I gave birth, "fine and easy."

The third time I did have the cesarean. Afterwards, I was in a recuperation ward with eight other women.

When it was time to give me antibiotics to prevent postsurgical infection, I told the nurse I was allergic to them.

"What are you, a doctor?" she said, and gave me the injection.

I went into allergic shock. When the night doctor came on, he saw what was happening and he yelled at me, "Why didn't you say you were allergic to antibiotics?"

"I told them fifteen times!"

But that was hardly the worst of it. In the two weeks I was there, half of the children in our ward died, more than half. We all lived in horrible fear that our child would be next. Every day when they made their rounds, the doctors would say to one woman or another, "Have you been informed yet that your child has died?"

Andropov's grip on Soviet society was felt immediately, but his grip on life soon proved weak. Andropov kept disappearing from public view though the police continued checking papers in movie theaters and the public baths. For a year and three months Andropov had the view from the very top. What he saw was a land so riddled with corruption and inefficiency that only a vigorous young man like his protégé, Mikhail Gorbachev, could ever hope to set things straight. But, when Andropov died in February 1984, he was not succeeded by his protégé. The new leader was Konstantin Chernenko, another semi-senescent Brezhnev mafioso. Chernenko saw no reason to break with his predecessors Brezhnev and Andropov concerning Afghanistan and the persecution of dissidents in general and Sakharov in particular. In fact, Chernenko twisted the dial a few degrees and in 1984 had Elena Bonner exiled to Gorky, too, on a charge whose obvious contrivance was itself a signal.

But the spectacle of the three old men doddering one after the other was an affront to the nation's pride. The joke everyone was telling had a Muscovite being asked to show his pass to view the body of the latest leader to die. "I don't have a pass," he says, "I have a season ticket."

And it was death's season. Death had taken Brezhnev, Andropov, and The House on Pushkin Street. Now, after a year, a month, and a day in power, it took Chernenko too.

The interregnum between Andropov and Chernenko had lasted a month, but there was only one day between Chernenko's death and the emergence of the new leader, Mikhail Gorbachev. Open-faced, anointed with a mystical birthmark, a vigorous fifty-four, Gorbachev was effortlessly modern. In all respects, he seemed the man to lead the Soviet Union back into the world and on into the twenty-first century.

Gorbachev, too, did not alter his predecessors' position on

either Afghanistan or Sakharov. Under a fourth leader Soviet soldiers continued to kill Afghan rebels and be killed by them, under a fourth leader Andrei Sakharov remained in exile.

Two things were clear by late 1985. Elena Bonner's heart condition required serious attention, and the KGB's control of Soviet medicine was so complete that it would be suicidal for either Sakharov or Bonner to be treated by them. He, they would never let out of the country; she, they had and might again. If they would not respond to civilized requests, he always had the weapon of the hunger strike, a chemotherapy that either kills the problem or the patient.

Reporters loiter on the lawn, waiting for a statement, a shot, a tear. They are waiting in front of a modest house in the Boston suburb of Newton. The street is empty as suburban streets are on weekdays, and the TV vans, logos brightly emblazoned on their sides, seem alarming as ambulances.

Inside the house, two old women are sitting in the breakfast nook drinking tea and smoking cigarettes. A small, black-and-white television is on, a car dealer exhorting in a language neither of them can understand. Natalya Viktorovna has kept her bargain and has come to America to be near her son and grandchildren. Her companion in the vigil is Ruth Bonner, Elena's mother, who came with the rest of the family to the United States in 1980. She was now in the last of her exiles, the strangest banishment of all, America, where you could buy whatever you wanted and say whatever you thought.

It is quiet now but any moment the phone can ring, a wire service wanting a statement, a station needing an update. All the other adults are away, lobbying senators, delivering speeches, doing everything to keep the spotlight on Sakharov and Bonner.

Through the window Ruth can see her great grandson Motya, age eleven, playing a game of driveway football with friends. When he was less than two years old, Motya had been mysteriously poisoned, no doubt by the KGB, and that had been the turning point. Shortly thereafter they all left the country.

The phone rings. Her cigarette now jutting up at the corner

of her mouth, Ruth answers, in Russian, with military crispness, "I'm listening."

The caller does not speak Russian. Ruth calls through the window to Motya, all of the great grandchildren thoroughly used to providing precise answers to newsmen. Motya comes running in, takes the phone, and answers, "Hike."

He shakes his head and laughs at himself, knowing that neither his great grandmother nor Natalya Viktorovna could appreciate what a funny mistake he has made. But, recovering his aplomb, he provides the necessary information, which is that there is still no information whatsoever—they do not know if Sakharov is still on his hunger strike, they do not know if Elena Bonner will be released for the bypass operation.

Fortunately, the next caller, though American, can speak Russian. He is working with an independent television production company that is making a documentary about the fight for Sakharov's freedom made by his family. They want to come over and tape a statement from Ruth. "Come."

As they set up their lights in the living room, the hot, blinding lights of the media, Ruth checks her hair and her dress, a black cough racking what's left of her lungs. As old as the century, she is eighty-five now.

Ruth goes out to face the lights, the cameras, the comically earnest and solicitous faces, leaving Natalya Viktorovna to man the phone. Ruth squints, then smiles, flattered in some way to be the center of attention, grotesque as it might be. Then that extravagance is gone and she is once again on the witness stand of history, located that day in her grandchildren's suburban living room: "My husband was arrested on May 27, in '37. And I was arrested on December 9, that same year, '37 . . ."

Listening from the kitchen, Natalya Viktorovna scrapes crumbs from the table with the edge of her hand.

"The last of the Pushkin Streeters, that's how we sign our letters to Natalya Viktorovna," says Galya, who had moved into Natalya's building after one visit. "There's about twenty or thirty Pushkin Streeters left, spread out from Kharkov to Chicago."

It's even a little like Pushkin Street in her kitchen tonight. Her daughter, Masha, home after a marriage that collapsed because of "all those Sakharovs," has three friends over, drinking tea, discussing issues, their attention sometimes drifting away toward the television, which has been on for most of the evening. Galya herself, the former field geologist, looks over at the television to watch the forecasts scroll by over images of Soviet cities, tomorrow's weather for one-sixth of the world.

The table is quiet now. Masha's friend Valya the musician is sipping tea; the Latvian photographer studying in Leningrad is nervously turning the pages of a magazine, blinking in images of the West; tall, handsome Anton, Masha's friend from high school, has a small pony tail and an impassivity of face that is absolutely contemporary. A damp, childish wonder is on his lips as he watches the forms and colors stream across the screen, enjoying them as an artist, as a set designer in a puppet theater and a former hippie, but a hippie whose mother had almost died in the Siege of Leningrad, a hippie who had served two years in the Soviet Army.

Masha is distracted, pensive. She knows what it is, the time between loves. There will be other loves. But no one wants other loves, just love. "Maybe I should go away for a vacation but I can't relax, I can't just lie there on the beach. I have to be doing something. That's why I like going to the potatoes."

The Latvian photographer who knows Russian very well does not know that expression and asks Masha what it means.

"Going to the potatoes?" Masha giggles into her hand but then looks over it at the others at the table.

It should be embarrassing, *says Masha,* it *is* embarrassing that the Soviet Union, which employs a quarter of the population in agriculture, not only can't feed the country, they can't even bring in the potato harvest without the help of people from the city. But I don't care, for me it's fun. For me it's a vacation.

If the weather's half-decent, there's nothing better than harvesting potatoes on a collective farm. All your problems just go flying right out of your head. You work for eight hours, following the harvesting machine. You pick up the ones it misses and put them in the box you carry. Or they might have you rake hay. The worst work is sorting rotten onions in a cold storage room. The best job is loading melons, you can eat all you want.

You stay in a barracks divided in half for men and women. We built a steam sauna for ourselves. In the nighttime we'd sit around an open fire, play guitars, and sing songs. Sure, sure, sure, it was all the result of bad economic planning, but it just wouldn't be true to say I didn't like it.

She laughs and shakes her head at everything, herself, the world, Russia, Pushkin Street. But the smile on Anton's full lips has turned into a wince and his finger instinctively pats the slight swelling on his neck. He says:

L eningrad is so polluted now, that I always get a headache if I spend any time walking around. You can't breathe the air here. I've heard that other countries won't buy the "Icarus" buses we use here because they're an ecological hazard. And now you hear health warnings on the radio all the time, Don't drink the water without boiling it, Don't take baths. And there was an article about a district in Leningrad province where gathering mushrooms was banned because the mushrooms were radioactive. The article said this was a result of Chernobyl, but some people said the radiation was from leaks in another nuclear power station. *Anton's grimace has now gone from one of pain to that of modern youth's distaste for the poisoned world into which they were born.*

Nobody I know is doing anything about it, *continues Anton.* Young people don't want to be involved in anything, everybody's caught up in their own problems, they're just about living day to day. They raised us to do nothing and that's what we do.

I couldn't get with the Punks and their slogan, "No Future." I feel like I ought to do something with my life, make some contribution, after all I am enjoying the blessings of society.

I'm still not sure about what I'm doing in life either. I paint. I do art. I used to go to those "apartment art" shows when the avant garde would rent a little space for a short time, never more than ten days. The cops always came and took the show down.

I always had problems with the cops when I was a hippie with the long hair and the leather shoulder bag. I was always being pulled in by the police and frisked for drugs. Then they'd let me go. In the hippie days, the older generation was very against us and would curse us left and right. But when they began to see that it was something that was everywhere and it wasn't really so bad, they got used to it and stopped paying long hair any attention.

I'm living the way I like to live now. I work three or four hours at the puppet theater usually four days a week, which gives me a lot of free time. I spend it on music, art, and videos. I used to swim in a pool but it's polluted now too. What I do now is run barefoot through the snow every evening. In ancient times everyone went around barefoot and we all had contact with the earth. Running barefoot through the snow puts you in touch with the cosmos and makes you hardier at the same time.

I'm not at all that mystical or anything, but I wouldn't say that I don't believe in God. Maybe God is real and so are flying saucers, why not?

I got baptized after I was discharged from the army. Not for any idealistic reasons, and not because I don't believe in Marxism, but just because I wanted that sense of my roots. A great deal has changed in Russia but for a thousand years the church has remained more or less the same. My father and I drove to a village outside Moscow where we have relatives, and one of them is a priest. I was calm as could be about the whole thing, walking into the church, but then I felt a little excitement, not religious but something out of the ordinary. And when I began reciting the baptismal, I experienced a great surge of emotion. It was as if my mind had divided into two. One part could see reality, just as it was, the priest with long hair and the censer. The other part was the soul. Suddenly, I felt the soul, knew it was there, but I couldn't tell what it was because the soul is a mystery, *says Anton, smiling now, his finger still tapping the swelling on his neck.*

Subcutaneous drips were being jabbed into both of Andrei Sakharov's thighs twenty-five times a day, his legs ballooning with pain. The state has power over the bloodstream. A clamp was applied to his nose, a lever jammed between his teeth to pry his jaws open. The state has dominion over breath.

But in the end it was Sakharov who had the power and dominion, the state acceded to his demands. Elena Bonner would be allowed to leave the Soviet Union on December 2, 1985. Still, it was not a victory without real cost—it meant that they would be apart, they who found each other so late in life that "every year must count for three." Dashing from operating theater to podiums in the United States, Elena Bonner was both vivid and spectral, for on a set day she would vanish back to Russia and exile.

The year 1986 began with an explosion and ended with a phone call. In April, physics erupted into history at Chernobyl, when Reactor Number 4 went haywire. Many people in the nearby city of Kiev, convinced it was the end of the world, behaved accordingly, raiding wine stores, debauching wildly.

The wind took the heaviest radioactivity in a broad northwest swathe that ran across Poland and Scandinavia, even reaching reindeer in Lapland and sheep in Scotland. Absolutely objective units of information were escaping the Soviet border and being registered on dozens of meters in laboratories across Europe. After a few days the new Soviet government of Gorbachev was forthcoming with hard data on what had gone so terribly awry in Chernobyl.

The incident was an object lesson in what was becoming increasingly clear at the top. Technology drives history now. A society that has alienated its scientists will not be able to compete in the twenty-first century. Sakharov was not only the greatest Soviet scientist, he was the symbol of the entire intelligentsia. To continue his exile would be as counterproductive as continuing the war in Afghanistan, and the two were of course connected.

On December 15, 1986, two electricians accompanied by a KGB agent installed a telephone in Sakharov's and Bonner's Gorky apartment. They were told to expect a call at ten the next day.

No one had called by twelve and Sakharov was about to go out to buy bread. Just then the phone rang, and it was Mikhail Sergeevich Gorbachev, informing him that he was free to return to Moscow and his "patriotic activities."

Sakharov expressed his gratitude but also pressed for the release of more political prisoners and gallantly objected when he felt his wife's name had been insultingly mispronounced by Gorbachev. They were off to a prickly start.

Still, returning Sakharov from exile was a clear signal, a clear move, though hardly an abrupt one, for Gorbachev had been in power twenty-one months by then. Time would tell how serious he was about freedom of speech and the restructuring of the political and economic system. In May 1987, Ruth Bonner returned from the last of her exiles to the apartment in Moscow she had been granted upon her rehabilitation in 1954, moving in with Elena and Andrei. *Glasnost* meant that Ruth could die in Russia.

The next year, 1988, was one of miracles, fitting for the one thousandth anniversary of Russia's conversion to Christianity. The occasion was allowed to be marked with church bells and services. Soviet troops returned from Afghanistan, the final political prisoners were released. In July of 1988 Sotheby's held its first auction in Moscow and a painting by Grisha Brushkin sold for a staggering sum, a painting that would have been confiscated or destroyed by the police just a few years before.

And in that same year of miracles, Ilya Jaffee, who had seen the Tsar three times, now saw Los Angeles for the first. And Boris Yampolsky, the old Zek who had avoided foreigners, now found himself in Manhattan suffering such vertigoes of scale and abundance that he was relieved to return to Russia and his little neighborhood grocery store, whose shelves were bare except for a few grey boxes of macaroni, all of it suddenly so dear, so infinitely dear.

It was even a year in which a special list of Jews to be

granted emigration visas was drawn up and made public. The name Yuri Chernyak was among the fifty, on what Yuri would call a wine list of vintage refuseniks.

And in November of that miraculous year, Andrei Sakharov and Elena Bonner traveled to Newton, Massachusetts, to be with their children and grandchildren, sitting at the kitchen table almost as if their lives had never been torn asunder.

Sakharov says good-night. Everyone, family and friends like Natalya Viktorovna, who has flown in from Detroit, wish him a good-night. In the hallway his eye catches a volume of poetry by Blok left opened on a table. He picks up the book and begins reading. A minute later he surprises everyone by reappearing in the kitchen doorway, book in hand, saying, "You must hear this wonderful poem by Blok."

Slightly embarrassed to find himself the center of attention, Sakharov quickly sits down and begins reading the poem aloud, his voice faltering with the rhythm at first but then catching it and riding it well past any shyness. At the other end of the table, Natalya Viktorovna bobs her head, gazing at him with the same dazzled delight she had felt the first time she saw him in the courthouse in Kaluga not even knowing his name.

*

But the year 1988 was for no one more miraculous than for Revekka. And it had nothing to with the fact that at the age of seventy-four she had her first apartment where she could care for Ivan Vrachov, seventeen years her senior, weak of sight and hard of hearing now.

There is a light bulb attached to Ivan Vrachov's telephone that alerts him to the ringing he can no longer hear, though he can hear the person on the other end when he picks up the receiver, perhaps because of the instrument's ability to funnel sound. As one of the last Leninists on Earth, he is very much in demand in these days of early *glasnost*. Suddenly, reporters want to hear his stories about making the revolution in Voronezh, shifting the capital from Petrograd to Moscow, defying Stalin to his face at a party congress.

At ninety-one he is in buoyant spirits, having outlasted them all and having found Revekka again. Like any Bolshevik, he is happiest and most alive in combat, and now once again he is free to fight for Lenin's party and Lenin's name, which he still cannot pronounce without lowering his voice.

Revekka's voice is one of the few voices he can still hear. She calls him to lunch, an omelet cooked in butter with fresh vegetables. The door to the little balcony is open and a breeze blows in a freshness from the massed green of the birches.

Revekka eats with her apron on, plump again and always glad to eat after those years of Gulag hunger that can never be filled. After lunch they have a nip of brandy and a few cups of amber tea.

"For years I fought for Papa's rehabilitation," says Revekka. "In September 1987 I was called into the military attorney general's office, which must have been one of the first to undergo *perestroika.*

"The prosecutor in charge of Papa's case was such a wonderful man that I'll pray that God grants him a long life, if God exists. That's how grateful I am to him. The compassion he showed, the genuine desire to be of help," says Revekka warmly. But then for an instant she goes blank with utter horror at what it is all really about. Then she reexerts control over emotion as her father had always enjoined. "In 1988 I was called into district party headquarters and handed a paper stating that Papa had been reinstated in the communist party. I had conquered my Everest."

Part Two

But great as the year was, it ended badly.

In December 1988, while Gorbachev was in New York to deliver a speech at the UN and to make official the list that contained the names of Yuri Chernyak and his family, plates beneath the earth in Armenia that had abraded for centuries suddenly could no longer wait another instant. Twenty-five thousand people died in ninety seconds.

Gorbachev raced home from triumph to tragedy. The quake's devastation revealed what the world already knew but, so dazzled by Soviet armor, had never seen clearly—that the USSR was a vast poverty, held together, like the buildings in Armenia, with cement cut with sand.

Four months later, and for the first time in seventy-one years, there were free elections in the Soviet Union, an event transforming subjects to citizens. And those citizens showed themselves as full of surprises as their new leader. The people were neither cynical nor apathetic. Just as they had been in the last free election of 1917, the people proved themselves to be pluralistic and leftist. One of those elected was Andrei Sakharov, who in two years had gone from Enemy of the People to Delegate of the People.

Since his return from exile, he had been besieged by all his nation's dire needs. A life of phone calls, telegrams, emergencies.

On this evening, dinner has been postponed by the arrival of the leader of Crimean Tartars who has flown in from Central Asia to see Sakharov, fearing a "bloodbath."

The word pains Sakharov, who flinches and sighs. "You know what Pushkin said in *The Captain's Daughter:* God save us from a Russian revolt, merciless, senseless." Quite tall, Sakharov has something of the English country parson about him, except for the Mongol slant of his eyes, which are both shy and fearless.

The leader of the Crimean Tartars, Rashid Dzhemilev, has steel-streaked black hair brushed straight back, a chevron moustache; he wears a double-breasted suit and walks with a war-wound limp to the table in the light, airy front room where Sakharov and Bonner receive official visitors. He is accompanied by his associate, a burly, copper-skinned man with the distracted attention of a bodyguard.

Having seen them to their chairs, Sakharov sits down where he has a pen and note pad ready. He wraps one ankle around the other, then wraps both legs around the leg of a chair. After placing one elbow on the back of his chair and the other elbow on the table, he seems to be leaning backwards and forwards all at the same time.

But there is nothing for Sakharov to note down because Dzhemilev is passionately recounting the injustice done to his entire people. Sakharov could not be more well aware that Stalin exiled that entire people from the Crimea to Central Asia, just as he had exiled other entire peoples for alleged collaboration with the Nazis.

Sakharov listens with nearly perfect patience. Still, he cannot help but touch the ballpoint pen to paper. One geometry gyroscopes out of the other, the science that he sacrificed but still would rather do.

"We have *glasnost* now," says Elena Bonner with a mischievous smile, "and so I feel free to ask you just what it is you want of Andrei Dmitrievich?"

"We want him to use his authority . . ."

"What authority?" interrupts Sakharov with an irked sigh. "I can write Gorbachev a letter supporting your demands. Do you have a list of demands?"

"We have five demands," says Dzhemilev.

"Good," said Sakharov, glad to be down to business. "What are they?"

"The demands are," says Dzhemilev, waiting with satisfaction as Sakharov takes a fresh sheet of paper to list the points, "return of the Crimean Tartars to their homeland; restoration of the Crimean Republic; state financial assistance in the relocation process; and the release of Crimean Tartars imprisoned for human rights activities."

"That's four," says Sakharov. "What's the fifth?"

"The fifth?" says Dzhemilev, looking away to review what he has just said. "I can't remember the fifth one, can you?" he says to his associate, who scowls as he thinks, shaking his head.

A faint beatitude of humor plays at the corner of Sakharov's lips. Then even the Tartars laugh, but only for a second, as if every pleasure were betrayal.

"Don't worry," says Sakharov. "We can consider ourselves fortunate if one of the demands is accepted, and the first is the most important, that your people be allowed to return home."

"No!" cries Dzhemilev. "It's been almost fifty years and my people cannot wait any longer! The government must satisfy all our demands, otherwise there may be a bloodbath!"

Still, the Tartars leave satisfied.

"My pie is ruined!" exclaims Elena in the kitchen when they sit down to dinner well after ten.

"No, it's fine," says Sakharov, eating her special meat-and-mashed-potato pie with appetite and pleasure.

When he finishes his portion, he takes the salad bowl and walks over to the stove, where he uses a long, wooden spoon to scoop some of the salad into a frying pan.

"Andrusha, heating your salad!" says Bonner, shaking her head with the exasperation that is only a form of love, for they had first met when she offered him some cold food at the trial of a dissident in Kaluga and he had refused, saying he liked all his food warm.

She is still shaking her head at him when he sits down and begins eating the warm salad out of the frying pan with the long wooden spoon. When he looks up at her, their eyes meet in the joy of gratitude.

*

The first free elections were held in late March 1989, but in the next month a peaceful demonstration in Tbilisi, the capital of Georgia, was broken up by troops using sharpened shovels and poison gas. Sakharov went to Tbilisi to investigate and attempt to persuade the army to overcome its national security objections and release the chemical composition of the gases used so that the injured could be properly treated. It took considerable persuasion before divulgence was made and it was the delay that would be remembered in Georgia.

The first congress of freely elected delegates took place in June of 1989. Russia was tipsy on *glasnost* champagne. Every radio and television in the country was on. Production fell 20 percent. To the terror of their passengers, speeding cab drivers could not help but let go of the wheel and clap their hands when their car radio broadcast sentiments they thought they'd never hear spoken in anything louder than a whisper. At the same time, in the capital of a superpower, rumor turned into fact, and Moscow was suddenly without matches or salt. Still, nothing could dim the country's exuberance, not even the hideous glow from Tiananmen Square.

The current was moving faster now and becoming turbulent. *Glasnost* was beginning to show its dark side. Authoritarian rule had not only suppressed freedom but a variety of hatreds as well. And they were reported on in the form of jokes, one of which ran: "Before *glasnost* I couldn't say this," said the personnel director to Rabinowitz, "but now I am free to tell you that you're not being hired precisely because you're a Jew."

The derangements Russia had suffered in the twentieth century have been incarnated in the group known as Pamyat, a word meaning "memory" but implying vengeance. They cannot believe that Russia's agony had been mere chance. It had to have been caused by an enemy. And it could only have been a secret cabal of Jews and Masons. Pamyat is a fringe group waiting for its hour, as the Bolsheviks had, as the Nazis had, the century marked by sudden streaks from the margin to the center.

It is a warm evening in late June 1989, the birthday of the great nineteenth-century poet Alexander Pushkin. The day had been marked with celebrations by his statue at the end of a long park of shade and benches in Moscow. The ceremonies done, the crowd remains to discuss and debate, the police numerous but very relaxed, signaling that their only task is to preserve public order.

The Pamyat people stand out in the crowd of two or three hundred. Some carry a black and yellow flag, some wear black or yellow shirts with epaulets, all have the shoulders-back attitude of young men who have vowed an oath.

A stocky Armenian in a black leather jacket is trying to demonstrate to a member of Pamyat that national hatred can lead only to chaos, degradation, and slaughter. The Pamyat member, a blond in his twenties with the washed-out look of a poor childhood, listens, venomous with patience, furious that at this stage they still must tolerate argument.

An impish man with a long, grey beard darts from group to group whispering inflammatory quips in people's ears, gone before they can turn around.

One speaker, a stout woman in a blue-grey raincoat, has won an audience with her outspoken hatred for the KGB, some of whom have to be in that crowd. She has begun to lose her voice but not her energy. "Those sons of bitches in the KGB have machines installed everywhere that beam a ray that destroys your will. I've seen them. I have three degrees. And I have worked in the fisheries of the North and I know what people suffer."

The young blond Pamyat member can no longer bear the sight of the Armenian and strides over to Pamyat's platform, two flags, a spotlight, and a mike, which he takes, saying: "Pamyat isn't against the Jews. We're against the secret organization of Zionists and Masons who attempted to kill Russia by imposing communism on it."

"Not that old tune again!" shouts someone from the crowd in the clear hope of getting a laugh, which he gets, along with catcalls, hoots.

"Fascist!" shouts someone else who is not at all looking for laughs.

Arguments break out.

"If he's a Fascist, so is Mayakovsky."

"Why Mayakovsky?"

"Didn't he write in one of his poems: 'I love to watch little children dying'?"

"That's isn't Fascism, that's futurism."

And, "Lenin was a Jew."

"No, that was Trotsky."

"Lenin, Trotsky, what's the difference?"

"Besides, Lenin had a Jewish grandmother, on his mother's side."

"See!"

"Listen, listen!" shouts the young blond, almost tearful with rage. "This is what you have to hear. It's from the official Pamyat publication." Now he reads, his voice capitalizing every letter just as the writer had done on the page:

THE TIME OF THE GREAT TRIAL IS APPROACH-ING! A TRIAL WHICH WILL BE MORE GRANDI-OSE THAN THE NUREMBERG TRIALS! THE IN-EVITABLE AND FINAL COURT OF NATIONS IS IN SESSION! THE TIME HAS COME TO PASS SENTENCE! THE DEFENDANT, ZIONISM, WILL RISE!

*

But *glasnost* was still brighter than it was dark. Freedom of speech spread by edict and example. For some people it only meant raising the volume of their voice. But not for Ilya Jaffee, who had always been accustomed to speaking from the top of his voice.

We broke the back of the economy! We waged a war against the people like the war Hitler waged on us!

But those insights don't come easy. I had to read through all fifty-five volumes of Lenin to finally understand what a swindler Stalin was, what a liar, what a traitor.

But I also realized that the basis of the basis of the system could still be saved. I drew up my six-point plan and began bombarding party officials with it. And under Gorbachev I've seen five out of the six points put into practice. But none of it means anything without point 6. Point 6 states that unless the means of production can be freely bought and sold, *perestroika* doesn't have a chance. There has to be a socialist market.

The other day I got a call from the Central Committee, from the head of Economics Section. He said, "Point 6 can't be put into effect before 1992." "Fine," I said, "then *perestroika* starts in 1992!"

"I don't believe a word of it, I don't believe in anything!" says Raisa Danilovna, reopening the wound to her pride that was inflicted when the secret police called her surviving the war treason to her country. "I don't believe in any of that *perestroika!* Nothing will come of it and I'll tell you why. The generation that's forty today grew up without ever once having done an honest day's work. They can't even see that's how a person is supposed to work.

"Perestroika, it's all talk and promises. I don't expect to see anything good happen. Things may get worse but they won't get better. And my life will end in confusion and disorder."

"I wish to insert a correction," says Ivan Vrachov to the Swedish journalist who has already replaced his tape recorder in its case and zipped it closed. They all have so many little cases and zippers. Vrachov waits with severe and concentrated patience until the tape recorder is out, running, and tested: "I wish to refute the contention of certain Western press agencies that the current Congress of People's Deputies is the first instance of any democracy in the Soviet Union. That isn't true. There was democracy here in the early years of the revolution. Our party congresses and Central Executive Committee conferences functioned as a parliament and were democratic. And that's a fact. However, in no case would I compare the first congress with the one now occurring under Gorbachev. We were elected by the party while now the deputies are directly elected by the people. Under much more democratic conditions, and with people speaking openly because of *glasnost.* End of correction."

To her amazement and chagrin, Praskovya has not woken to heaven but to the communal apartment on Sretensky Boulevard. She goes to the kitchen to boil water for tea. Her eyes are too weak to make out the face on the small black-and-white TV but she recognizes the Soviet leader's voice.

Still, *says Praskovya,* under Gorbachev it's better. Talking feels nicer.

I never liked that Brezhnev though, a nasty smile on him.

And I didn't grieve over Stalin. Not that I didn't like him.

A friend of mine went to Stalin's funeral and got caught when the mob went wild. She came back all raggedy and missing a shoe, I couldn't stop laughing, she was such a sight.

But I'm an illiterate woman, what do I know. I can't even remember all those leaders, there's been so many of them . . .

But when I used to go to market there'd be cabbages and little pickles, that I remember. You could stand there all day just sniffing the air. Now even in a dream you wouldn't dream of eating pickles like that. How come? How come there used to be cabbage and pickles and that nice picklely smell in the air?

Elated to be leaving Russia, Yuri Chernyak grows serious when predicting the future:

There's a Russian saying—Making and breaking are two different things. The human being was broken here, for sixty or seventy years the very structure of the human being was broken. To remake something has to take longer than to break it. It will take decade after long decade to remake anything here.

Moses led his people out of Egypt and then through the desert for forty years. The desert has ideal, laboratory conditions, no outside influences. Under those ideal, laboratory conditions it took forty years to change people's mentality from that of slaves to that of free men. And it can't take any less than forty years here where the conditions are hardly ideal. And Gorbachev is no Moses, not yet anyway.

Gorbachev is the light of my life, *says Boris the Zek,* and if it's all going to come to naught again, may God not let me live to see the day.

Of course Russia has been almost totally destroyed. So many people killed, so much destruction over seventy years. There are still human beings here, the Solzhenitsyns, the Sakharovs, and in that sense the nation is immortal. There are still human beings here but human society has been destroyed in Russia.

The philosopher Berdaev said that the Bolsheviks put iron hoops around the collapsing barrel of the Russian empire. And now the barrel's falling apart again. What's to be done? What kind of democracy can there be in Russia where there never was any respect for law?

As for me and others like me, we don't give a good goddam even if they screw the whole thing up all over again. We don't need sausage, just give us a pound of bread a day and we'll even go out and work the fields. Just publish the writers and don't throw us in jail. That's all we ask.

"Still," says Andrei Sakharov, smiling like a man who has just been kissed, "still, these are astonishing times."

Part Three

It is a pollen-gold afternoon in the last July of the 1980s. Andrei
Sakharov and Elena Bonner have traveled again to the United
States to visit their family, absolutely without fanfare, another good
sign in itself, for rights are never secure until they run at least as
deep as habit. At a small desk wedged into one corner of a guest
bedroom, Sakharov is writing a supplement to his memoirs, covering the years after the phone call from Gorbachev, whom he continues to find intelligent but worries that he is not entirely free of
the mentality he seeks to change. He writes about the "astonishing
times" with a new radiance and his usual deliberation. Some bitter
stories do end very sweet in Russia.

Elena Bonner is taking the sun on a chaise longue in the
backyard and the light on her white sundress is the washed-out
white of old summer snapshots. She is at peace except for a bad
cough. In the far corner of the yard, one shoulder hunched like a
bird in bad weather, Natalya Viktorovna is enjoying a solitary
cigarette and remembering how her husband fell in love with her.

"It was in Leningrad, in the restaurant on the top floor of the Hotel European. They still did everything in the old style there. Every table had its own waiter who would anticipate your every desire. At one point a dish of fried potatoes was served and I immediately began eating them with my bare hands. I always loved eating with my hands. And later he told me that I'd done it so spontaneously, that I was so uninhibited by the elegance of the restaurant, that it completely won his heart and he knew he had to marry me."

In the fall of 1989, the world oohed and aahed like one great crowd at the visionary light show in the skies over Eastern Europe. It was all the more wonderful because not a single prophet had foreseen communism melting into nothingness in the space of weeks. No madman had envisioned the Berlin Wall becoming a dance floor. Suddenly, the fairy tale seemed the most realistic genre as poets went from prisons to presidencies.

Andrei Sakharov had lived to see the triumph of the idea for which he stood and which gave him the strength to withstand the Soviet state. But exile had wounded his health. And on December 15, 1989, death again proved how cruel its democracy is.

Today

Part One

Masha and Anton are out in search of a chicken to buy. It is a warm spring day in Leningrad and they stroll with easy absorption in each other, high school classmates who stayed in touch, friends. For some reason, today Anton is not wearing the simple pigtail that identifies him as a soldier in the army of the new sensibility. His hair is loose, down to his shoulders, and he looks more like the hippie he once was, hitch-hiking through Siberia with the Beatles echoing in his brain. He winces slightly and touches the boil on the side of his neck with the tips of two fingers.

Masha notices. She is almost relaxed today, able to enjoy the sun on her bare arms, throat, and upper chest. In a red scoop-neck top, jeans, light sandals, her sunglasses sometimes down, sometimes on her hair, she could be from any country. But her face is lit with the happiness of curiosity, which is rare in any country, but was not rare on Pushkin Street.

After passing through narrow streets where decades of grime has so darkened the details on the Russian Art Nouveau buildings and gate grilles that only a careful eye can detect them, they walk a long, tree-shaded park to the river. Near a theater a rock group is singing a medley of rock songs and old-favorite folk songs as part of a drive against alcoholism.

The chicken is for Anton. Masha is just keeping him company and at the same time keeping an eye out for anything that might make a suitable present for her friends who are to be married soon. Anton is not invited to that wedding. Mostly, they have different worlds now except for the one they have together.

They cross the Neva on a mighty arc of a bridge, then amble alongside the iron railing by the water.

Out of the corner of her eye Masha checks to see if it's still there. It is. One small, wrought-iron, double-headed eagle, the imperial insignia, had somehow survived the revolution's fury to destroy the old. She always checks, and she always smiles, reassured by the imperfection that is survival.

They are now parallel with the battleship *Aurora,* which fired the first shot of the revolution. A huge, old-fashioned toy of a battleship with a big red star on its smokestack, the *Aurora* is anchored in all its teak and brass glory across from the Hotel Leningrad, which is strictly for foreigners (with certain exceptions) and whose doormen are people who have retired from work in which sizing people up quickly by eye was very much part of the job. Immediately to the left of the hotel is another pale grey modernity, a residential building for important party people whose first-floor grocery, reason would dictate, would be well supplied. They might well even have a few chickens.

Masha looks at Anton's white T-shirt, the words NEW YORK and pictures of planes, skyscrapers, and cockroaches in Constructivist black.

"I've got an idea," she says.

"Let's hear it."

"Let's have a Pepsi in the hotel."

He smiles with the gratitude of the adventurous to the one who has thought up the next adventure.

"We don't look Soviet at all!" says Masha with a vehemence

already tinged with anger that they must resort to ingenuity and daring to enter a hotel in their own country.

The cab drivers and criminals who congregate in front of the hotel pay them no more attention than they would to a Swede with a slender Austrian wife.

All the hotel's several front doors are locked, and everyone must pass through a single door where a uniformed doorman watches people pass or suddenly asks to see a hotel pass. Just before they walk through the door, Anton whispers a joke in Masha's ear and she is smiling with such mirth as she enters that she has to seize her mouth and nose with her slender fingers. The doorman has not caught any glint of mistrustful Soviet alertness in their eyes.

They walk around the vast, marble lobby. The little glass-topped wooden stands selling magazines, souvenirs, and cold remedies look oddly makeshift, out of place. In the ground-floor bar a group of Finns is starting to grow loud at a table covered with glasses, bottles, ashtrays. The barman tells Anton he can buy Pepsis for rubles in the snack bars on the odd-numbered floors, the evens only take foreign.

Something about the hotel makes them feel both ashamed and scornful, and angry to be feeling that blend of shame and scorn yet again. They almost decide against the Pepsi just to be back out in the open air but, now that she thinks of it, Masha really would like a cold drink.

One of the counter girls comes out of the little back room where they drink tea, smoke, and gossip, quickly serves Anton and Masha their Pepsis, then disappears through curtains to resume the conversation at the point where it had been so rudely interrupted.

"What's that on your neck?" asks Masha.

"I don't know. A swelling."

"Do you have penicillin?"

"I have penicillin and I have a hypodermic but I can't get any clean needles. Needles have disappeared. Everybody's afraid of AIDS."

For a little while neither of them say anything. The swelling on his neck, the lack of needles, the doormen with the sharp grey eyes, have reminded them once again that their country might be a place they will one day have to leave for good.

"Is your theater going on tour in Canada?" asks Masha.

"Looks like it. And everybody wants to go. You wouldn't believe the games that have started."

"I'd believe them. I see them every day."

"I can't play them."

"Neither can I. Still, you never know, they might take you along just because they really need you."

"In a pinch."

"Let's go," says Masha.

They finish fast.

Waiting for the elevator, they see the key attendant watching television at her desk. Gorbachev's face fills the screen. A passing maid pulling a vacuum cleaner says, "Poor Mikhail Sergeevich, he looks so tired lately."

Glad to be back out in the powdery light of the open space by the river, they head for their original destination, the party residential building, to which the local intelligentsia have given the name of a Turgenev novel, "A Nest of Gentlefolk."

The first-floor grocery is long, clean, and dim. Its several sections each have their own cashier seated across from them. The customer chooses a product, is given a bill, walks over, pays the bill, and returns to the counter to collect the merchandise, hoping that a line has not formed in the meantime.

Masha and Anton go from section to section. Since they are both tall they can look over the small crowds into the display cases, which, apart from a few types of cheese, display nothing Masha and Anton cannot buy in their local stores.

Finally, they join the short line at the vertical glass-front rotisserie. They lean to the side for a glimpse of the chickens and spot them—black, their thin ribs in clear relief. Masha squeals in mock horror, then dissolves in giggles. The man in line beside Anton asks, "What do you think those chickens died of?"

Anton looks at the chickens, sniffs, and, deadpan, replies, "Hunger."

*

Masha has arrived in time for one cigarette before the wedding, five minutes by the embankment, the city shimmering both in water and in air as the dying light darkens the pastel palaces. It is not Leningrad here, but Petersburg, though the address could not have been more idiotic: the Palace of Matrimony on Red Navy Embankment.

"I always regretted not having a church wedding. My husband's parents were in the party, reason enough to make a church wedding out of the question. Still, in a way, that's good, it makes the marriage seem less real now that it's over.

"I hate Soviet weddings. They're so empty and vulgar, so sugary and false."

Masha joins the last flurry of guests entering the palace, once no doubt a count's townhouse.

Walking up the grand stairway, she winces at a burst of static from a worn cassette of wedding marches played by an unseen tape deck.

The presiding official from the city soviet is a plump, peroxide blonde in a business suit and a red sash covered with glittering pins—Lenin in profile, a torch flaming red. She exhorts the bride and groom to assume not only the vows of love but their civic responsibilities as parents-to-be, for children, yes, children are our future.

Everybody seems constrained, the army people in their well-brushed uniforms, the party people in their best bureaucratic blue, and especially the bride's and groom's friends, people in their middle twenties.

But the bride and groom are not constrained. They have an identical lightness to the blond of their hair and the blue of their eyes. They look at each other throughout the ceremony with the happiness that believes it has the power to make others happy. And it does, for when they are pronounced man and wife, the bride flashes with such bridal radiance that even those only waiting to get a jump on the line in the cloakroom downstairs are stirred for a moment by youth and love.

Darkened by twilight, the architecture is now only inky silhouette, a tragic elegance of line.

A half an hour later in the line for the cloakroom in the restaurant where the reception is to be held, Masha notices, then makes eye contact with, two men, one whose hair is wild and shaggy. The person with him, blond and round-faced, seconds the contact rather than actually making it. The message is nonverbal but clear enough for that: We'll sit together and somehow get through this evening, which promises to be dreadful.

They're ahead of her in line, they'll grab good seats, meaning good escape points, and save one for her.

Masha touches her hair as she walks through the smoking room and past a small dance floor in the banquet hall, where she spots them right away at one end of the two parallel tables set perpendicular to the head table, which is raised a few feet on a dais. Covered in linen and glinting with good silver, all three tables have been lined end-to-end with bottles—Georgian red wine, Georgian white, iced Russian vodka, Soviet champagne. Nearly every other square inch is occupied by appetizers—red caviar, vinaigrettes, herring, pâtés. And there is plenty of bread, dark and light, each basket covered sacramentally with a clean napkin.

After introductions—the one with shaggy hair, bad skin, and lupine elongation of nose and mouth is Nikolai, his placid round-faced companion is Vanya—they exchange commiserations about the ceremony like people stranded while traveling and determined to make the best of it. It also isn't long before they are exchanging phone numbers because the two men are from a rock group she has heard of, and since she works for Soviet television on the most popular show produced in Leningrad, they might well have some business in the future.

They stop talking to watch the pleasant ripple of people being seated. Napkins are opened, chairs adjusted, the offering scanned. Interrupted conversations resume, new ones begin. Those with a thirst are already pouring themselves a drink, some start with champagne, some go right to vodka. Masha, Nikolai, and Vanya toast their fortuitous meeting with champagne, but it is synthetically sweet in just the same way the ceremony was, and they wash the taste out of their mouths with cold vodka.

No sooner is everyone settled than a short, bald man speeds

into the room. Pumping his short arms, he scatters stragglers like tenpins, then comes to a sudden halt between the two tables. Facing the dais, he claps his hands thunderously and his shout "Attention, Comrades!" silences the room at once.

"What a troll," says Masha with amusement and distaste. "It's so old-fashioned to have a master of ceremonies. As if people even needed to be told how to enjoy themselves."

She cannot bear his aggressive humor. He seems to intentionally tell jokes that are old and crude, jokes that will not elicit laughter but only groans of recognition that life is that way too, crude and old, never fresh or fine. But the master of ceremonies is eliciting no laughter at all and very few groans of recognition, except among the older army men. This he takes as a personal affront. And the anger of humiliation marshals his energy to defeat his insulter, the audience.

"He doesn't even know he doesn't belong here," says Masha.

"How could he know," says Nikolai.

"Attention, Comrades! In keeping with tradition, the bride's family will rise and toast the groom's parents," commands the master of ceremonies, using the authority of his own voice and that of tradition.

On the dais the bride's family rise, plain people with the blurred look of the deeply tired. The bride's father says a few words that come out awkwardly and make the atmosphere awkward as well. But toasts must be drunk to and round-faced Vanya is just filling their glasses with clear vodka that is kept in ice.

They clink glasses and smile at the encouraging clarity of the sound, then take the vodka in one gulp.

Masha and Vanya immediately chase theirs with herring, Nikolai savors the arctic astringency in his mouth, then says, "Vodka's the only thing of ours foreigners will pay money for."

"Furs," adds Vanya.

"Vodka and furs, it could be the thirteenth century," says Masha, and they all laugh at Russia.

The room had been subdued after the first imposed toast, but after a time the hum begins arising again, some always less able

to endure awkward silences than others. But now every time that
hum reaches a certain frequency the master of ceremonies is there
between the tables, clapping his hands, commanding attention.
He's got the crowd figured: First, take charge of the room; second,
try different jokes; if jokes fail, enforce a toast.

The jokes always fail and toasts are enforced. "The groom's
parents will toast the bride." "The husband will toast the bride's
parents."

"They would probably be making perfectly fine toasts if it
weren't for him," says Masha.

"Shall we get out of here?" asks Nikolai.

"Not yet."

But the master of ceremonies has made a drastic miscalcula-
tion! Every encumbrance of a toast has been followed by a tall shot
of cold vodka, and somewhere between the third and the fifth shot,
all the white electrical charges flashing in all the nervous systems
reach critical mass.

Seeing that he is about to lose final control, the master of
ceremonies knows his only hope is in the magic words "It's bitter!"
which tradition says can be cried out by any guest and which when
cried out, are a command for the bride and groom to kiss, to make
life sweet again with love.

"Attention, Comrades," he says, looking from table to table
to dais with a broad smile, "I would like to point out that—IT'S
BITTER!"

The bride and groom rise reluctantly, not wishing to kiss at
his call. But they have no choice except there and then to overthrow him, which they do not do. All they can do is make the kiss
as insincere as the toast, that insincerity itself a tenderness.

Suddenly, a dark-haired man in his forties stands up and the
room quiets, but with respectful attention now. He fills his chest,
extends his arm toward the bride and groom, and begins singing
an old folk song about marriage that is both dignified and saucy.
The beauty of courage and of song now command the air and the
master of ceremonies scuttles from the room, head down and
brows knit. And when the singer is done and has accepted the

applause, he has the right like no other in the room to throw back his head and call out—IT'S BITTER!

To redeem their previous kiss, the bride and groom fall into a shamelessly passionate embrace, and life is very sweet again.

And it stays sweet for the rest of the meal, which is interrupted only by toasts that arise spontaneously, or from someone's need for a drink so great it inspires moving words that people cannot help but wish to drink to.

It is only after dessert, when people have begun shifting in their chairs, that the master of ceremonies launches his counterattack. At the keyboard on the small dance floor, he flicks on the mike with a scratch of static. Wasting no time on talk, he goes right into a dated dance tune designed to honor the older generation by allowing it to have the dance floor first. Several couples rise to dance; Masha, Nikolai, and Vanya also rise but only to drink a last vodka and flee the room. As they pass the dance floor the master of ceremonies smiles at them with hearty contempt, then turns away as if he hadn't seen them at all.

The plush red curtains of the smoking room act as something of a baffle on the music. Low and comfortable chairs are arranged in groupings around ashtrays, clean but impacted with grey ash.

Masha and Vanya take seats, Nikolai stands beside them leaning against Masha's chair. He accepts a Marlboro from Masha after lighting hers with a lighter that comes flaming out of his pocket.

For a while they don't talk. Nikolai's attention is on the music. Vanya recedes into a gloom that looks comically out of place on his round and simple face.

"Vanya, what's wrong?" says Masha with a coo of concern.

"I've done things I can't live with. Do you know what that means—things you can't live with? Sometimes it goes away and I think it's gone for good but then it always comes back. And when it comes back you always know it's going to keep coming back again and again, and there'll never be any end to it, never. I can tell what you're thinking—what did he ever do that was so terrible?

I'll tell you what I did—I went to work for the KGB! BUT ONLY TO EARN HARD CURRENCY SO THE BAND COULD BUY SPEAKERS!!''

He begins to weep. Masha, with amusement and compassion, begins to console him. But he does not want to be consoled too quickly, for that would imply insufficient regard for the magnitude of his transgression and of his repentance.

When his tears stop, he looks up. Nikolai is gone. He has heard what he had been waiting to hear—the silence of the keyboard, the master of ceremonies called away by some administrative detail. That silence is very brief, for Nikolai is at the keyboard now, driving one generation from the dance floor while drawing another with his Soviet heavy-metal rock 'n' roll, his voice a howl of fury, boredom, contempt, vitality, and a loneliness like that of a Siberian wolf left by a space mission on Mars.

Masha and Vanya come racing through the plush red curtains right onto the dance floor, which is filling fast. The master of ceremonies reappears only to scowl and vanish. Bottles of vodka grabbed from tables are passed from hand to hand on the packed floor, which instinctively parts for the bride and groom, who spin until she is only a white blur at the heart of the dancing. And, in a voice greater than the music and the howling, the man who stood and sang now calls out, "IT'S BITTER! BITTER!"

Part Two

An early morning in the early nineties. The hallway is lined with moving cartons. Lusya walks among them, massaging her jaw. It is the KGB family who has found an apartment and is moving out. At least there'll be some peace in the place.

She goes to the kitchen, where Praskovya is yawning in front of the stove, waiting for her kettle to boil. Being alone with Praskovya is even better than being alone, her large innocence a comfort. But either way it won't last long, someone else will come into the kitchen, her own children, the other family that still lives there, the new family of strangers about to move in.

Picking at what's left of the children's breakfast, Lusya rubs her jaw and knows that she going to have to decide very soon. "If I go to the state dentist, the root canal will be free, but I won't get any anesthesia. If I go to a private dentist, I can get a shot but I have to pay for it. And how can I take from the money we're saving for our own place. I can stand the pain. I have always been able to stand pain. In school I used to be beaten up all the time. I only had one friend, a girl who lived next door. We'd play at home but in school she'd beat me up too. She'd say, 'I'm doing this so no one'll guess.' So no one would guess she was my friend.

"Everyone beat me up but I wasn't angry with any of them. I never told on any of them. I totally accepted the whole thing as natural. When I grew up my friends insisted I free myself of all that inhibiting passivity. I worked at it, and some I just lost along the way. And now that I've accepted Russian Orthodoxy, I'm killing myself to get some of that humility back!"

She shakes her head. "Russians are masochists." But then beaming a wicked radiance, she adds, "Sadomasochists!"

Praskovya is pouring herself tea. The air in the kitchen has a laundry dampness to it even though very little wet clothing is hanging overhead.

"We're never going to get our own place," says Lusya. "It's ten years to get on the list and another ten once you're on. I'll have started getting old by then. That's the story of everybody's life here, by the time they get what they were waiting for they're too far gone to even appreciate it. I don't want this horrible nightmare of a communal apartment to be my children's memories of home. I don't want it to be their experience of home, which is the most important thing in the world, the thing that makes us human."

Praskovya takes her cup over to a small black-and-white television set, which she turns on. Drinking her tea, she stands with one ear toward the television as if it were a bird cage whose chirps keep her company.

Lusya begins listening to the report on secessionist Lithuania, when her three-year-old daughter comes in with a crayon drawing for her mother's approval and, having gotten what she came for, leaves.

"It wasn't that I made a conscious choice to devote myself to raising the children. It's just that one day I realized that nothing else gave me that same feeling of the fullness of life. To give them a home, to protect them against this society, this totalitarian society with a president, in this little breathing space before the next horror. Sometimes, I have some doubts about what I've done, especially now when the children have started growing up, and I ask myself what I'll do when they're gone. But who knows, with a little luck, I'll be a grandmother by then.

"Still, I have no regrets. I feel absolutely fulfilled. I have no complexes about staying home and taking care of the children and the house. And I have absolutely no regrets!

"How could I when my spiritual awakening came during my first pregnancy. I was pregnant with Pasha when all of a sudden I had a feeling that was almost cell-deep—if it had been any deeper, it would have been unendurable. I experienced a state that surpassed any understanding. It was a mighty emotional certainty: God exists in the universe and there is a life after death."

Lusya hears footsteps in the hallway and goes to see if it is the new neighbors, the new strangers. But it is Pasha running out to play, Pasha who had been a visitation in her womb. He flashes her a quick, dark-eyed smile and is almost out the door before she can inscribe a quick, miniature sign of the cross in the air.

Inwardly, she follows him down in the elevator still marked DEATH TO KIKES AND TARTARS, still rank with urine, through the hallway tattooed with rock 'n' roll graffiti, and out onto Sretensky Boulevard.

But Pasha cannot be followed as he slips into the absolute present of the street and the day where a white-bearded civil veteran with a cane and suit-front full of medals passes a band of savage Punks with red and green Mohawks, and where an Asiatic soldier, his pants tucked neatly in his boots asks directions from an old woman who is like nearly everyone else rushing from store to store in search of food.

A street drunk, a man from the bottom of black Soviet poverty, walks down Sretensky Boulevard, side-by-side with his woman, a ragged drunk herself. He curses her, she accepts his curses. Without breaking stride he punches her in the face and without breaking stride, without flinching, she accepts it. A few heads turn, a few feet halt, but people are too busy keeping alive for even this distraction.

There is an urgency in the air along with the dust of crumbling architecture, diesel fumes, strong cheap tobacco, the urgency of surviving the day and what is yet bound to come.

Just as Russians know in their bones when it's time to start hoarding matches and salt, they know that their country must now either be reborn or die.

Arriving with such rapidity, the future is even more dazzling than ever. Its surface can reflect any vision, any miracle, dark or bright—nuclear civil war, weary collapse, a Russia with liberty at last.

There were three revolutions in Russia in the twentieth century—the revolution of 1905, the February Revolution, and the October Revolution. Now there is a fourth.

Over the centuries, Russia has had three incarnations—pagan Russia, Christian Russia, Soviet Russia. Now, the fourth revolution is giving birth to a fourth Russia and it too will yet amaze the world.

Index